THE DICTIONARY OF
ESPIONAGE
Spyspeak into English

Joseph C. Goulden

New Foreword by
Peter Earnest
Executive Director,
International Spy Museum

DOVER PUBLICATIONS, INC.
Mineola, New York

For the Bearess of the Flagship,
Who speaks spook and other languages
As well; with love from your
Perpetual Shipmate...

... for Lacey, who brought 78 pounds of unabashed Black Lab
love and affection into The Fam...

... and for friends who were Masters of The Game and mentors
for a novice: Sam Halpern, Cameron John La Clair, Jr., James
R. Lilley, Cord Meyer, Robert W. Page, David Atlee Phillips,
John Waller, and John Walker. Thanks, guys!

Copyright

Copyright © 2012 by Joseph Goulden.
Foreword copyright © 2012 by Peter Earnest.
All rights reserved.

Bibliographical Note

This Dover edition, first published in 2012 is a revised and updated
republication of the work originally published by Stein and Day,
New York, in 1986.

Library of Congress Cataloging-in-Publication Data

Goulden, Joseph C.
    The dictionary of espionage : spyspeak into English / Joseph C. Goulden ; new foreword
by Peter Earnest.
        p. cm.
    Originally published: The dictionary of espionage : spookspeak into English / Henry
S.A. Becket. 1986
    Includes bibliographical references and index.
    ISBN-13: 978-0-486-48348-1
    ISBN-10: 0-486-48348-7
    1. Espionage—Dictionaries. I. Becket, Henry S. A. Dictionary of espionage. II. Title.
III. Title: Spyspeak into English.

UB270.B35 2012
327.1203—dc23

2011040245

Manufactured in the United States by Courier Corporation
48348701
www.doverpublications.com

Foreword

We use language and words to describe the world around us—and sometimes to shape it to serve our own ends.

"The belt was his favorite child development tool." That's Mafia underboss Tony Soprano talking about his father. Blunt, funny, and often profane, Tony and his crew of tough-talking New Jersey mobsters burst onto the American scene in early 1999 and almost overnight became a hit on American TV. The colorful, violent world of *The Sopranos* gave Americans a window into the personal lives and workings of a criminal gang and their families.

Week after week, we crowded around to peer through that window in order to savor a world few of us knew or would ever experience. We relished every noisy confrontation, every beating, and every threat to "whack" a rival. We loved listening to them, to their jargon, and to their crude attempts at sophistication.

At the height of the show's popularity, there were reportedly bona fide criminals and mobster wannabes who adopted some of the Soprano's jargon and mannerisms. It was the Sopranos language: how they talked and what they said that was at the heart of their culture. Copying them wouldn't make you a mobster, any more than Goulden's *Dictionary of Espionage* will make you a secret agent. But you can sound like one.

James Bond, George Smiley, Jack Ryan, and all the books, movies and TV shows spawned in the latter years of the Cold War opened a wide window into the shadow world of espionage, spies, and double agents. Even more light was shed by the vast amount of information revealed by the media, the memoirs of practitioners, and even the classified documents released to the public (albeit often reluctantly).

Goulden's Dictionary will take you one step closer to that world, whether you just want to write about spies or you want to be one. Goulden has known more spies and more about clandestine operations than many of the real spies he writes about. He's a stickler for accuracy and has one of the most sensitive, built-in BS-detectors in the nation's capital.

As a young, newly recruited CIA case officer in the mid-1950s, I was assigned to the "Farm," the Agency's legendary training site in Virginia (cf. Goulden). The "clandestine ops" training, the new language and jargon, indeed the whole way of thinking had an extraordinary impact on our young minds. Assuming a student alias, participating in immersive training in nighttime cross-border operations, recruiting and debriefing agents, and practicing how to conduct and elude surveillance—all of which was so engrossing and intense that it was indeed like entering another country and mastering a new language and vocabulary: that of the Cold War Intelligence Officer and his arcane craft.

The Dictionary of Espionage brings back vivid memories of those exciting days and of first encountering that new language. Now you too can enter that world and enjoy a lively tour through the plain talk, double talk, and euphemisms of Spyspeak as rendered by its practitioners.

PETER EARNEST
Executive Director,
International Spy Museum

Introduction to the 2011 Edition

For the last twenty or so years, I have been the primary reviewer of intelligence and espionage non-fiction books for *The Washington Times*, thanks to the generosity of the late Colin Walters and his successor as book editor, Carol Herman. Listing the scores of titles I reviewed during these years would serve no truly useful purpose. When a particular volume proved of special value in defining a term, it is listed as a "source" under that heading.

I began accumulating books on intelligence and foreign affairs in 1956, while a student at the U.S. Amy Intelligence School, Fort Holabird, Maryland (in a sequence so low-grade, I must add, that I was not issued a cloak, much less a dagger). Over the years my holdings grew to many thousands of volumes. The bulk of this collection now reposes in the library of the International Studies Program at Virginia Military Institute, Lexington, Virginia. When ISP ran out of shelf space, the overflow was directed to the library of the George C. Marshall Foundation, on the VMI campus in Lexington; the Institute of World Politics, a graduate level school on national security in Washington; and the National Security Program at DeSales University, Center Valley, Pennsylvania.

Given that my own collection is now scattered to four libraries, a work of continuing value to me in doing this update was *Spy Book: The Encyclopedia of Espionage*, by Norman Polmar and Thomas B. Allen, Random House (2nd edition), 2004. I drew upon this Polmar-Allen to confirm dates and names of persons involved in various intelligence matters. *Spy Book* would be a valuable cornerstone volume for any intelligence collection.

Persons eager for more good—and authoritative—intelligence reading are directed to online issues of *Studies in Intelligence*, the CIA's in-house journal, produced by the Center for the Study of Intelligence. For years, *Studies* was published in classified form and was not available to anyone outside the intelligence community. Online articles date to 1992 and include many that have been declassified (some still carry the SECRET or CONFIDENTIAL marking). The subject matter varies widely: articles on episodes in the history of intelligence, how-to pieces on tradecraft, and various theories of intelligence analysis. The CIA website also has a "reading room" section of declassified documents which could keep one reading for weeks, even months. The Center for Cryptologic History of the National Security Agency, also offers a wealth of online reading, albeit highly technical.

* * *

Because of contractual obligations to another publisher at the time, I used the pen name "Henry S. A. Becket" for the first edition of *The Dictionary of Espionage*. This "cover name" survived less than 24 hours after publication. Now I am happy that Dover has given me the opportunity revise the book and to correct some errors under my own name. I give special thanks to my friend of more than four decades, Paul A. Dickson, who shepherded the book through Dover, and to my pal Peter Earnest, a retired Agency operations officer who now runs the International Spy Museum in Washington. Comments can be sent to JosephG894@aol.com.

JOSEPH C. GOULDEN
Washington, DC
January 2011

A Prelude

How hath the spy dwelt so long amongst us? What is his utility to the state and the citizenry? How is he considered—and known—by the people he serves, often at the risk of his life? He is at once rogue and useful fellow. We survive by his information, yet we taunt and abuse him, and we have scant knowledge of his theories and his tactics; yea, we do not even speak his tongue. So let us examine our society's surrogate, commencing with his origins and purposes, and then proceeding to the manner by which he addresses his very own.

Introduction

Spies speak their own language. This is no accident. Agents practice a secret craft, and they wish and they try to keep it that way. The purpose of a priestly private language is several fold. It fends off outsiders, or at least leaves them uncertain as to what is being said around them. Learning the language is one of the first lessons addressed by an apprentice agent. Of training at the CIA's facility at Camp Peary, Virginia, during the early 1950s, longtime Agency officer Joseph Burkholder Smith explained, "At the same time this vocabulary was taught, we were warned never to use it except among ourselves and with agents under secure circumstances, because its use would identify us as spies. Obviously, learning the language of espionage was partly a familiarization with the tools of the trade *and partly an initiation rite.*" (Emphasis added.) Another espionage veteran, the pseudonymous Christopher Felix*, said much the same in his memoir: "The purpose of secret operations [is] obscured by the existence of a professional lingo which—like all technical language—is used by professionals for greater precision and misused popularly to the confusion of the layman."

These men, however, were trained decades ago, in an era when the world's intelligence agencies still operated in relative secrecy. Such is no longer the case. Intelligence is spawning its own professional and popular literature (indeed, the two officers cited above have published accounts of their espionage experiences). The public reads the language of spydom in hundreds of thriller novels annually. The Church Committee of the U.S. Senate, which poked through CIA's closets for two years during the 1970s, was so intrigued with the peculiar language used in the American intelligence community that it felt compelled to include a fourteen-page

---

*A pen name for James McCargar, who worked for a super-secret State/Defense/Department unit known as The Pond. *See* POND.

glossary in its final report. Spyspeak is now part of the daily babble that comes to our ears.

But does the lay citizen understand what he is hearing or reading? I think not. Nor, for that matter, did veteran CIA officer David Atlee Phillips, who in retirement formed the Association of Former Intelligence Officers* in an attempt to promote better public understanding of intelligence issues and functions. During the ongoing debate on how a democratic and "open" society should conduct secret operations, Phillips told the Church Committee, "subject matters and issues were being obscured—if not lost—in an esoteric jargon borrowed by Congress and the media from the intelligence subcultures. As with most trade talk, intelligence terminology such as *clandestine operations, covert action* and *black box* is highly technical and has developed nuances not easily inferred from the words themselves." Spyspeak is a lively and derivative language, and one that is constantly evolving, and rival services borrow and adapt one another's terminology. They have also reached into antiquity for the precise word for a practice they wish to describe.

A good example: In 1974, in his book *Tinker, Tailor, Soldier, Spy* the British novelist John le Carre sent his indefatigable counterintelligence officer George Smiley in quest of a Soviet agent who had penetrated British intelligence. Le Carre called this agent a "mole."

The word struck popular fancy, even within the intelligence community, and officers soon used the word as their very own, although even such an esteemed CIA veteran as William Hood confessed that he had never heard it used pre-le Carre. Then Walter Pforzheimer, retired CIA legislative counsel and in his day the foremost intelligence bibliophile in the world, poked into history and discovered that the crafty le Carre actually was using a term some 350 years old. Sir Francis Bacon had written, in a 1622 biography of King Henry VII, "Hee was careful and liberall to obtaine good Intelligence from all parts abroad...Hee had such Moles perpetually working and casting to undermine him."

---

*An alternative name, the Association for Intelligence Officers, was adopted in 2009. Either designation is correct, per Elizabeth Bancroft, the AFIO executive director.

But how did le Carre come to use this ancient term in his novel? Robert Burchfield set out to determine the origin of the term for the Oxford English Dictionary. He reported that le Carre told him that "as best his recollection served him" he found the term in a glossary attached to the Canadian Royal Commission Report on Soviet espionage prompted by the defection of GRU cipher clerk Igor Gouzenko.*

Burchfield continued his pursuit, as he reported in the *Daily Telegraph* of London in 1987. Aha! He found a far more current use of the term "mole" in an intelligence context. In 1964 writer Geoffrey Bailey published a book on the Russian security services, "The Conspirators", that reported that in 1935 the Russians recruited a Captain Fedossenko as a double agent and gave him as an alias "The Mole."

The Dictionary of Espionage is an attempt to interpret the language the espionage community uses in talking to and about itself. Much of the information in the following pages was gleaned from officers, both active and retired, who served the world's major spy organizations. There are also some sidetrips into intelligence trivia, the oddball facts with which operatives entertain themselves while at rest. These are scattered through the text under the heading, "Safe House Interlude." (A "safe house" is a place where an intelligence officer can forget about spying for a bit in confidence that the adversary will not come knocking at his door.) Tradecraft dictates that I not give formal acknowledgments to the persons who contributed to this book. The major printed sources are found in the bibliography.

HENRY S. A. BECKET
April 30, 1985

---

*Perhaps. But the copy of the Canadian report that I possess, dated June 27, 1946, contains no such glossary.

A

ACCESS PERMIT

The document that gave Soviet intelligence agents permission to deal with classified material in the course of their work. The permit spelled out specific security procedures. According to A. I. Romanov, a former Soviet intelligence officer who defected, the gist of the permit was as follows: "If I am handed a secret document, I must sign for it in a special book, giving date and time of day, in the presence of the person responsible for the safekeeping of such documents. I must not allow this document to be out of my sight even for a moment, must not put it in my pocket, on a table, or in my briefcase, must not make a copy of it or write down any extracts from it, nor discuss its contents with anyone at all. After reading it, or, as they used to say in the NKVD, absorbing it, I have to hand it back personally to the man who issued it."

The exchange was formally noted in a control ledger, with stamps and documents. The agreement noted that the penalty for violations could be death. U.S. and Soviet intelligence schools followed a parallel course in impressing fledgling agents with the seriousness of security: a marginal student in each class would be detected in a security violation and rather noisily dismissed from the school. This happened at midcourse of my training at the Army Intelligence School in Baltimore in 1956; the poor wretch who left a classified manual atop a filing cabinet was sent to Fort Dix for infantry training—a fate whose discomforts were not lost on the rest of us.

ACCOMMODATION ADDRESS

A location where an agent can receive mail, even though he does not reside there or have any visible connection with anyone who does. Small European shops traditionally have received mail for transients, for a minimal fee. The FBI utilizes established corporations, where mail directed to a particular individual or department is shunted to a designated pickup point. Because of the mail pilferage endemic to the U.S. postal system, Soviet agents could not rely upon post office boxes as accommodation addresses, according to a counterintelligence expert on KGB affairs. The KGB utilized the plethora of "private post offices" that offer rentals for $10 or so monthly, with no requirement of identification.

The KGB used one such service for more than a year in the 1960s, not knowing that the supposed owner actually worked for a U.S. intelligence agency. Much of the material transmitted through this particular drop was said to be "low-grade," but the agency did acquire several "useful leads." The mail service eventually closed because of circumstances beyond the control of the agency. The business also served as a copy shop, which made duplicating the intercepted mail all the easier.

ACTIVE MEASURES (*aktivnyye meropriyatiya*)

A Soviet term used to refer to operations intended to influence or otherwise affect other nations' policies. According to a CIA internal memorandum published in 1982, active measures, both covert and overt, consist of a broad range of activities, including "manipulation or control of the media; written or oral disinformation; use of foreign Communist parties or organizations; manipulation of mass organizations; clandestine radio broadcasting; economic activities, military operations, and other political influence operations.... These operations have a common aim: to insinuate Soviet policy views into foreign governmental, journalistic, business, labor, academic, and artistic opinion in a nonattributable fashion." (*See* DISINFORMATION.)

AGENT

In current usage, a person who engages in spying or the support of those who do, or who seeks to detect them. Oddly, the word is one that professional intelligence operatives almost never apply to themselves. A CIA man working abroad as a spy would call himself an "officer," although the persons who worked for him (non-CIA men or women) would be called agents.

In the American context, the differentiation began during World War II, when the Office of Strategic Services drew a careful distinction between its own people and others. According to OSS manuals, an *operative* was "an individual employed by and responsible to the OSS and assigned under special programs to field activity." An *agent*, by contrast, was "an individual recruited in the field who is employed or directed by an OSS operative or by a field or substation."

FBI draws no such distinction; its officers are not only agents, they are *special* agents, and they so introduce and identify themselves. The late director J. Edgar Hoover insisted upon the distinguishing adjective as a means of setting his men apart from run-of-the-mill cops (Hoover didn't hire female agents until near the end of his reign.) The Dallas trial lawyer William F. Alexander delighted in opening his cross-examination of FBI witnesses: "Well, *special* agent Jones, what's so *special* about you?"

AGENT ENVIRONMENT

See OPERATIONAL CLIMATE.

AGENT-IN-PLACE

Perhaps the rarest and most valuable of intelligence persons—the agent who offers his services to a foreign power, but agrees to continue in his position so that the information he passes is current and valuable. Fatalism is presumed by both sides, for agents-in-place face horrible fates if detected. By reliable account one KGB traitor was thrust into a roaring furnace, feet first, while more than a hundred of his colleagues watched. The lesson was obvious.

AGENT OF INFLUENCE

A person not directly under control of an intelligence agency, but willing to work on its behalf. As former CIA operations officer David Atlee Phillips told the Church Committee, "He might be a radio commentator or a local Bernard Baruch whose park bench opinions carry political weight. The agent of influence might be the foreign minister's mistress. Most covert activities utilizing the agent of influence are useful to American ambassadors in achieving low-key but important objectives of U.S. foreign policy. These activities are known in intelligence jargon as 'motherhood,' and revelations concerning them would not shock or disturb the American public."

Because of widespread government corruption, agents of influence are easily acquirable in Latin America. The Spanish colonial tradition was that the king (of Spain) "owned" the government, hence he or his subordinate is entitled to payment for any routine service. Officials who routinely accept the *mordida* (little bite, or payoff) for doing their jobs see no harm in taking money from an intelligence officer: if the agent wants the information, and has sufficient pesos, the information is his. In one Latin country in the 1960s, an agent so cultivated such a "friend" that every document that entered or left his office was routinely copied and given to the CIA station. The cost was the equivalent of two bottles of Scotch monthly.

Another former CIA officer, E. Howard Hunt, defined the agent of influence as "either a government official so highly placed that he can exercise influence on government policy or an opinion molder so influential as to be capable of altering the attitudes of an entire country." In the case of a Soviet agent of influence, "though his politics may be of the left, he is not—and cannot be known as—a Communist."

The KGB used the same term as CIA, a literal translation from the Russian *agent vlyiyania*. A large portion of covert KGB intelligence work in the United States and elsewhere was devoted to handling such agents, who were not spies in the classic sense, and often did not even realize they were being used by a foreign power. But KGB singled them out for cultivation because of their ability to exert influence in their societies—professors, government officials, politicians, journalists, labor leaders, financiers, and industrialists. The approaches were low-key. The KGB officer would, for instance, suggest to an American businessman that United States trade policy means loss of profitable USSR markets to the Europeans; could he not say something to his friends in Washington about a change? Or a "visiting Soviet academician" might have a background lunch with Washington journalists, and argue that a shift in American bargaining positions on arms talks would bring commensurate concessions from the USSR. His statement would be publicized as a "softening" of Soviet position that should be matched by the United States. (Both these "examples" actually happened.)

"The run-of-the-mill influence agents recruited by the KGB in the capitalist world must by now run into the hundreds," the CIA Soviet specialist Harry Rositzke wrote in 1981. "It is difficult to determine in many cases the variety of motivations that induce them to 'cooperate' with their Soviet friends. Political and commercial opportunism plays a part. Some may have genuine political sympathies with the Soviet side of the Cold War confrontation.... Some no doubt have been blackmailed."

AGENT PROVOCATEUR

A person who insinuates himself into an organization with the aim of inciting it to acts that would make its members subject to punishment. In 1950s CIA usage, such an agent was a "tree-shaker," a person who would join an organization with the intent of seeing if its timetable could be accelerated, and what its actual plans were. An agent provocateur is an archvillain of labor and revolutionary history, and the genre does have an odious tradition.

AGIT-PROP

Agitation and propaganda, generally used in reference to Communist and Front Group activities. Agit-prop involves the dramatic portrayal of an issue—mass marches, exhortatory speeches, and events crafted to attract media attention. For instance, in 1967 the underground newspaper *East Village Other* intended to drop two hundred pounds of flowers on the Pentagon from an airplane to signify support of an anti-war march. An agent in the New York FBI field office answered an advertisement for a pilot, and kept up the pretense to the point where the publisher arrived at the airport with the flowers. No pilot, no flight, no dropped flowers. As the field office boasted in a memo to FBI headquarters in Washington, the agent thus was able to prevent "agit-prop activity as it relates to dropping flowers over Washington."

Another agit-prop stunt went awry in Washington in July 1982. Opponents of the regime in El Salvador had fatigue-clad soldiers "enact" the seizure of innocent peasant women by jumping from a truck downtown and grabbing persons (accomplices) from a crowd. The organizers did not bother to inform the Washington police of the stunt: when the soldiers grabbed the women, they in turn were quickly grabbed, handcuffed, and spread-eagled by officers.

ALL-SKATE

See FLOATING CONTACT.

AMAN

Israeli military intelligence.

AMTORG

A Soviet trading corporation set up in New York in the 1930s. In one sense, Amtorg was a genuine commercial enterprise that did hundreds of millions of dollars in business with leading American corporations. But this brisk activity also gave invaluable cover to hordes of Soviet intelligence agents. Amtorg provided these agents with jobs as "legal cover," and assigned them to visit various cities and industrial plants, as would any normal commercial travelers. They spied, bought documents, recruited agents—in sum, worked with a free hand. Of the seven hundred to eight hundred Amtorg employees in the mid-1930s, perhaps half were also members of the American Communist Party. There were occasional spy scandals and resignations by loyal and unwitting Americans who had gone to work for Amtorg. (One such person, Basil W. Douglas, one-time Amtorg vice-president, said angrily after his resignation: "I have seen information regarding the army and naval defenses of the United States that has been gathered by Amtorg's agents and transmitted to Russia.") But given the vast scope of Amtorg's economic activities, American officials tended to excuse such transgressions as "minor matters."

ANGELS

Popular derogatory name for agents of the Sandinista secret police of Nicaragua, circa 1984. The angels controlled *turbos divinas,* "divine mobs," who circled the homes of opponents of the Sandinista regime at night, beating sticks against cans and chanting threatening slogans. The *turbos* learned the harassing tactic from the Somoza secret police.

ANNUITANT

A retired CIA employee who receives a regular pension (an "annuity") and remains available for special assignments if needed.

A commission headed by former Senator John Tower used the term in its report on the abortive Iran arms negotiations of 1986, describing retiree George Cave as a "CIA annuitant and expert on Iran who went to Terheran as *Parsi* translator during the talks.

ANOMALIES

A counterintelligence term for unexplained problems or conflicting information that arises in an investigation. A veteran CI officer told me, "It's like that unexplained knock in your car engine that comes and goes without any discernible reason."

APOSTLES

A lively Oxford literary club of the late 1920s and early 1930s that attracted Communists and a good number of homosexuals. Two of its most prominent members were the Soviet spies Guy Burgess and Donald Maclean.

ARCOS

The Soviet trade mission in London during the 1920s, formally the All-Russian Co-operative Society, Limited; closed after its exposure as a spy center. Arcos played much the same role in Britain as its sister organization, Amtorg, did in the United States. (*See* AMTORG.)

ARMORER

KGB deep-cover agent whose chief purpose was to pass smuggled weapons to terrorists and other groups who worked for the Soviets, either wittingly or unwittingly.

ASSASSINATION

On December 4, 1981, President Reagan promulgated Executive Order 12333, titled, "United States Intelligence Activities." A key sentence read, "No person employed by or acting on behalf of the United States Government shall engage in, or conspire to engage in, assassination." Journalists and Congressional investigators have spent millions of man-years searching for a verifiable instance of a "CIA murder," to no avail. The Church Committee of the 1970s, to its acute dismay, found that various "CIA plots" for murdering Fidel

Castro and other leaders emanated from the White House. Given that both Democratic and Republican presidents were involved, the committee let the issue slide.

ATTORNEY GENERAL'S LIST

A list of subversive organizations first compiled by the Justice Department in the 1930s as a guide to evaluate applicants for Federal employment. Both the criteria for inclusion and the names of the groups have changed frequently over the years. In 1965, the U.S. Supreme Court ruled that requiring individuals to register as members of the cited groups was unconstitutional, as a violation of the privilege against self-incrimination. Thus federal agencies were forced to individually evaluate information regarding membership in allegedly subversive organizations based on raw data furnished by the FBI. The Nixon administration rewrote guidelines for the attorney general's list (in 1971) to redefine "subversive." Executive Order 11605 reads in part:

> ...totalitarian, fascist, communist, or subversive, or which has adopted a policy of unlawfully advocating the commission of acts of force or violence to deny others their rights under the Constitution or laws of the United States or any state, or which seeks to overthrow the government of the United States or any state or subdivision thereof by unlawful means.

ATTORNEY GENERAL'S PORTFOLIO

The Justice Department's secret plans during the early years of the Cold War for emergency detention of citizens and aliens in time of national emergency. The key element was the FBI's so-called "Security Index" of names of persons to be detained. The Portfolio also contained specific federal facilities at which the persons were to be held and draft "national emergency" orders to be signed by the President giving legal authority to the arrests. According to FBI internal memoranda disclosed by the Church Committee, the FBI would have broad discretion over who should be listed for detention.

AUNT MINNIES

Photographs taken by professional photographers, journalists, amateurs, or tourists that show a place of interest to an intelligence topographer. These are named after the proverbial "maiden aunt" whose half-obscured head does not block the view of a winding road or a beach or the quaint little whitewashed church that an artillery targeting officer might find of value. OSS had a special section during World War II that scoured antique and secondhand shops for Aunt Minnie postcards.

AUSSTEIGEN

In German, "getting out"; in espionage usage, getting out from under the cover of a Soviet passport and acquiring new travel documentation falsified by the astute "cobblers" in a Berlin "workshop" run by Soviet intelligence. (*See* COBBLER.) "Getting out" enabled an agent to travel without having to cope with the special attention that customs and border officials often gave to Russians. The agent surrendered his old passport in exchange for the new. When his journey is completed, he makes the exchange again. According to visa stamps, he spent the entire period in Germany.

AVANPOST

KGB term for a foreign spy cell involving two or more networks. KGB operational procedures would dictate that there be no overlap between the networks, for security reasons.

B

BABBLER

An electronic device that emits what appears to be simultaneous gibberish in at least a dozen languages, used as a counterbugging measure.

BACKSTOPPING

An array of bogus cover identifications issued to an operative that will stand up to fairly rigorous investigation. An agent who is backstopped is first given a birth certificate (either contrived or that of a dead person); then he proceeds to obtain the myriad identification certificates required in a modern society—from Social Security card through driver's license and credit cards to library cards and voter registration. These cards are "real" in the sense that the issuing agency thinks they are being given to a real person. A backstopped agent also has a phone number and mailing address that are "covered" by someone who can pass as a legitimate business or personal associate.

Full backstopping is such an expensive and time-consuming process that CIA tries to avoid it in favor of "flash-alias" documentation. This type of documentation consists of counterfeits produced by the Identification Section of Technical Services Division. Technicians there are able to manufacture seemingly legitimate papers ranging from an American Express card to a Libyan driver's license. (As flash-alias credit cards are not real, an agent carrying one uses it only for identification; he must pay cash for meals and hotels.)

BARGAINING COUNTER

An arrested agent who is stored in prison until the proper time arises to barter him for the release of a jailed operative from one's own side. During the Cold War, KGB satellites such as the East German Stasi had the nasty habit of locking up innocent Westerners on trumped-up spy charges who could then be used for trading purposes, either for its own agents or someone from the KGB or another friendly service. A good example was the American graduate student Frederic Pryor, arrested in East Berlin in 1961 and falsely accused of being a CIA agent. He was freed as part of the exchange of U-2 pilot Francis Gary Powers for KGB agent "Rudolf Abel" (in reality, the British-born Willie Fisher) in 1962.

BARIUM

KGB term for false information that is fed to a suspected source of leaks of classified material. As is true for the barium solution used in gastrointestinal examinations, the course of the "barium material" was watched as it flowed toward Western intelligence. Different "doses" of information are given to different officials; the dose that is detected in the West means the end of the spying career of the person who transmitted it.

BAZAAR INTELLIGENCE

Marketplace rumors and gossip, generally with about as much credence as the source would imply. But bazaar intelligence is not to be dismissed out of hand: if prices of basic commodities suddenly soar, the first signs of serious popular discontent will be detected among shoppers.

"A BETTER WORLD," "A WORLD ALL FULL OF BLISS"

Israeli euphemisms for the destination of murdered enemy agents. Similarly, to "send a person on vacation" means to injure him, but nonfatally; the extent of the injury depends on whether the vacation is to be "brief" or "long."

BfV (Bundesamt fur Verfassungsschutz)

Federal Office for the Protection of the Constitution, the West German counterintelligence agency. Functions of *BfV* roughly paralleled those of the FBI.

BIGOT LIST

A listing of the names of all persons privy to the workings of a particularly sensitive intelligence mission. The bigot list is intended to maintain tight control of the circulation of secret documents, to ensure that everyone reading them has a true "need to know."

The term began in World War II, when officers being sent to Gibraltar in preparation for the invasion of North Africa had their orders stamped "TO GIB." Later, when planning commenced for Operation OVERLORD, the Normandy invasion, the letters were reversed to read "BIGOT" and used to list persons with a need-to-know sensitive details of the invasion. (*See* WITTING.)

BIOGRAPHIC LEVERAGE

CIA euphemism for blackmail—literally, the use of known derogatory information from a person's past to coerce him or her into doing the Agency's bidding.

THE BIRD

See FORT HOLABIRD.

BIRDWATCHER

A slang word for a spy used by some British intelligence officers in the 1950s. An officer with a penchant for bird-hunting contrived a sublanguage for his subordinates. A birdwatcher who went into the field, for whatever purpose, was called a "poacher," and he was controlled by a "gamekeeper." The target was the "bag." The assistants were "beaters," who flushed the quarry, and "stalkers," who tailed it once it was running.

BLACK TRAINEES

Foreigners brought to the United States for training at Camp Peary or another CIA facility, and who are often not made aware that they are in the United States.

BLACK BAG JOB

An FBI term for warrantless surreptitious entries for purposes other than microphone installations; i.e., physical search and photographing or seizing documents. The FBI realized it was breaking the law with such raids. As an internal memorandum stated in July 1966, "Such a technique involves trespassing and is clearly illegal; therefore, it would be impossible to obtain any legal sanction for it. Despite this, black bag jobs have been used because they represent an invaluable technique in combating subversive activities of a clandestine nature aimed directly at undermining and destroying our nation." Targets (there were hundreds) ranged from the Ku Klux Klan to Socialist groups. Director J. Edgar Hoover finally ordered the black bag jobs halted in 1966, apparently because of fear of exposure. Numerous Bureau memoranda given the Church Committee warned of FBI embarrassment should the illegal break-ins be revealed. (Also called "surreptitious entry.")

BLACK BAG OPERATION

In CIA terms, an under-the-table operation such as passing funds to a foreign political party.

BLACK BOXES

Inanimate technical methods of spying, ranging from room bugs and telephone taps to satellite reconnaissance.

BLACK FORGERY

Material that is produced so that it appears to be of enemy origin.

BLACK PROPAGANDA

Operations in which the source of the disseminated propaganda is shielded or misrepresented so that it cannot be attributed to the source responsible for it. During World War II, for instance, German intelligence sent letters to French soldiers, purporting to be from hometown neighbors, claiming their wives were committing open adultery or had venereal diseases. Black propaganda is an activity that has now fallen under another umbrella term, "disinformation."

CIA officer E. Howard Hunt did a casebook black propaganda stunt while in the Mexico City station. Hunt learned that a Communist front group planned a reception honoring a Soviet visitor. He obtained an invitation, had a printer run off 3,000 copies, and distributed them all over Mexico City. Since the invitation offered free drinks and a luncheon, the response was so massive that refreshments were swiftly exhausted, and the Communist hosts had to bar the doors, to the outrage of the "invitees" waiting outside. Both the Mexicans and the Soviets went away with sour feelings about one another.

BLACKMAIL

The use of derogatory information to compel a person to work for an enemy intelligence service. Blackmailers have run the gamut of human frailties. One example from among hundreds:

Alfred Frenzel, a member of the West German *Bundestag,* or Parliament, had been a member of the Communist Party in prewar Czechoslovakia, but thought he had thrown off this past by claiming an exemplary war record. He boasted of being a pilot among exiles fighting the Germans for the British, whereas he actually served as a cook. (So firm was Frenzel in details of his story that he won a libel suit against a political opponent who accused him of embroidering his record.) But the Czech secret service knew better, and blackmailed Frenzel into passing along top-secret NATO annual planning reports. He was sentenced to fifteen years' hard labor for espionage in 1961; then he was swapped for a woman journalist arrested by the USSR on trumped-up charges in 1966.

BLIND DATING

An agreement by an intelligence officer to meet another person at a place of that person's choice. The greatest risk is that the officer can be kidnapped by the other side. The recommended procedure is that a first meeting be held at a relatively public place, such as a square, business district, or park, where neither party can be jeopardized.

BLIND MEMORANDUM

A memorandum written on blank (i.e., no letterhead) stationery with no signature nor indication of origin. Intelligence agencies frequently use the blind memorandum as a means of making an informal record, yet without assigning any individual responsibility for its content. Since such memoranda do not contain a file number, they can be destroyed with impunity in the event of threatened disclosure in legal proceedings (or by a Congressional committee).

BLOWN AGENT

An intelligence operative whose identity becomes known to the opposition. "Blown" also is used to refer to any aspect of an operation whose security has been compromised, be it a safe house, a secret radio frequency, or a letter-drop.

BLOW BACK

False propaganda planted in a foreign country that is picked up by news organizations and reprinted as fact—or a semblance thereof—by newspapers in the nation of origin. William Colby, one-time director of central intelligence, told the Church Committee in 1977 that material the CIA distributed abroad was often "blown back" into the United States as the truth. Although Colby did not deign to say so, American media could avoid blown back news by doing their own reporting, rather than repeating what is reported abroad.

BLUE BADGER

The color of the pass used by a direct employee of the CIA. Contract employees carry green passes, hence they are "green badgers." The color difference extends to parking permits as well. The proliferation of "green badgers" post-9/11 is obvious to anyone making a casual observation in the vast Agency parking lot.

BLUE CUBE

The mountain-top building near Sunnyvale, California, in the Silicon Valley that from the start of the space age through the 1990s, was the command center for military spy satellites. Nine stories tall, and covering an entire city block, the building's baby blue exterior prompted the nickname.

Formally, the facility is Onizuka Air Force Base, named for Colonel Ellison Onizuka, who died in the Challenger explosion. Although the mission of the "Blue Cube" was known throughout the Silicon Valley, the Pentagon for years denied that it served as the control center for satellites. And even when its function was admitted, the military did not reveal that the Blue Cube was run by the still-secret National Reconnaissance Office, rather than the Air Force. (The operations have since been shifted to an air base in Colorado.)

BND (Bundesnachrichtendienst)

The West German Federal Intelligence Service concerned both with foreign and domestic intelligence. Successor to the Gehlen Organization; created by CIA, although now feistily independent.

BOFFIN
Communications technician (British).

BOLSHOY CHIREY
Russian for "big boils," an internal KGB epithet for senior officers, whose tempers and pressures were such that they are apt to "burst at any moment."

BOOK MESSAGE
A CIA message that goes to each station and installation in the world. A book message announces personnel changes of general interest and declarations of policy.

BORDER CROSSERS
Agents who attempted to sneak across the border separating Western Europe from the Soviet Bloc countries. CIA wasted much time—and many European-born agents—with border crossings in the late 1940s and early 1950s. The few agents who managed to get past the border guards seldom were able to send back any information of value. Border crossers are now found primarily in blood-and-thunder spy novels. (*See* LINECROSSERS.)

BOYEVAYA GRUPPA
"Combat gangs," KGB squads trained—and authorized—to kill or abduct targets abroad, as required. (*See* WET SQUAD.)

BRAINWASHING
A term that came into wide use—or misuse—during the Korean War as descriptive of changes that Chinese Communist interrogators made in prisoners' minds through psychological manipulation, physical mistreatment, and drugs. The word suggests Oriental cunning and offered an "answer" as to why many American POWs decided to sign anti-U.S. manifestoes on such subjects as germ warfare and war guilt.

The first public use of the term was in a Miami News article headlined, "Brainwashing: Tactics Force Chinese into Communist Party," bylined by one Edward Hunter, who claimed wide-use of psychological manipulation of the Chinese populace. A propaganda specialist for the OSS during World War II, Hunter ostensibly was working in Asia as a journalist. In reality, journalism was a cover for his employment as a psychological warfare specialist for CIA. Hunter later wrote several widely-received books on the "brain-washing" of American POWs in Korea. The robotic performance of defendants in the notorious Soviet "show trials" of the 1930s was cited as further evidence of Communist "mind control."

But Colonel Allison Ind, who spent much of his Army career as an intelligence officer in the Far East, rejected the term. "What we call brainwashing is quite simply sales psychology driven to its absolute limits in conjunction with an atmosphere which increases receptivity: isolation, doubt as to one's own people, apparent sincerity on the part of the operator." The Dutch-born psychiatrist Dr. Joost A. M. Meerloo used yet another term, "menticide," or "murder of the mind."

A number of authors, citing CIA documents on psychological experiments, have claimed that "brainwashing" was actually an Agency creation, and linking it to Communist conduct was a propaganda effort.

In any event, an official glossary of the U.S. Department of the Army contains a definition of brainwashing: "to erase an individual's past beliefs and concepts and to substitute new ones."

BRIDE

The decoding, by the United States and British intelligence, of thousands of wartime Soviet messages to agents stationed abroad. The highly secret operation began in 1945 and was possible because of the discovery of a partially burned Soviet code book in Finland during the last days of World War II. The decoded messages revealed deep Soviet penetration of the British and U.S. intelligence services, and also gave information on such famed espionage figures as the Rosenbergs, executed in 1953 for wartime atomic espionage. Only the barest hints of Operation Bride's findings have become public. One longtime Western counterintelligence specialist told me, "The full story would knock the globe off its axis by three degrees." Bride was an outgrowth of the widely publicized Operation Verona.

BRIGADE 2506

The anti-Castro invasion force in the 1961 Bay of Pigs Operation. Each Cuban freedom fighter who came to the CIA-sponsored training base in Guatemala was assigned a number, commencing with 2000. Soldier 2506 fell to his death in a mountain training accident; his friends honored him by using his number for the name of their brigade.

BRITISH SECURITY SERVICE (MI5)

The agency responsible for internal security in the United Kingdom, roughly equivalent in function to the Federal Bureau of Investigation. It is popularly known as MI5, in the media and elsewhere. As was stated by a Crown Minister in 1945, when the government was deciding upon MI5's postwar role, "The purpose of the Security Service is the defense of the Realm, and nothing else."

MI5 began its current existence in 1909 paired with MI6, know known as the Secret Intelligence Service, working under the Defense Ministry with a combined "staff" of two men. (In reality, equivalent work had been done in Britain for several centuries.) The security service suffered so many scandals during the past three decades—including incessant hunts for apparently non-existent moles—that it has a dubious reputation in many circles. John le Carre used MI5 as the basis for his George Smiley novels, renaming it "The Circus."

Recommended reading: *Defend the Realm*, by Christopher Andrew, Knopf, 2009. It is a rare "authorized" work that is a warts-and-all account of MI5's first century.

BROTHERLY ORGANIZATIONS

Ostensibly independent cultural and political groups in a target country that gave aid and comfort to the Soviet Union. (KGB term.)

BUCKET JOB

When the New York field office of the FBI began trailing Nazi spies around the city in the 1930s, members of surveillance teams worked such long and irregular hours that agents joked about "bringing dinner to work in a bucket." The teams eventually took on the name "bucket squads," and their surveillances came to be known as bucket jobs. An agent working on a surveillance is "in the bucket," or "carrying the bucket."

BUG

The wiring of a room so that any sound made therein can be heard and recorded.

Because of tight controls on movements of foreigners, Communist Bloc intelligence services could practically ensure continuous electronic "coverage" of targets. According to the defected Czech agent Josef Frolik, "A number of Prague restaurants—the better ones—are permanently equipped with audio devices at certain tables. Waiters in such establishments are trained to recognize persons of interest from photographs. In the event such a person comes to the establishment, the waiter will seat him at one of the tables equipped with a monitoring device; such tables are usually marked as having been 'reserved.'" The waiter would then announce that the other party has cancelled, and after seating the targets, he'd go to the telephone and alert the "hotel detail" of the intelligence service, which would activate the monitor by remote control. As Frolik notes, "Any kind of checking which a CIA officer may have engaged in prior to meeting a contact or an agent thus [becomes] useless. Because he entered the restaurant at random and did not discuss the location beforehand with his contact or agent, just let an analyst try to find out where a mistake had occurred or at which point the operation was blown."

Diplomats of all nationalities assume that their embassies are bugged by the host country, despite Article 27 of the Geneva Convention that guarantees the "protection of free communications" for all diplomats.

Counterintelligence specialists responsible for finding and dismantling bugs are aptly called "exterminators."

BUREAU SPECIAL

An FBI investigation carried on outside the framework of usual Bureau procedures, with no files or records being maintained. Bureau specials generally involve illegal or politically sensitive affairs—for instance, the wiretaps installed on numerous Washington journalists and National Security Council officials by White House order in 1971.

BUREAU CENTRAL DES RENSEIGNEMENTS ET D'ACTION (BCRA)

A French Resistance organization that combined intelligence-gathering with sabotage during World War II; it worked closely with the British SOE and the American OSS. The exiled General Charles de Gaulle chose Andre Dewavrin to build and then direct BCRA.

BURN

An intelligence agent who is deliberately sacrificed in order to protect a more valuable and productive spy. British counterintelligence has long suspected (but never conclusively shown) that two prominent Soviet agents were burned to preserve other spies: Klaus Fuchs, of nuclear secrets infamy and John Vassall, an Admiralty functionary forced to spy for the Soviets after being photographed in a homosexual orgy. The British theory was that Fuchs and Vassall were put into positions where they were sure to be detected, thereby halting searches for other spies in the areas where they worked.

BURST TRANSMISSION

As former DCI Richard Helms explained to columnist William Safire of *The New York Times* in 1988, "Sometime back, the technicians discovered how to send a hell of a lot of words in a very quick broadcast, making it hard to intercept and decipher. Say you are an agent in a house in the center of Moscow and you want to communicate with your headquarters. You wouldn't want to stay on the air long enough for the triangulation of listening bands to locate you. With a burst transmission, you can pass along information instantaneously, making you harder to trace."

Safe House Interlude One

Who Are These Spies?

"Who are these CIA people, after all? They are the men and woman living next door, down the street, or across town—they are normal Americans who have gone through an extraordinary experience to get into the Agency in the first place.

"These are people serving his country very well and very loyally and very patriotically, in some cases under very difficult circumstances. But too often they are reviled and cast as second-class citizens. If this is the way the public wants to deal with its intelligence professionals, then we ought to disband the Agency and go back to the way we were before World War II. Otherwise, it is up to the citizens of this country, the Congress and the President to support these people and to support them adequately, or else there is no reason to expect them to do these kinds of dirty jobs. It isn't fair, it isn't right, and it won't work."

—Former DCI Richard M. Helms, in a 1988
television interview with David Frost.

∞

"I today went out and hired me a base fellow."

—Journal of Sir Francis Walsingham, who was in
charge of intelligence for Queen Elizabeth the First.

∞

"These [CIA] officers who must depend on cover to conduct their business abroad are obliged to continue the cover at home. A routine life is not possible for them even when living in the Washington area. They must pretend to be somewhere else when a creditor or visitor telephones them at the office in Langley on an 'outside' line...If troubled they may not select their own psychiatrist, but instead visit one cleared and approved by CIA. They—and their families—must lie constantly. They cannot tell the truth to bankers, neighbors, lodge brothers or delivery boys. I lied even to the Boy Scouts of America when filling out an application to be a Scoutmaster. They must lead a double life at home so that cover will be intact when they are next assigned overseas. It is a vexing existence."

—David Atlee Phillips, who ended a long CIA career as chief of the Western Hemisphere Division, in his 1978 memoir *The Night Watch*.

∾

"We of the Game are beyond protection. If we die, we die. Our names are blotted from the book."

—Rudyard Kipling, in his book *Kim* (1901), explaining the rules of the Great Game to the Indian lad Kim, who was an aspiring agent.

∾

"It is part of the CIA director's job to be the fall guy for the President."

—Longtime CIA officer Harry Rositzke in his book *CIA's Secret Operations* (1977).

C

C

The single-letter term, written in green ink, used on correspondence by the person who serves the director of the British Secret Intelligence Service, SIS, or MI6. According to British historian Keith Jeffery, who published an authorized history of SIS in 2010, the original "C" was the service's first director, Mansfield Cumming, a career navy officer, who signed papers with the "C" beginning January 10, 1910, the year SIS was founded. As Jeffery points out, "the practice of writing in green was a naval tradition, by which officers in charge of branches or services used it to indicate their superior status." Although Cumming used a different colored ink from time to time during SIS's early years, he was consistent in choosing green from 1916 on—a tradition followed by his successors to this day.

(I owe thanks to Dr. Jeffery for a good deal of the SIS material in *Spyspeak*. See his *The Secret History of MI6*, Penguin Press, 2010.)

CABLE VETTING

British euphemism for a procedure whereby security agencies would routinely scrutinize private cables and telegrams dispatched from or received in the United Kingdom via the post office (which runs the British telegraph system) or private cable companies. The practice was authorized under the Official Secrets Act of 1920 and continued until revealed by the Daily Express in February 1967.

CAMP 020

A highly secret interrogation that the British security service (MI5) utilized to interrogate and confine suspected German agents during World War II.

Camp 020 was at Latchmere House, a rambling Victorian mansion amid acres of dense woodland near the Surrey village of Ham Common, originally bought by the War Office as a hospital and recuperation center for officers shell-shocked during World War I.

Prisoners taken to Camp 020 effectively disappeared for the duration of the war: the British omitted it from the lists of POW camps given to the International Red Cross for neutral inspection. (Likewise, the Germans did not list their interrogation centers with the IRC.)

Interrogators at Camp 020 relied upon a variety of psychological and other techniques to break prisoners. Under the "soft" approach, a prisoner would be treated with cocktail-party hospitality during which interrogators would reveal what they already knew about the agent and his mission and German intelligence in general. Occasionally German agents already "doubled" would appear and urge the new captive to tell what he knew. In the "hard" approach, the agent would be thrust into solitary confinement, his only contact with the outside being a guard who (for example) might casually comment: "This cell is empty because we shot the previous fellow last night. Have you been told when you are scheduled for the firing squad?" Unconfirmable stories abound about dummy firing squads and torture. According to MI5 historian Nigel West, some German prisoners suffered breakdowns and attempted suicide; only one, however, died in Camp 020—an elderly German who suffered a heart attack during an air raid.

CAMP PEARY

The CIA training facility on a narrow neck of land between the James and York rivers near Williamsburg, Virginia. A Seabee (navy construction battalion) training camp during World War II, Peary passed to CIA in the early 1950s. It then consisted of ramshackle wooden barracks and administrative buildings; by the 1960s red brick buildings gave it the appearance of a small New England college. In its early days, Peary was known as "Camp Swampy"—the terrain had much brackish water—and carried the official cryptonym ISOLATION. (CIA's Office of Training had the misconception that the location and purpose of the facility were deep secrets.) Agency people called Peary "The Farm."

There is no public access, so don't even try. But if you wish to see trainees at play, seek out Pierce's Pitt Bar-B-Que just off Highway 64 on a Friday night. (A full rack of ribs will run you around $12.)

CANARY TRAP

Making minor and innocuous changes in copies of documents which are circulated to multiple sources, as a means of identifying leakers.

CASE-DEATH

An intelligence operation that fails for no discernible reason. The immediate suspicion is a security breach.

CASE OFFICER

In CIA usage, the person in charge of agents who collect intelligence and perform other clandestine duties. He is the key figure in CIA's Clandestine Service—the "ultimate link between the giant bureaucracy in Washington and the information it wants to collect, and the actions it wants to see taken," as former case officer Joseph Burkholder Smith has written. Contrary to the field agent, the case officer has no direct contact with the opposition. He is responsible for keeping the operation on course, and supplying the agent with the necessary resources (monetary and otherwise) to carry it out.

Under ideal circumstances, the agent's only contact with the intelligence agency is through the case officer. Involving other persons dilutes the case officer's necessary authority and gives the agent a chance for second-guessing. A "horrible example" cited in CIA case studies was the Bay of Pigs. Although Richard Bissell, then the CIA deputy director, was primary case officer, the Cuban exiles with whom he worked—and whom he supposedly controlled—also had access to Adolf Berle, Jr., a State Department official, and Arthur M. Schlesinger, Jr., of the White House staff. This diffused authority was one of many weaknesses that caused the operation to fail.

CASSEROLE

Informer; a French intelligence term.

CATTLE GUARDS

Euphemism for the paramilitary soldiers of fortune hired for anti-terrorist operations by the government of South Africa. Ostensibly recruited to protect herds on outlying South African farms, the cattle guards in fact go as far north as Angola in quest of black "terrs" who with outside support are attempting to overthrow the government.

As of mid-1984, the pay was $600 to $900 per month, plus room and board and round trip air fare from Europe to Johannesburg.

CAUTERIZATION

Removing compromised agents to safety. CIA had to "cauterize" scores of agents, contract employees, and informants in Mexico, Ecuador, and Uruguay when turncoat officer Philip Agee of the agency's Western Hemisphere Division revealed their identities in his 1974 book, *Inside the Company: CIA Diary.* The process also involved terminating every operation of which Agee might have knowledge. Agee's mischief cost the United States government uncountable millions of dollars.

CEI

CIA term for an operational error that is a "career-ending incident."

CENTER, THE

KGB term for headquarters at 2 Dzerzhinsky Square in Moscow. Also called "Moscow Center."

CENTRAL INTELLIGENCE GROUP (CIG)

The first post-war attempt to create a single agency to coordinate all U.S. intelligence efforts. Pesident Truman established CIG by executive order on January 22, 1946, directing that "all Federal foreign intelligence activities be planned, developed and coordinated so as to assure the most effective accomplishment of the intelligence mission related to the national security." CIG would work under a National Intelligence Authority (created in the same order), to be composed of the secretaries of war, army, and navy, and his "personal representative," who turned out to be his Chief of Staff, Admiral William Leahy.

Truman's order was intended to quiet a vicious bureaucratic war over control of intelligence being waged between the military, the Justice Department (i.e., FBI), the State Department, and the Treasury Department. Intelligence had been left in limbo since the preceding September, when Truman peremptorily shut down the wartime Office of Strategic Services. OSS functions were scattered between the State Department and the military.

Unfortunately, the order was silent on whether CIG should actively collect intelligence on its own and conduct operations, or simply work with materials gathered by the existing departments. The activist view was pressed by those who felt that CIG should not simply be a "coordinating sewing circle" dependent on existing agencies. The issue remained unsolved until creation of the Central Intelligence Agency a year later, which was assigned both collection and analytical functions, plus the catch-all authorization that CIA shall perform "such other functions and duties related to intelligence affecting national security as the National Security Council may from time to time direct." [Section 102(d)(4) National Security Act of 1947].

For more than half a century, historians have referred to OSS having been the "wartime predecessor" to CIA. A case can surely be made for the broad accuracy of this statement, but the short-lived CIG is seldom mentioned. In fact, its structure—and many key officers—were transferred intact into CIA. The building it occupied, an old Navy medical facility on C Street Northwest in Foggy Bottom, became CIA's first headquarters.

CHAMFERING

A technique for opening sealed mail—essentially, a sophisticated version of a kitchen tea kettle but designed for mass usage. British intelligence taught the technique to six FBI agents just before the start of World War II to enable them to open Axis diplomatic mail entering and leaving the United States. Suspended right after the war, the program resumed under CIA sponsorship in the early 1950s. (*See* FLAPS AND SEALS.)

CHEKIST

Member of the *Cheka*, the Soviet secret police founded in 1918 by Felix Dzerzhinsky. The *Cheka* eventually evolved into the KGB, whose agents are still known to many Russians as Chekists (although not out loud).

CHENG PAO K'O

The Chinese counterespionage service used to watch Chinese abroad (both Chinese citizens and the so-called "overseas Chinese") and foreign agents. A separate service, the *Chi Pao K'o*, does internal security.

CHICKEN FEED

The "information" that doubled German agents were permitted to feed back to Berlin during World War II, under control of British intelligence. Chicken feed, while not necessarily inaccurate, was nonetheless inconsequential; it was intended to demonstrate that the German spies were obtaining authentic information. Chicken feed was a "mixture of truth, wherever possible," notes Ewen Montagu, a British disinformation officer, "and falsehood where the truth could not be told and where the falsity would not be detected or the detection, when it came, would not matter."

The British MI6 term for such misleading information during World War II was "foodstuff."

CHIEF OF OUTPOST (COO)

The CIA officer in charge of a field office that is subordinate to the CIA station in a country.

CHIEF OF STATION (COS)

The CIA officer in charge of the main Agency office in a foreign country—the "station," in popular usage. The station is usually located in the capital of the host nation, and generally has a presence in the American embassy. But other elements, particularly the covert side of the business, are likely to be housed elsewhere in discreet locations that are not always known to the host government.

CHURCH COMMITTEE

The Senate committee that investigated American intelligence during 1975–76. Formally, the Senate Select Committee to Study Governmental Operations with Respect to Intelligence Activities. The Senate created the committee on January 27, 1975; its final report was issued April 26, 1976. The chairman was Senator Frank Church, Democrat of Idaho, who was itching to be the Democratic nominee for president, and saw the hearings as a chance to reap favorable by publicizing perceived misdeeds of CIA and other elements of the intelligence community.

The impetus for the hearings was the decision by DCI William Colby to reveal to *The New York Times* many instances where CIA actions skirted close to illegality (and in fact crossed the line on several occasions). He ordered the in-house compilation of a paper that became known as "the family jewels," a term that suggested many persons in CIA felt the misdeeds should be private.

In any event, Church famously opened the proceedings by declaring that CIA was a "rogue elephant"—a judgment rendered before he heard a single witness. Another senator, Fred Harris (D., OK) declaimed, "We've got to dismantle this monster." In due course, Church and Harris were compelled to eat a copious serving of crow. As his committee's final report admitted, "All the evidence at hand suggests that the CIA, far from being out of control, has been utterly responsive to the instructions of the President and the Assistant to the President for National Security Affairs."

In his memoir (*A Look over My Shoulder*, 2003) former DCI Richard Helms commented, "The published hearings of the Senate and House committees weighed some twenty pounds. My impression was that these hundreds of thousands of words were more useful to the KGB and to some of our other adversaries than to the American taxpayer footing the bill."

Colby's disclosures, both to the *Times* and then in his committee testimony, caused a breach between him and Helms that lasted the remainder of their lives. Several times, I attended events where both men were present. They seemed to go out of their ways to avoid any possibility that they might have to speak to one another, or even acknowledge the other's presence.

CHUZHOI

Russian for "alien"; to Soviet intelligence, a person who was serving a Soviet agency for other than ideological or political reasons. "Usually the term is applied to those who are spies by profession, avocation, or for gain," David J. Dallin notes.

CI-NICKS

CIA term for counterintelligence officers of their own organization. Officers in the clandestine service often feel the ci-nicks (pronounced see-niks) gather much information that is never put to operational use.

CLANDESTINE OPERATION

An operation conducted in secrecy, but with no effort to disguise its nature. If a U.S. submarine surfaces off the coast of Iran at night and an agent paddles ashore on a rubber raft, the operation is concealed by natural circumstances, but it is exactly what it appears to be. A cruising patrol boat, or a fisherman, could chance upon the scene and destroy the necessary secrecy. Hence the hazardous nature of clandestine operations. (*See also* COVERT OPERATION.)

CLANDESTINE SERVICES

Commonly used name for the espionage arm of the CIA, first known as the Directorate of Planning, then as the Directorate of Operations; supplanted by the National Clandestine Service in the bureaucratic shuffling of the intel community following 9/11. (*See* NATIONAL CLANDESTINE SERVICE.)

CLASSIFIED INFORMATION PROCURES ACT (CIPA)

A law that permits evidence in criminal proceedings that might be classified to be heard in camera by a judge, who rules whether it can be used in open court. The legislation was intended to cope with trials in which defense lawyers used a tactic known as "gray mail" to dissuade prosecutors from taking national security cases to trial. In essence, they would threaten to use classified material as part of their defense. Under the act, a judge has the authority to review the subject material without a jury present and rule over whether it can be used.

CLASSIFICATION

A system whereby information pertaining to national security is categorized according to its sensitivity. The definitions have varied frequently over the years. As of this writing (September 2010) the most recent standards were spelled out in Executive order 13526, signed by President Barack Obama on December 29, 2009.

"TOP SECRET" shall be applied to information, the unauthorized disclosure of which reasonably could be expected to cause exceptionally grave damage to the national security that the original classification authority is able to identify or describe.

"SECRET" shall be applied to information, the unauthorized disclosure of which reasonably can be expected to cause serious damage to the national security that the original classification authority is able to identify or describe.

"**Confidential**" shall be applied to information, the unauthorized disclosure of which reasonably could be expected to cause damage to the national security that the original classification authority is able to identify of describe.

The Obama executive order splled out the categories of information that are subject to classification:

(A) Military plans, weapons systems, or operations;

(B) Foreign government information;

(C) Intelligence activities (including covert action), intelligence sources, or methods, or cryptology;

(D) Foreign relations or foreign activities of the United States, including confidential sources;

(E) Scientific, technological, or economic matters relating to the national security;

(F) United States government programs for safeguarding nuclear materials or facilities;

(G) Vulnerabilities or capabilities of systems, installations, infrastructures, projects, plans, or protection services relating to the national security, or

(H) The development, production, or use of weapons of mass destruction.

Crispin Black, a British expert on intelligence matters, wrote in the *London Mirror* in August 2010, "as in nature, where the most dangerous animals are brightly colored, the brighter the color the more secret the intelligence. The ones for the prime minister and the queen are bound in scarlet and gold." For US intelligence agencies, SECRET documents contain a yellow cover; TOP SECRET, Red.

New York Times columnist William Safire redefined "confidential" as "if this gets out, it's no big deal."

CLEAN

A piece of intelligence apparatus—an agent, a safe house, a letter-drop, or whatever—that has never been used operationally and hence is unknown to the adversary. An astute case officer keeps a stock of clean agents for emergency use; once one is needed, the reason is frequently so urgent there is no time to do the necessary recruiting and security clearance. Such an agent might be used only one time.

COBBLER

KGB term for an intelligence technician who entered false entry and exit stamps in a passport. The term came from the Soviet habit of calling false passports "shoes." Hence anyone who worked on the shoes was a cobbler.

COCKROACH ALLEY

The cluster of wooden "temporary" buildings on the Mall in Washington that housed CIA's first offices in the late 1940s. Buildings I, J, K, and L shuddered in the slightest breeze, and they smelled; officers walked cautiously over the rotting floors.

CODE NAMES

An alias adopted by an intelligence operative to conceal his or her identity.

COINTELPRO

FBI term for the bureau's "counterintelligence program" of the 1960s directed at anti-war and other radical groups, ranging from run-of-the-pulpit pacifists to black militants and white supremacy groups. COINTELPRO utilized a plethora of techniques, ranging from leaking a militant's criminal record to the press to writing spurious letters intended to wreck domestic lives.

Under COINTELPRO, which lasted from 1956 through 1971, techniques the FBI had developed for use against hostile foreign agents were adopted for use against perceived domestic threats to the established political and social order. The Church Committee called COINTELPRO "a sophisticated vigilante operation aimed squarely at preventing the exercise of First Amendment rights of speech and association, on the theory that preventing the growth of dangerous groups and the propagation of dangerous ideas would protect the national security and deter violence."

COLD APPROACH

An attempt to recruit a foreign national as a source without any prior indication that he might be receptive to such an offer. Risky, at the least; disastrous, at the most. A person who rejects a cold approach will report to his government, which will loudly protest the attempt to "bring your Soviet-American clash to our nation." (Also known as a "cold-pitch recruitment.")

COMINTERN AND COMINFORM

The Communist International (Comintern) was established by Lenin in March 1919 as a means of giving Moscow tight control of communist parties in other nations. As Lenin declared, "The founding of the...Communist International heralds the international republic of Soviets, the international victory of communism." Its existence meant that "the victory of the Proletarian revolution on a world scale is assured." Trotsky, Lenin's militaristic colleague, called the Comintern the "General Staff of the World Revolution."

American Communists were quick to affiliate with the Comintern. At a meeting in Chicago in September 1919, only a few months after the founding, two parties were formed: the Communist Labor Party, and the Communist Party of America. After bitter doctrinal fighting, they merged in 1929 into the Communist Party, USA (CPUSA).

Because the CPUSA regularly ran candidates for president of the United States, adherents tried to pass it off as "just a political party" that was part of the American democratic political process. Subservience to the USSR was denied as a matter of course, a disclaimer accepted as gospel by many persons on the American left for decades.

But persons joining the CPUSA were required to sign a loyalty oath which stated: "I pledge myself to rally the masses to defend the Soviet Union, the land of victorious socialism. I pledge myself to remain at all times a vigilant and firm defender of the Leninist line of the party, the only line that ensures the triumph of Soviet power in the United States.

Lenin correctly foresaw that the American party could pass itself off as simply another political group. He stated, "We must (a) In order to placate the deaf-mutes, proclaim the fictional separation of our [the Soviet] government...from the Comintern, declaring this agency to be an independent political group. The deaf-mutes will believe it. (b) Express a desire for the immediate resumption of diplomatic relations with capitalist countries on the basis of complete non-interference in her internal affairs. Again, the deaf-mutes will believe it."

Lenin continued, "They will even be delighted and fling open those doors through which the emissaries of the Comintern and Party Intelligence agencies will quickly infiltrate into the countries disguised as our diplomatic cultural and trade representatives."

At a Comintern Congress in 1920, delegates were instructed to support "armed insurrection" against non-communist governments in order to replace them with communist regimes.

In a directive sent to the American party soon after its founding, the Comintern made plain that Soviet espionage was a priority item: "We call the attention of the comrades to the necessity of creating illegal underground machinery side by side with the legally functioning apparatus." The goal was "the destruction of the bourgeois state machinery"—that is, democratically-elected governments.

During World War II, when Stalin temporarily allied the USSR with the West to fight Hitler, with much fanfare he ordered the Comintern dissolved, thus officially abandoning his years of advocacy of a "world revolution." Never truly dormant, it came to public life again in 1947 with a new name, the Communist Information Bureau.

Source note: I first read documents pertaining to Lenin's strategy for use of the Communist International while a student at the Army Intelligence School at Fort Holabird, Maryland, in 1956. To understate, the blinders came off my eyes, forever. Alas, the hundreds of pages of material on the subject that the army gave me then have long since gone walk-about. Fortunately, the same documents are covered in considerable detail in *Dupes: How America's Adversaries Have Manipulated Progressives for a Century*, by Dr. Paul Kengor, ISI Books, 2010. (*See* USEFUL IDIOTS.)

COMINFIL

An FBI acronym for a 1960s program to counter Communist infiltration of such organizations as the NAACP and the civil rights movement. The initial technique was to inform a leader of the group about the attempted infiltration and to name the Communist agent. Later, however, the FBI targeted both the Communist infiltrator *and* the organization for embarrassment. For instance, a friendly newsman would be given information about Communist infiltration in a civil rights march, with the express purpose being to discredit both the organizers of the march and the participants. SANE and the United Farm Workers were two early targets.

COMING IN DARK

A CIA officer who operates in a foreign country without the knowledge of the local chief of station. This breach of protocol is not a matter of rudeness, but as a means of giving the Chief of Station deniability in case the operations goes wrong. The chief can tell the host agency, truthfully, "I did not know what those &&Ŷ%$$ in Langley were thinking about when they did this stunt, but believe me, I knew nothing about it, and I shall make your displeasure known."

COMMUNICATIONS INTELLIGENCE (COMINT)

"Communications intelligence" in the United States falls under the purview of the National Security Agency (NSA). COMINT is formally defined as "technical and intelligence information derived from foreign communications by other than the intended recipient"; in other words, by intercepting electronic and other communications. (The language is from a National Security Council Intelligence Directive.)

In a monograph published in 2008*, NSA historians Robert J. Hanyok and David P. Mowry noted that since revelations of the World War II Ultra successes by the Allies (notably through F. W. Winterbotham's classic *The Ultra Secret*) "the public has been exposed to numerous arcane terms associated with the business of intercepting messages and the making of codes and ciphers. Unfortunately, from the early literature on the Ultra story through today, there still exists among many scholarly and popular writers the tendency to confuse or incorrectly mix these terms."

Thus Hanyok and Mowry compiled a glossary of terms involving sigint and coding that are commonly used in relating to effort to "read other persons' mail," which in essence is what the craft is

---

* *West Wind Clear: Cryptology and the Winds Message Controversy: A Documentary History, Center for Cryptologic History, NSA, 2008. Available free upon request to the NSA History Office.*

all about. This section, including terms relating to coding and the breaking thereof, is drawn heavily from their history, and I tip my hat in admiration of how they managed to put highly technical work into terms intelligible to the layman.

Signals Intelligence (or SIGINT) "is often used synonymously with COMINT. Signal intelligence, though, includes a broader range of omissions as targets. SIGINT includes the intercept, processing and reporting of intelligence derived from noncomunications signals such as radar and navigational beacons."

Electronic intelligence (ELINT) "was to develop so-called countermeasures to such signals, exemplified best by the use of the famous British 'window' or chaffs—strips of aluminum that reflected German radar signals and obscured their tracking of Allied bombing missions over Europe."

Cryptology. "The study of the making and breaking of codes and ciphers."

Cryptography. "The study of the making of codes and ciphers."

Code. "A method in which arbitrary, and often fixed, groups of letters, numbers, phrases or other symbols replace plaintext letters, words, numbers, or phrases for the purposes of concealment of brevity. To **encode** is to transform plaintext into a code form. To **decode** is to break the code back to its underlying plaintext. A variation of a code is known as an '**open code**' or **codeword**. This occurs when a seemingly innocuous or ordinary word, words, phrase or number is used in a message or transmission to convey certain information or initiate an action previously agreed upon by the sending and receiving entities. The true meaning of an open code or codeword, as opposed to its literal or accepted meaning or connotation is supposed to be denied to anyone else who might be listening other than the intended recipient.

"Before World War II, codes came in the form of pages, tables, or a book. On each page of the **codebook** or table, a plaintext word or phrase is aligned opposite its code unit or code group equivalent. Codebooks were arranged alphabetically or numerically in order of the plaintext, making it easier to encode a message. To facilitate decoding by the intended recipient, a second codebook was used that was arranged alphabetically or numerically by the code group. This procedure of using two separate books, known as a **two-part**

code, was intended to complicate the cryptanalytic recovery of the codebook, a process known as '**bookbreaking**.'

"A **cipher** is a method of concealing plaintext by transposing its letters or number or by substituting other letters or numbers according to a **key**. A **key** is a set of instructions, usually in the form of letters or numbers, which controls the sequence of the **encryption** of the text or the **decryption** of the cipher back to the original plaintext. A cipher that results from transposing text is known as a **transposition cipher**. A cipher resulting from substitution is known as a **substitution cipher**. Transforming plaintext into cipher is called **encryption** Breaking cipher back into plaintext is called **decryption**."

COMMO

CIA's Office of Communications. COMMO provides communications between CIA headquarters and its offices abroad, and "between headquarters and sensitive agents abroad with whom regular contact is impracticable or a threat to their security." Much of this traffic is now via satellite.

COMPANY

Common reference by CIA personnel to their employer. Insiders never use the article "the" when referring to CIA; they simply say the initials. Other euphemisms are "The Agency" or "Langley," the latter the suburban Virginia community in which the CIA's headquarters buildings are situated.

COMPROMISE

The detection of an agent, a safe house, or an intelligence technique by someone from the other side.

COMPUTERIZED TELEPHONE NUMBER FILE (CTNF)

An FBI file created in 1970 (and since discontinued) that included phone numbers of "black, New Left, and other ethnic extremists."

COMSEC

Acronym for "communications security," the method of protecting communications by providing the means of enciphering messages and by establishing the security of the equipment used to transmit them.

That nations—and intelligence services—now put the most routine of communiques into code has sound historical logic. During the Mexican Revolution, insurgent Francisco (Pancho) Villa happened to capture a federal troop train as he was driving north toward the key city of Juarez. But the five seized cars were not enough to transport his entire army. So Villa had a telegrapher tap out a signal to the federal commander in Juarez: "Engine broken down at Moctezuma. Send another engine and five cars." Villa signed the message in the name of the train commander he had captured. When the "relief train" arrived—and was promptly captured—Villa shot off another bogus message to Juarez stating that a large force of rebels was approaching from the south and asking instructions. The Juarez command ordered him to retreat posthaste. Villa did so, pausing periodically to telegraph cheering messages about the "federal escape." His captured train rolled into Juarez unmolested, and he seized the city virtually without a shot.

CONCEALMENT DEVICE

An item which could reasonably be found in a person's possessions and withstand a cursory examination while concealing material within (e. g., coded messages, secret writing materials, files, et cetera). The CD itself can be deposited in *the dead drop* or cache and to provide protection when the material is later retrieved. Examples of such devices would be a pack of indigenous cigarettes, an asprin tin, a pen, even a wad of chewing gum. CIA officers have been known to leave artificial "dead rats"—very realistic creations, including a rank odor—containing messages alongside roadways and in alleys with confidence that no one will disturb them.

CONFIDENTIAL SOURCES

A broad range of persons who supply an intelligence agency with information that is available to them because of their position. The FBI Manual of Instructions, the basic procedural guide for special agents, lists as examples "bankers, telephone company employees, and landlords." CIA's pool of confidential sources includes customs and immigration personnel at international airports. (At the Mexico City airport, for instance, travelers bound for Cuba are routinely photographed for the local CIA station.) Hotel personnel are also valued confidential sources for agencies, as are friendly newspaper writers and editors.

CONSENSUAL ELECTRONIC SURVEILLANCE

Bugging or wiretapping where one party to the conversation consents to the monitoring. The Supreme Court held in 1971 that this type of monitoring does not violate Fourth Amendment rights (*U.S. v. While, 401 US 745*). Nonetheless, Justice Department guidelines initiated in 1972 require that the attorney general or his designated deputy approve all consensual electronic surveillances conducted by the FBI.

CONTROL

Physical or psychological pressure exerted on an agent or group to ensure that the agent or group responds to the direction of an intelligence agency or service.

CONTROL SIGN

A deliberate error of spelling or text used by an agent in communicating with superiors by radio or in writing when he (the agent) has come under hostile intelligence control. (Also called "danger sign.") An example: The agent garbles a word in the text corresponding to the week of the month in which he is transmitting— the second week, the second word; the third week, the third word. Variations are endless.

CO-OPTEES

Soviet diplomatic personnel serving in a foreign embassy who were not KGB officers, but who did the KGB's bidding when ordered.

CORPORATIONS

KGB term for foreign Communist parties, members of which were called "corporants."

COUNTERESPIONAGE (CE)

One of the more frequently misunderstood terms in the espionage lexicon. The word "counter" suggests that CE is concerned solely with defending against enemy intelligence operations—finding agents and arresting or otherwise neutralizing them. "Quite to the contrary," notes intelligence veteran Christopher Felix, "CE is an offensive operation, a means of obtaining intelligence about the opposition by using—or, more usually, attempting to use—the opposition's operations. CE is a form of secret intelligence operation, but it is a form so esoteric, so complex and important, as to stand by itself."

For a CE operative, the ideal (although rarely achieved) situation would be to winnow his way into the heart of the opposition's ongoing espionage operations: to know what information is being sought, and how and from whom, and what is being found. Through diligence and patience, the CE operative could achieve a position of influence enabling him to control operations against his own country.

The highest form of espionage chess, CE is a blend of wits, intuition, and balance: to maintain his cover, the penetration agent must face the possibility of doing damage to his own agency to maintain credibility. It is not unkind, or inaccurate, to state that CE specialists tend toward paranoia; that the mental juggling required to keep track of double and triple agents, and who has been fed what information for what purpose, is perhaps the most demanding intellectual task of anyone in the business.

The story is told of a CE agent for a Western intelligence organization (not CIA) who reported he had been offered a deputy directorship of the opposition group he had penetrated. "Take it," his chief counseled. "Maybe I should," the CE agent replied, "for I think I've gone about as far as I can in my own organization." He spent the next hour convincing his own chief that he was only joking.

COUNTERGUERRILLA WARFARE

Operations and activities conducted by the armed forces, paramilitary forces, or non-military agencies of a government against guerrillas.

COUNTERINSURGENCY

Military, paramilitary, political, economic, psychological, and civic actions taken by a government to defeat subversive insurgency within a country.

COUNTERINTELLIGENCE

Those actions by an intelligence agency intended to protect its own security and to undermine hostile intelligence operations.

COUNTERINTELLIGENCE CORPS (CIC)

The longtime security police for the United States Army, reorganized in 1970 into the US Army Intelligence Command and subsequently into the Defense Investigative Service. Under either name, the group protects Army installations from intruders of a security nature (the military police worry about vandals; the CIC about spies). CIC is also responsible for security clearances for military personnel in sensitive assignments. Through the mid-1950s CIC did the bulk of counter-Soviet work in Western Europe, only to be supplanted by CIA. Officers from the fledgling CIA frequently infuriated CIC people by claiming affiliation with the army unit if they got into trouble. Support personnel (notably female secretaries) carried the loose cover of "DAC"—Department of the Army Civilian.

Whatever the bureaucratic label of the moment, to its veterans CIC retains a proud identity. A statute of its symbol, a Gold Sphinx, stood proudly in front of the headquarters building at the then-headquarters, Fort Holabird, on the western fringe of Baltimore. When in uniform, CIC persons for years wore no insignia of rank—only replicas of the Golden Sphinx on their lapels. This insignia has been replaced by a composite of the sun's rays, a rose, and a dagger, "symbolizing the search for information, trustworthiness, and danger," according to CIC veteran Bruce A. Trinque of Niantic, CT. The Fort Holabird training facility—formally, The US Army Intelligence School—is now at Fort Huachuca, Arizona. (*See* THE BIRD.)

COUNTERRECONNAISSANCE

Measures taken to prevent observation by a hostile foreign service of an area, place, or military force. At its lowest form, counterreconnaissance consists of putting signs outside sensitive government installations prohibiting photography. There is a yarn in intelligence circles, perhaps apochryphal, but probably not, of an innovative FBI agent who tired of tailing two KGB agents ("legals") on a days-long drive around nuclear installations in Tennessee. He "borrowed" a truck and rammed the side of their car when they parked for the night at a motel, damaging it so badly they had to return to Washington by bus, their mission scrubbed.

COUNTERSURVEILLANCE

The process of ensuring that an agent is not being surveilled when he sets out to keep an appointment with a contact. Soviet tradecraft calls for the agents to move about for at least two hours before the contact, changing from subways to cabs to foot, and traveling in no pre-set pattern. If he suspects he is being followed, he has a variety of options to shake himself free—for instance, darting into a busy department store that has many floors, many elevators, and many exits. If a meeting is especially sensitive, the agent might be trailed by colleagues who will watch for signs of a surveillance. Former CIA Soviet expert Harry Rositzke has called New York City "the best place in the world to slip a surveillance," what with its crowded streets, vast parks, and intricate subway system.

The subject of a surveillance operates at an advantage. Maintaining a round-the-clock watch requires at least twelve agents from the rival service—a manpower investment that is difficult to sustain.

Soviet practice in Washington was to "scatter" upward of two dozen known KGB and GRU operatives from the embassy on Tunlaw Road Northwest within minutes of one another. Some darted for Virginia, others for Maryland, still others drove aimlessly around the District of Columbia. The intention, obvious to FBI surveillance teams, is that one of the agents intended a meeting, and the dilution of the surveillance effort increases the chance for success. The "scatter" moves generally came at dusk, when heavy traffic hampered effective surveillance.

The Czech State Security Service (STB, by its Czech-language initials) had a much-admired (and copied) surveillance system. The unnamed mastermind who drew up the basic system had the Prague street system adjusted—one way streets—so that cars driven by

Western diplomats followed predictable routes to and from the center city from their residences or embassies. Czech agents routinely attached homing devices to diplomatic cars.

According to Josef Frolik, who defected to CIA from Czech intelligence, "Surveillance teams utilize all possible camouflage systems. Their vehicles have rotatable registration plates, the roofs of vehicles can change color by removing a plastic foil, luggage racks are installed on vehicles or taken off, vehicles can have Austrian, West German or Swiss tags; vehicles marked 'driver school' or 'rescue service' are used; other vehicles have easily removable markings indicating various enterprises and institutions.... Individuals conducting surveillance on foot are disguised as villagers, soldiers, mailmen, forestry workers. Every surveillance team has their clothing in one vehicle where the person... can change clothes, or put on his glasses, pick up a suitcase or other pieces of luggage. For a time, use was even made of a 'blind' person with a cane and a seeing-eye dog..."

COURIER

A messenger responsible for the secure physical transmission and delivery of documents and material. Even journalists are sometimes so foolish that they will agree to mail a letter abroad for someone who purports to be a friend. Such dupes are afforded the courtesy of being described as "unwitting couriers."

COUSINS

The term British and American intelligence officers use for one another. But to the Israelis, "cousins" has a sharply different meaning. When a Mossad agent refers to a cousin, he means an Arab, a reference to the common Semitic origin of the Israelis and the Arabs, both descended from the patriarch Abraham.

COVER

The role played by an intelligence officer to conceal his true purpose for living or traveling abroad. "The best cover is that which contains the least notional and the maximum possible legitimate material," maintains intelligence veteran Christopher Felix. An oft-cited example of nigh-perfect cover was that of Richard Sorge, the Soviet spy who lived in prewar Tokyo in the guise of a German journalist. (The only blank, and one not detected until Sorge's arrest, was his whereabouts the years he was training in Moscow.) Sorge's cover was so good that he managed to work in Tokyo for nine years, gathering reams of intelligence from the German embassy and elsewhere for transmission to Moscow.

Sorge's warning of the imminent German invasion of the USSR in 1941 was among many alerts ignored by Stalin, who scrawled an obscenity across his cable report and tossed it aside.

Poor radio security finally undid Sorge, who was hanged. (Sorge even managed to maintain his cover after a drunken escapade that ended with him crashing a motorcycle into the wall of the American Embassy. Although severely injured, and either in a coma or delirious for several days, Sorge said not a word inconsistent with his cover role.)

British businessman Greville Wynne, a counterintelligence officer during World War II, was given a vague instruction by an old intelligence friend in 1955 that it might be useful if he developed business contacts in Eastern Europe. From 1955 to 1960, Wynne did just that, establishing himself as a commercial traveler and salesman for a number of British industrial plants on trips to a number of Communist Bloc nations, including the USSR. Not until 1960 did Wynne come into direct contact with the agent-in-place he was to handle—Colonel Oleg Penkovsky, perhaps the most important spy ever to work for Western intelligence. Further, their first contact was at a meeting with Soviet trade officials, which Wynne arranged in the course of building contacts in the USSR; not until later was he informed that the entire operation had been tailored to bring him into seemingly casual contact with Penkovsky. Wynne's superb—and natural—cover lasted almost two years, until he and Penkovsky were arrested.

By reliable estimate, Soviet intelligence agents filled 60 to 70 percent of the "diplomatic" slots in USSR embassies in Washington, London, Paris, Tokyo, and Mexico City. New arrivals seldom kept their cover beyond a few weeks; they were "burned" by FBI surveillance and in-place informants in the Soviet Embassy. One story, perhaps apochryphal—but perhaps not—is of the FBI agent detailed to cover a minor American diplomat who had arranged a meeting with a KGB contact in a motel parking lot in suburban Virginia. Another agent reported by radio that the KGB man had been involved in a traffic accident en route, and could not possibly make the rendezvous. But despite the hour, and the cold, wet rain, the American diplomat showed no signs of leaving the parking lot. In shivery frustration, the FBI man finally rapped on his car window and announced, in a borscht-circuit Russian accent, "Boris no come, you go home, he call you maybe tomorrow." Several weeks later, the KGB man and the diplomat were caught in the espionage equivalent of *en flagrante;* the Russian was expelled, the American was permitted to resign. The surveilling agent filed a somewhat less than complete report on his penultimate surveillance and was subsequently promoted.

COVER BOY
British jocular term for an American felt to be concealing intelligence activities behind a cover job, governmental or otherwise.

COVER FOR STATUS
As defined by former CIA officer Joseph Burkholder Smith, "an activity that explains by some believable story, other than the truth, why a spy sees the people he does, is surrounded by the accoutrements he possesses, lives the way he does, and so forth…" Smith had such cover in Indonesia in the 1950s by posing as a representative of a New York firm that was to create a chain of bookstores. His concurrent "cover for action" was to actually run a bookstore that he could use to meet agents he recruited locally. The projects proved such a financial disaster that CIA dropped them in short order.

COVER NAMES
The pseudonym assigned an agent for security purposes. This name is used in general files, and the person's true identity is recorded only in a tightly secured central security registry. No particular rule is followed in choosing such names, but the British permit themselves occasional whimsy. An agent who worked with the famed Dusko Popov was of such girth that his control officer dubbed him "Balloon." Popov himself, a Lothario who enjoyed entertaining two women in bed at the same time, was titled "Tripod," for obvious reasons. A German agent doubled by the Twenty Committee operation (see p. 245) was code-named "Tate" because

of his resemblance to Harry Tate, a popular music-hall comedian of the era. Edward Chapman, safecracker-turned-spy, told so many conflicting stories when offering his services to MI5 (as a defecting Abwehr agent) that he was named "Zigzag."

Several CIA veterans have told me, over the years, that cover names used by the agency have been computer-generated for decades. British intelligence long used a different system, in what seems to this outsider to be sloppy tradecraft. MI6, for instance, found itself working in uneasy competition with the Special Operations Executive (SOE) during World War II. One clash was over code names. As the MI6 officer Sir Claude Dansey wrote in a memo, "....the Greek alphabet, names of motor cars, names of precious stones, big game, fruit and colours are reserved for S. I. S." The dangers of such cover-name symmetry seem obvious—but again, I speak as an outsider.

A persistent myth popular with spy novel writers from time to time has it that the Secret Intelligence Service selects cover names from outdated issues of the London phone book. T'ain't so, an MI6 retiree tells me.

Soviet tradecraft called for frequent changes of code-names assigned agents. To confuse Western counterintelligence agencies, male agents often were assigned female code-names and vice versa.

COVER ORGANIZATIONS

Organizations created solely to provide cover for a covert agent (unlike "organizational cover," where an existing, legitimate organization is so used). These organizations can range from the one-man law office of Peter Ward, the fictional agent of many E. Howard Hunt spy novels, to the Gibraltar Steamship Company, a major cover group for the Bay of Pigs invasion. (The Bay of Pigs, indeed, grew so vast that the Agency created a subsidiary of a car-rental agency in Florida so that it would not have to account for the movements of all the vehicles.) Cover organizations have imitated virtually every type of business and private group, from labor unions to newspapers and export-import companies. A main requirement is that the cover organization provide the agent or agents working for it with plausible reasons to travel and keep odd hours. (There can be embarrassments. A CIA officer worked in Mexico in the 1960s under cover provided by a major international cotton trading company. At a party one evening he encountered a German who, during casual conversation, remarked that he was in the "cotton business." The German, however, proved to know nothing about cotton. The CIA man made some quiet inquiries and discovered that the Germans had set up a minor intelligence shop in Mexico City under the guise of a cotton company.)

Cover organizations have a long history. During the American Revolution, the French wished to help the colonists fight the British, but not openly. So at the urging of Pierre Auguste Caron de Beaumarchais, a poet, playwright, and independently wealthy man, the government created a "private" trading firm, Hortalez and Company. Acting through Hortalez, the French government literally opened its doors and arsenals to the revolutionists; by one estimate, 90 percent of the arms used in the Battle of Saratoga came through the company. (Unfortunately, de Beaumarchais had to sue the government to be reimbursed for his out-of-pocket costs; not until 1835 did the U.S. Congress pay his heirs' last claims.)

An essential rule is that a cover organization have authentic enough underpinnings—say, an office, however so meager, and a listed telephone—that a few routine phone calls won't expose it as a myth. In 1960, two United States students, arrested in the USSR, claimed they were researchers traveling for an "educational fund" in Baltimore. A Baltimore newspaperman sought to locate the fund, with the anticipation that its officials would deny any involvement in espionage. Not a trace of the "fund" could be found. The students spent several months in jail before the Soviets turned them loose. They were, in fact, on a journey that involved low-level espionage.

COVER RULES

In selecting cover for its officers working in enemy territory, the Office of Strategic Services stressed what it termed "The Five Freedoms of Cover," to wit:

- Freedom of Action—What can he do?
- Freedom of Movement—Where can he go?
- Freedom of Leisure—How much time will he have for his "hobby"?

- Social Freedom—What kinds of people can he associate with?
- Financial Freedom—How much money can he spend?

As an OSS training manual stated, "Selection of cover for an agent must be based on two primary considerations: (a) the cover must be safe, and (b) it must provide opportunity for him to fulfill his assignment."

COVER STORY

A plausible explanation employed to explain an operation that goes awry. For instance, the U-2 spy plane shot down over Russia in 1959 was officially explained (at first) as a weather reconnaissance craft. A press release from the National Aeronautical and Space Administration (NASA) stated, "An NASA U-2 reseearch plane, being flown in Turkey on a joint NASA-USAF Air Weather Service mission, apparently went down in the Lake Van, Turkey area at about 9 A.M. (5 P. M. E. D,T.), Sunday, May 1."

The bitter lesson of the U-2 is that the cover story had best not be told until an agency knows exactly what counterinformation is held by the other side. The Russians held not only the wreckage of the U-2, with cameras intact, but also the live pilot, Gary Powers.

COVERT OPERATION

An operation using a cover story to conceal the real purpose of the agent's mission. If the CIA sneaks an agent into Iran under the guise of being a businessman, and he steals away for a few hours to do his business, he is operating covertly. In contrast to a "clandestine" operation, no effort is made to shield a covert operation from view; the agent relies upon his wits to avoid detection. (As summarized by Christopher Felix, longtime intelligence officer, "In brief, the working distinction between the two forms of secrecy (i.e., clandestine and covert) is that a clandestine operation is hidden, but not disguised, and a covert operation is disguised, but not hidden."

Joseph Burkholder Smith, longtime CIA officer turned historian after retirement, cites President James Madison's attempt to wrest Florida away from Spain in 1811 as the United States' first covert action. The same techniques were used time and again in Latin America: "The common pattern it established, from which the others were cut, consisted of a preliminary propaganda phase—working up excitement in and about the target—then the organizing of a 'patriot government' opposed to the group we wished to get rid of, then an armed attack by the 'patriots' on the nearest legitimate authority over which the targeted group held sway, then an appeal to the United States government to assume control and restore 'order,' a call which the United States...usually answered."

Historically the United States government has found ways to conceal funding for intelligence and other covert activities. In the Florida operation, for instance, President Madison had Congress appropriate $2 million "to defray any expenses which may be incurred in relation to the intercourse between the United States and foreign nations." Even this euphemistic language was hidden in a secret Presidential message to Congress. The money was intended as a bribe to Napoleon of France to pressure Spain to cede the desired territory. Representative John Randolph of Virginia challenged the President and his men for having Congress "do all the dirty work which would otherwise have soiled their fingers." Randolph failed; Madison got his covert funds. The plan failed, however, when Napoleon refused cooperation.

CREDIT CARD REVOLUTIONARIES

Sarcastic FBI term for the middle- and upper-income persons who gave support to anti-war and leftist groups during the late 1960s and early 1970s. (Actress-activist Jane Fonda, for instance, gave an American Express card to an organizer for Vietnam Veterans Against the War to finance his cross-country travels.)

CRYPTOMATERIAL

All material—including documents, devices, equipment, and apparatus—essential to the encryption, decryption, or authentication of telecommunications.

CRYPTONYM

A false name assigned to a covert agent; also, a cover name for a secret operation. During an operation, an agent is never referred to by his true identity, even in the supposed privacy of a headquarters office. One reason is the ever-present fear of electronic surveillance; another is to accustom case officers to speak of the person by his cover name, so that its use becomes second-nature. For further security, the cryptonym is changed frequently as an operation progresses.

For administrative convenience, CIA cryptonyms—operational code names—use a two-letter digraph at the beginning of the word. The digraph can designate either a geographic location or a general subject matter. During the Korean War, the letters TP indicated activities directed against Communist China. (For example, TP-STOLE was the cover name of an operation involving the hijacking of a Scandinavian freighter carrying medical supplies to the enemy.) During the 1960s, MH indicated matters relating to internal U.S. security. Hence MH-CHAOS came to denote activities directed at anti-war protesters.

There are instances where intelligence officers select names on impulse. For instance, when cipher clerk Igor Gouzenko defected from the Soviet embassy in Ottawa in 1945, his handlers referred to the "Corby case"—apparently because of the brand of Canadian whiskey favored by the officers.

CRIME RECORDS DIVISION

The FBI's euphemistically titled public relations arm. The division, in the headquarters division in Washington, is responsible for high-level media contacts. One of the more tightly guarded items in the crime records division was the list of reporters considered to be "friendly media," who wrote pro-FBI stories. At the field office (i.e., local) level, the FBI relied upon what it called "confidential sources"—press friends—both to pass along information to which they were privy as reporters, and to write about the bureau in a friendly fashion.

CRYPTANALYSIS

The breaking of codes and ciphers into plain text without initial knowledge of the key used in the encryption.

CRYPTOGRAPHY

The enciphering of plain text so that it will be unintelligible to an unauthorized recipient.

CRYPTOLOGY

The science that embraces cryptoanalysis and cryptography, and includes communications intelligence and communications security.

CRYPTOSECURITY

That component of communications security that results from the provision of technically sound cryptosystems and their proper use.

CRYPTOSYSTEMS

The associated items of cryptomaterial that are used as a unit and provide a single means of encryption and decryption.

CULTIVATION

The process of establishing rapport with a possible source of information or a potential defector. Cultivation commences with a show of friendship and a tangible offer—say, a dinner or even an all-expenses-paid or discount trip to the foreign country. Soviet "diplomats" in Washington constantly offered such bait to Americans whom they considered of potential value. During the 1960s journalists in Washington who covered national security affairs learned to report "cultivation approaches," such as dinner invitations, to the FBI's Washington field office. A phone call would save them the bother of having an FBI agent come to ask, "What did Soviet Counsellor Ivanov talk about at his house when you and your wife were there for dinner the other night?"

CUSTODIAL DETENTION LIST

In the words of FBI Director J. Edgar Hoover in 1940, "a suspect list of individuals whose arrest might be considered necessary in the event the United States becomes involved in war." Hoover had American citizens in mind, as well as aliens. Hoover's list was never used. When Attorney General Francis Biddle ordered it destroyed in 1943 (claiming the concept was "impractical, unwise and dangerous"), Hoover simply changed the title to "Security Index" and his agents kept adding names to it. The existence of the renamed list, understandably, was a closely guarded secret within the Bureau.

Later, the file was known variously as the "Reserve Index" and the "Communist Index." The latter designation indicated the shift in emphasis from coverage of Nazis to Communists. But persons the FBI considered to be active Soviet espionage agents were not listed for fear of security leaks. By 1951, more than 15,000 persons—the bulk of them members of the Communist Party (U.S.A.), plus a handful of Puerto Rican nationalists—were on Hoover's list as prospects for detention in the event of national emergency.

CUSTOMERS

The various government departments that use information and analyses produced by intelligence agencies.

CUT-OUT

The go-between, or link, between separate components of an intelligence organization—for instance, the person who maintains contact with a clandestine agent on behalf of the handler controlling him. The existence of the cut-out makes it unnecessary for the clandestine agent to know the exact identity of persons superior to him in the organization. There are two basic types of cut-out systems:

- In the *block* cut-out, the contact knows the name of each agent working in an individual operation or cell;
- In the *chain* cut-out, the contact knows only one agent; any others are recruited sequentially, with agents knowing only the persons directly above and below him.

The cut-out permits oral contact when direct physical contact or a written communication would be dangerous. The cut-out also enables the case officer's true identity to be concealed from the agent, thereby lessening the danger of exposure. If the KGB arrested an agent working in East Germany, for instance, all he knew is that he received money and instructions from a man named "John" who was speaking on behalf of an unknown person named "Carl." Often the agent is not even certain which intelligence agency employed him (other than that it is Western or Soviet Bloc).

D

D-NOTICE, DEFENSE-NOTICE

A British system for "voluntary"—but enforceable—censorship of the press. The Defense-Notice is a formal letter circulated confidentially to mass media editors warning that certain information should remain secret. The information is usually material protected by Britain's Official Secrets Act and which is in danger of disclosure. The D-Notice is issued by authority of something called the "Services, Press and Broadcasting Committee," composed of four government and eleven press representatives. A D-Notice normally originates with a government agency such as MI5 or MI6 that fears one of its secrets is about to be published. It is circulated to committee members and then issued under the name of the secretary, a permanent civil servant. In emergencies, the secretary can issue a D-Notice on his own authority. The secretary is also available to offer "guidance" at all hours on whether particular information should be published. A D-Notice can remain in effect for a specified period of time or indefinitely.

The D-Notice itself is considered a confidential document. But some examples have leaked over the years. In 1967, the *Spectator* published two D-Notices dating to the 1950s. One asked the media to make no references to "secret intelligence or counter-intelligence methods and activities in or outside the United Kingdom." Included were any references whatsoever to the identity or numbers of intelligence personnel or the organizations they served or their bases, recruiting, or training. Another D-Notice—a "standing request"—asked newspapers to make no reference to "cyphering work carried out in Government communications establishments...[or] to the fact that on occasions it is necessary in the interest of defense for the services to intercept such communications."

British intelligence has also used D-Notices to prevent trade embarrassment. When George Blake went on trial as a Soviet spy in 1961, a D-Notice asked that editors not reveal he had worked for MI6 as well as the GRU.

DAJNAVNA SIGURNOST (DS)

Bulgarian secret police who were directly controlled by the KGB. The subservient *DS* drew such high-risk assignments as the attempted assassination of Pope John Paul II. *DS* was headquartered at 30 General Gurko Street, Sofia.

DAMAGE CONTROL

The means by which an intelligence organization attempts to minimize the harmful results of an operation that aborts. The agency must learn as rapidly—and accurately—as possible exactly what agents and facilities might have been compromised to the other side, and thus lost.

One index of an agent's toughness is his ability to pass back to his control the exact information he has given under interrogation. Heinz Felfe, acting head of the Gehlen Organization's counterintelligence department, was arrested in 1961 and convicted of being a Soviet double agent for at least a decade. Since most of his work for Gehlen had dealt with Soviet affairs, both sides had a keen interest in knowing (a) what he had done and (b) what he had told. Felfe said little under interrogation. While in Karlsruhe, the West German prison for top-security prisoners, he managed to send to the Soviets a precis of his "confession"—what his interrogators had asked, and how he had responded. (Questions often indicate the amount of independent information an intelligence agency has concerning a suspect and his ring.) Felfe smuggled his reports from prison via bales of the German popular magazines *Freundin* (The Girl Friend) and *Film Revue,* which were addressed to subscribers by prisoners under contract. Other messages went to his mother in East Germany in secret ink writing.

The mischief—a weak word; call it *disaster*—of a traitor was illustrated during the 1960s espionage trial of Hans Clemens, a turncoat counterintelligence official in the Gehlen Organization. The judge asked Clemens, "Did you tell the Russians where the *BnD* [the West German intelligence organization] has its espionage schools?"

Clemens smiled broadly and replied, "You mean *had* their espionage schools."

The judge, unmoved by the levity, stated during sentencing, "Codes had to be altered, agents exchanged, old and tried contacts severed, live- and dead-letter boxes abandoned, couriers and courier routes altered. Much of eleven years of development work had to be scrapped."

DAME

Acronym for a course entitled "Defense Against Methods of Entry," taught at the Army Intelligence School, Fort Holabird, Maryland, during the 1950s. Of the three-week course, two weeks and four-and-one-half days were devoted to teaching fledgling agents how to pick locks and break into safes. As a sort of afterthought, the last afternoon of the three weeks concerned defense methods against lockpickers. Persons who completed the course were never concerned about losing their car or locker keys—each was given a set of sophisticated picks upon graduation. (*See also* LOCK STUDIES.)

DANCER

A detainee—circa the Iraq/Afghanistan war period—who during interogation veers between periods of cooperation and resistance. It is a form of passive resistance designed to slow the pace of an interrogation. By being overly resistant, the detainee thus skates around some of the unpleasant techniques interrogators were known to use in detention facilities.

DANGER SIGN

See CONTROL SIGN.

DANGLE

A person who approaches an intelligence agency in such a manner that he is asking to be recruited as an agent to spy against his own country.

Harry Rositzke, long a Soviet specialist for CIA, has written, "The worst mistake any service can make is to recruit as an agent a man who has been 'dangled' before it by a hostile service. The basic rule of thumb in the business of recruiting is to suspect anyone who takes the initiative in making contact with an intelligence officer."

A KGB manual warned its U.S.-based operatives against FBI attempts to dangle supposed recruits. It notes that "the person being dangled either attempts to interest us in his intelligence potential or he takes the initiative and offers to pass us certain secret materials."

Such dangles "display a disproportionate interest in money..." KGB also cautioned against "persons with liberal views who have contacts with Soviet installations."

Edward Jay Epstein, one of the more intelligent non-fiction writers on espionage and intelligence, describes a dangle as "someone who, while loyally taking orders from his own intelligence service, feigns disloyalty to his country to attract the attention of the other side, like the bait on a fish hook."

DASE

Acronym for a course entitled "Defense Against Sound Equipment," taught at the Army Intelligence School during the 1950s. As was true of the DAME course at the same school (see above), most of the instruction involved methods of bugging rooms and tapping phones, with defensive techniques taught in by-the-way fashion. Some of the techniques taught at Holabird in 1956 were revealed as "dazzling new technology" during Senate investigations of private investigators of the 1960s. One rule of thumb in bugging is that any method discussed in the press is already outdated.

DEAD DROP BOX, DEAD-LETTER DROP

A location where a message can be concealed by an agent for retrieval by another party.

The system devised for Colonel Oleg Penkovsky seemed superfluously elaborate. He would first paint a black mark on a certain street post, then put his communication in the designated hiding place (one used was a space behind a radiator in a lobby between a butcher shop and a shoe store); next, telephone two Moscow numbers and, when a person answered, hang up. A former intelligence officer says, to the contrary, the phone calls were necessary: Penkovsky might be detected painting the spot on the post, and depositing the letter. The phone calls were the extra security, for without them no British intelligence agent would pick up the dead drop letter. (*See* DUBOK, LETTER-DROP.)

DCI

Director of central intelligence. The officer who commands the CIA and other components of the intelligence community. A frequent media error is to refer to this person as the "CIA director," a title that does not exist, and one that ignores a good deal of his job. In any event, creation of the post of "director of national intelligence" after 9/11 mean a substantial loss of oversight authority. (*See* DNI.)

DECEPTION

According to an essay on analytical tradecraft by CIA officer Jack Davis, who spent four decades in intelligence work, "Deception can be defined as the manipulation of information by a foreign government, group, or individual to get U.S. intelligence analysts to reach an erroneous conclusion. Deception often works because it gives busy analysts what they are seeking—seemingly reliable information on which to base a conclusion."

Davis wrote that deception operations can be divided into two closely related subjects: "(a) Denial—measures taken to protect secrets through concealment, camouflage, and other activities that degrade collection systems, including the information analysts receive from open sources, diplomatic channels, clandestine assets, and technical collection; and (b) Disinformation—operations to feed analysts false or partly false information through the use of double agents and manipulation of diplomatic and media as well as intelligence channels."

In a 1957 Special National Intelligence Estimate (SNIE 100-2-57 that originally bore a TOP SECRET classification, the CIA wrote, "The capability of Communist governments for undertaking operations of deception is greater than that of most other governments because (a) they exert a higher degree of control over the information respecting their countries which becomes available to the outside world, and (b) they need not refrain from deception because of concern that their own general public may be puzzled or misled by operations primarily intended to deceive foreigners.

A more succinct definition, "Luring your opponent into doing voluntarily and by choice what you want him to do," is offered by Christopher Felix, penname for veteran intelligence operative James McCargar. The most historically significant example was the "bodyguard of lies" (Churchill's phrase) the Allies posted around the Normandy invasion of June 1944—first, to convince the Germans that the landing would take place elsewhere; second, that the first landing was a diversion, and that the main strike would come days later, to the north.

As summarized by Sun Tzu, the legendary Chinese military thinker, "All warfare is based on deception. Hence, when able to attack, we must seem unable when using our forces, we must seem inactive; when we are near, we must make the enemy believe we are far away; when far away, we must make him believe we are near." (*See* ELECTRONIC DECEPTION.)

DECLARED OFFICER

An intelligence officer, most often from CIA, who operates under embassy cover, but whose true status is made known to the host government.

DECRYPT

To convert encrypted text into plain text by use of a cryptosystem.

DEE-SID

See DIRECTOR OF CENTRAL INTELLIGENCE DIRECTIVE.

DEFECTOR

A person who, for political or other reasons, has repudiated his country and who may be in possession of information of interest to an enemy government.

Handling of a potential defector is one of the more demanding tasks of intelligence. Agents must first establish that the defector is not a "plant" sent over by the rival service. Then an attempt must be made to persuade the defector to "stay in place"—that is, keep his old job in his country—and pass along current information, with the promise of being given asylum in due course. Given the psychic traumas of defection, convincing a person to stay in his country as an active spy is a strong challenge. It can work: The CIA convinced Soviet Colonel Oleg Penkovsky, for instance, to continue working in a high military position for almost two years after he announced his willingness to defect. More often than not, the defector refuses and demands asylum.

Neither the United States nor any other Western country

automatically "opens the door" to a volunteer defector. Expense is one factor, for defectors must be subjected to lengthy debriefing, and then be "relocated" under a new name and given a living subsidy for a period of several years. A former CIA official who worked in three Western European stations states, "If you've already spent hundreds of thousands of dollars—and years of man-hours—on a guy who walked in from the Soviet air ministry, what do you say when a guy from the desk next to his shows up? Is he worth the investment?" Rank is one determinant. Any Soviet or bloc military figure of the rank of colonel or above apparently was accepted without question; majors and captains would be required to produce evidence they could be of intelligence value. A KGB or GRU agent of any level was given sanctuary (although they could expect prolonged isolation and interrogation under drugs, as a necessary means of establishing their bona fides).

The Soviets routinely covered up high-level defections by putting out stories to the effect that "Colonel General X" died in a plane crash, rather than admit he fled to the United States or Great Britain. British intelligence and CIA produced no less than twenty "dead Russian officers" in the flesh in 1961 to convince Colonel Oleg Penkovsky that many of his trusted past colleagues had cast their lot with the West and had survived and flourished. Western intelligence publicized only a minute fraction of the defectors who come across in any given year, thus the KGB was seldom *absolutely* certain of the whereabouts of an officer who disappeared.

If the West decided to "surface" a defector and publicize the fact he had "come over," and hint at the value of the information he carried, the Soviets responded with character assassination. Their press depicts the defector as a man who stole money, abused his family, had psychological problems, or whatnot. The author unwittingly accepted such "disinformation" as truth in writing about an Eastern Bloc military defector in the 1960s. An Eastern European diplomat gave me such a deliciously salacious—and convincing— account of the "real reason" the man defected that I published it. CIA friends quickly told me I had been hoodwinked. I saw the maligned man at a social function years later, but did not have the nerve to apologize. I was told he dismissed the story as "a tribute to my virility which I truly do not deserve."

DEFENSE INTELLIGENCE AGENCY (DIA)

The Department of Defense agency responsible for producing military intelligence for the four services. Secretary of Defense Robert S. McNamara created DIA in 1961 in an attempt to produce a coordinated intelligence effort by the services, rather than the bifurcated reports and estimates he saw during his first months in the Pentagon. DIA worked better than most intelligence professionals expected; it now has a budget and a bureaucracy (partly civilian) rivaling that of CIA.

DEFENSE INTELLIGENCE OBJECTIVES AND PRIORITIES (DIOP)

A single statement of intelligence requirements compiled by DIA for use by all Department of Defense intelligence activities. The DIOP in effect, is the "master shopping list" for American military intelligence. Because it tells what the Pentagon *needs*, rather than *knows*, a DIOP is a closely held document.

DEMORALIZATION

A means by which KGB salvaged some good from a failed operation. As defined by former American intelligence officer Edward Van Der Rhoer, "When an operation has outlived its usefulness or has finally been exposed, the KGB seeks to terminate it in such a way that maximum demoralization occurs on the other side, with accompanying loss of confidence of people in their government. If citizens at large believe that their government is infiltrated at many levels, if they find their leaders incompetent or venal, national stability is bound to be adversely affected." Van Der Rhoer cited as an example the Soviet gloating over the disclosure that a key aide to Chancellor Willy Brandt of West Germany was an agent of East German intelligence, a KGB surrogate. The loss of the agent was a blow to KGB—but in retribution, it so shattered public confidence in Brandt that he was forced out of office in 1974. A continuing demoralization campaign concerned the Philby-Burgess-Maclean spy ring, which seemed to reappear in the British press every two years with cyclic regularity.

DENIABILITY

The deliberate use of euphemisms that gives the President of the United States (or another high official) grounds for denying knowledge of covert activities discussed at a meeting that he attended. (I use the United States because the Soviet leadership, with its controlled press, did not have to bother with explanations of *any* of its activities because the public knows nothing other than what it is told.) During 1960, for instance, President Eisenhower spoke so strongly about Patrice Lumumba, an erratic Congolese rebel, that Robert Johnson of the National Security Council staff heard his words as "an order for [Lumumba's] assassination." But when he wrote of the meeting, he carefully excised any mention of Eisenhower's statement. Larry Devlin, CIA chief of station in The Congo, refused to carry out a White House order to kill Patrice Lumumba, who was murdered later by rivals acting independent of CIA.

Given the veiled language employed when persons have "deniability" in mind, William Colby, the former director of central intelligence, has written that matters can easily go beyond desired bounds: "... [In] the macho atmosphere of secret operations, a substratum of the violently inclined will always tend to discount normal moral restraints or exceed their original instructions in the heat of action, and any encouragement from above can launch them into horrendous behavior, and once launched, they are difficult to recall or control."

In discussing "deniability," intelligence officers hark back to Henry II's query about Thomas Becket: "Who will free me from this turbulent priest?" The cleric shortly thereafter was killed in Canterbury Cathedral. But: did the king actually *order* the murder? Or did his courtiers put their own interpretation on his outburst?

Actually, "deniability" in certain circumstances is permitted under United States law. In 1948, the National Security Council, with the approval of President Truman, through NSC Directive 10/102, created the Office of Policy Coordination (OPC) as CIA's covert action arm. OPC was authorized to practice "economic warfare, preventative direct actions including sabotage, anti-sabotage, demolition, and evacuation measures," as well as "subversion against hostile states." NSC 10/102 further directed that these covert activities be "so planned and executed that any U.S. Government responsibility for them is not evident.... and that if uncovered the U.S. Government can plausibly deny any responsibility for them."

DENIED AREA

A country with such strict internal security that foreign intelligence agents dare not contact informants in person. By CIA definition, this included the Soviet Union, Cuba, and (to a lessening degree) the People's Republic of China. In a denied area, agents rely upon dead drops and clandestine radios to maintain contact and to pass information.

DEPARTMENTAL INTELLIGENCE

The intelligence that U.S. government departments and agencies generate in support of their own activities. Such intelligence is not routinely shared. For instance, the FBI might run across information of value to the Drug Enforcement Administration. Rather than forward it in comradely fashion (both agencies *do* work for the same government), the FBI would be apt to barter and elicit information of equal value from DEA.

DESTABILIZATION

The process of undermining, to the point of collapse, a foreign government through overt political and economic actions. Although the term is said to be of CIA origin, as descriptive of the efforts to overthrow President Salvador Allende of Chile in the early 1970s, former CIA officer David Atlee Phillips attributes its first use—and subsequent introduction into the American political lexicon—to Representative Michael Harrington, a Massachusetts Democrat and a vocal critic of the agency. Harry Shlaudeman, formerly number-two man in the embassy in Chile, had been questioned by Harrington during Congressional hearings in April 1974. Shlaudeman then telephoned Phillips, CIA's chief of Latin American operations, and asked him: "He [Harrington] kept asking me about the 'destabilization' of the Allende regime. Have you people given Congress anything to indicate that 'destabilizing' was the plan?" Phillips assured Shlaudeman he had never heard of the word. Proceedings of the hearings (before the Latin American subcommittee of the House Foreign Affairs Committee) show that Harrington used the word "destabilization" three times before attributing it to William Colby, the director of central intelligence. Despite this history, "There is nothing that will change the current usage of 'destabilization,'" Phillips recognized in his memoir.

DETERRENT TAIL

Watchers who deliberately let their quarry know they are being followed to scare them out of achieving their purpose.

DEVELOP

To cultivate a sympathizer into becoming an active espionage agent, generally on ideological grounds.

D.G.S.E.

See S.D.E.C.E.

DIRECCION GENERAL DE LA INTELIGENCIA (DGI)

Cuba's intelligence service, originally organized and directed by Eastern European Bloc services, particularly the East Germans. DGI did surrogate work for the Soviet KGB throughout the world. Its United States outpost was run through the Cuban Mission to the United Nations in New York with a strong substation based in the Cuban Interests Section of the Czech embassy in Washington. As was true of other Communist Bloc nations, DGI was slavishly subservient to KGB.

DNI

Director of National Intelligence, a position created in the post-9/11 period when the White House and Congress decided a new cabinet-level office was needed to oversee both the CIA but the entire U.S. intelligence community. Many critics felt the position—and the bureaucracy created to support it—added a needless lawyer of oversight, given that the DCI had long been tasked with the same responsibility for oversight.

DIRECTOR OF CENTRAL INTELLIGENCE DIRECTIVE (DCID, or DEE-SID)

A directive issued by the director of central intelligence that outlines general policies and procedures to be followed by intelligence agencies under his direction. A dee-sid is generally more specific than a National Security Council Intelligence Directive ("nee-sid").

DIRECTORATE "S"
The KGB wing that was responsible for directing the work of "illegals" abroad.

DIRTY TRICKS, CZECH STYLE
In 1962 a West German tank regiment arrived in Wales, Great Britain, for training in NATO exercises. Alarmed at the growing military cooperation between West Germany and the United Kingdom, the KGB, through its Czech subsidiary, decided to create the public impression that the German soldiers were anti-Semitic Nazis. The Czech agent stationed in Wales received orders to paint swastikas on Jewish graves and vandalize Jewish graveyards. The British press accused the Germans of responsibility for these ghoulish acts.

DISCARD
An agent betrayed by his own service in order to protect another, more valuable, source of information.

DISINFORMATION (*dezinformatsiya*)
A KGB term denoting a variety of techniques and activities to purvey false or misleading information, including rumors, insinuation, and altered facts. CIA cited numerous case histories in a 1982 report on Soviet active measures, ranging from the spread of a rumor that the United States was behind the seizure of the Grand Mosque in Mecca in the late 1970s, to forged "top secret" documents showing that the United States intended to use nuclear weapons against the territory of its NATO allies. Disinformation was a key element of Soviet "active measures."

DISPATCHED AGENT
An operative who seeks out a rival intelligence agency and claims he wishes to defect, when in actuality he is attempting a penetration. If the operative arouses suspicions, he is subjected to intense

and prolonged interrogation. One such suspect was Yuri Nosenko, a former KGB officer who in 1964 appeared at a CIA office abroad with a claim that he had "handled" Lee Harvey Oswald when the Presidential assassin resided in the Soviet Union. Although Oswald himself, at the U.S. embassy in Moscow, confessed having told the Soviets everything classified he had learned during his years in the Marine Corps, Nosenko insisted that Oswald in fact had not even been interrogated. The CIA counterintelligence section refused to believe such an unlikely claim, and so from April 1964 to December 1968 Nosenko was held in solitary confinement and subjected to devious psychological pressures. CIA finally concluded that he was a bona fide defector.

Nosenko was eventually given a new identity and a position as a CIA "consultant." Many persons within the Agency continue to entertain doubts about his authenticity, asserting the KGB "sent him over" to persuade the U.S. government that the Soviet Union had no role in the Kennedy murder.

DISPOSAL

CIA term for the dismissal of a non-career agent, usually a non-American who has worked for American intelligence for diverse reasons. Intelligence veteran James MacCargar thought the term "unnecessarily macabre." Disposal can be done either directly—the case officer or the cut-out tells the agent his services are no longer required; or indirectly—the case officer simply breaks off contact without saying a word; or maliciously—the case officer uses Agency facilities to tarnish the reputation of the ousted agent or arranges for his arrest on either real or contrived charges. No firm rules govern disposals, for each agent is different. (*See* TERMINATE WITH EXTREME PREJUDICE, EXECUTIVE ACTION.)

DISSEMINATION

The distribution of information or intelligence products in written, oral, or graphic form to departmental and agency intelligence consumers. The extent of distribution depends upon the sensitivity of the material involved. Much U.S. intelligence bears the admonition "NOFODIS," for "no foreign distribution."

DOCTOR

KGB term for the police. If an agent suffers an "illness" (i.e., he is arrested), he goes to the "hospital" (jail).

DOORKNOCKER

An agent assigned to do personnel security interviews, to ascertain whether persons needing a security clearance have no nefarious activities in their past. The process begins when the person in question completes a background information form listing such essentials as date and place of birth, parents, educational background, employment history, and (this is where things get tricky) professional and personal references.

Each of these items must be verified by an investigator either from the military intelligence services (if the subject is under arms), the Civil Service Commission (if the subject desires to be a bureaucrat), or the FBI (if the subject wishes to work for the Bureau or in an industrial installation that requires security clearances for employees).

A doorknocker is the foot soldier of the security system and behaves and is treated as such. He often has no information other than the bare notation that the subject lived at such-and-such address for two months, fifteen years earlier, when his father worked for a pipeline company. The impulse is to jot "NV"—"not verifiable"—on the form and go have a beer, but superior powers sprinkle the day's work load with "setups"—tests to ensure that the doorknocker is doing what he should.

Doorknockers must endure such other indignities as amorous housewives (who are happy to have a stranger come around unannounced at mid-morning), dogs that bite, people who hate the government and anyone associated with it, and old ladies with cookies and milk and boundless conversation. Whatever the indignity, the doorknocker must elicit a yes or no answer to the key question: "Do you recommend [name of subject] for a position of trust and responsibility with the United States government?"

DOUBLE AGENT

A person who goes to work for one secret service and then changes his allegiance to a rival; he purports to serve both his conflicting masters. Given enough money, he might do just that. The double agent is sometimes confused with the "mole" or "penetration agent," a person whose loyalty lies with the rival power but who joins another cause for duty purposes.

Intelligence archives include a self-definition of "double agent" by a person who served as such: Colonel Stig Wennerstrom of the Swedish air force, who over a twenty-year period worked for Nazi Germany, the USSR, and the United States. In Wennerstrom's confession, he described a double agent's function: "The one side has an agent whom it deliberately tries to work in as an agent on the other side, of course without the other side knowing anything about it." And, Wennerstrom added, this is "the most advanced and dangerous kind of work an agent can do, both for the agent himself and for the two parties."

DOUBLED

A doubled agent is said to "work under control," or "in harness." He will "play back" bogus messages to his home controller—using texts provided by his captors.

DOUGHNUT, THE

The headquarters building of the British Government Communications Headquarters at Cheltenham, so termed because of its shape. (GCGH was known formerly as the/Government Code and Cypher School, or GCCS.)

DRAGON LADY

Nickname for the U-2 reconnaissance aircraft, so named, according to former pilot Charles Espinosa, because "you never knew what to expect when you took it into the air, no matter how seasoned a pilot you were." (*See* U-2.)

DRY CLEANING

Various techniques a surveillance subject uses to shake off his pursuers or to establish whether he is being followed. Walking a haphazard route, with many turns and changes of course; darting in and out of elevators, department stores, and subway cars; scurrying through obscure exits of churches or cafes—the methods of dry cleaning are as varied as a skilled agent's imagination can contrive.

(During a foot surveillance exercise in downtown Baltimore in the 1950s, the author followed a well-dressed subject who went into a jewelry store and spent almost an hour pricing expensive watches. I attracted so much adverse attention as an obviously impecunious youth in his early twenties, clad in a sports shirt and chinos, that the salesmen made signs they were ready to call the cops. When the subject finally left the store, he looked at me—now lurking behind a newspaper across the street—and gave a broad wink. I was not amused.)

DUBOK

Literally, a "little oak" in Russian; in KGB usage, a hiding place for messages. The KGB equivalent of a dead letter drop. The possibilities were limitless.

According to Igor Gouzenko, a Soviet cipher clerk who defected to the Canadians in 1946, the GRU and KGB are particular about the use *of duboks*. As Gouzenko told the Royal Canadian Mounted Police, "The favorite places for a *dubok* are telephone booths (behind the phone box); toilets (inside the water tank); some abandoned stone structure with plenty of splits between the stones—old fences, graveyards, etc. In most cases all places are selected in such a way that access to them is easy but not conspicuous. Sometimes they [Soviet case officers] may use a trick such as this: The contact man sits down on a bench in a casual and relaxed pose. Unnoticed, he may pin a letter under the bench with thumb tacks, then, minutes later, leave the place. Agents may come half an hour later and pick it up. So those who are watching the agent's every movement—even the most unsuspicious and relaxed movements—should check them right away."

KGB people also referred to a letter-drop as a *taynik*.

DUD

A person who makes contact with an intelligence agency with the declared intention of passing information, but who never appears again. *(Blind-gaenger,* to the West German intelligence services.)

DYNAMO SPORTS CLUB

KGB's "team" in track and field and other sporting events in the Soviet Union.

Safe House Interlude Two

Spy Lucre

"Gold is the only reward for a spy."
>—Napoleon, in rejecting the Legion of Honor
>for famed French Spy Karl Schulmeister, whose
>exploits led to Austrian defeats in two crucial
>battles; he received money rather than a medal.

∾

Despite what Napoleon proclaimed, a principle of intelligence is that an agent must be paid, regardless of the depth of his ideological motivation. But the approach is dictated by the nature of the person. If he is an out-and-out rogue, willing to betray his country, the questions to be resolved are "How much?" and "How?" whereas the "idealistic" agent is hooked by first being persuaded to accept "expenses," then "payment for your time."

The KGB and its successors were especially strict in enforcing the pay-principle. As the Soviet espionage expert David Dallin has written, "An agent who works without pay feels independent and can give up his spying activities whenever he desires; he might reconsider his decision and reveal his activities to the authorities, minimizing his guilt by stressing his 'idealistic motives.' A paid agent, however modest his remuneration, is a *serving* person, a subordinate, a dependent individual…receipts bearing his signature can be produced and used to coerce him if he should desert the secret service. He is firmly in the hands of his employer." Even Sam Carr, the Canadian Communist who worked for the GRU until exposed by the defector Igor Gouzenko in 1946, was not averse to putting Soviet money in his pocket; his "control card" noted, "financially secure but takes money."

When Whittaker Chambers protested to his Soviet superior about the demand that he give presents to persons who were "Communists on principle," the superior replied, "Who pays is boss, and who takes money must also give something." When Chambers warned, "you will lose every one of them," the superior replied, "Then we must give them some costly present so that they will know that they are dealing with big, important people." One of the persons eventually accepting a handsome rug was Alger Hiss, who later was convicted of perjury for denying involvement in Soviet espionage. The gift rug was part of the evidence used to prove Hiss's guilt.

One Soviet agent who did refuse taking money was Harry Gold, the Philadelphia chemist who was a key courier in the wartime atomic secrets spy ring. But he did accept the Order of the Red Star, which would be "held for you" in Moscow. Save for glory, the award carried one material benefit: lifetime free rides on buses in Moscow. Gold spent 20 years in prison, thus he never had the opportunity to flash his medal at a Russian bus driver and enjoy a free ride.

Accountants have long been the bane of intelligence officers. During the Civil War, a Treasury Department bean-counter challenged an item submitted by Union General Benjamin Butler during fighting around Baltimore: "Fifty dollars for hand organ and monkey." Butler explained: "The rebels were close-mouthed and I could get no inside news as to their doings. One day I saw a crowd gathered around a man with a hand organ and a large dancing monkey. I noticed that the organ grinder looked much like a certain smart Irishman in my own corps.

"That evening I called the Irishman to headquarters. I knew him well, and I was sure I could trust him. I gave him the money to buy the hand organ and the monkey, together with the very clothes that their owner was accustomed to wear. Dressed in these, I sent him out as a spy....He traveled all over the surrounding country, and the information he brought back was invaluable in the campaign. It was worth thousands of dollars to the Union Army." Butler was reimbursed the $150.

"Cicero," the valet for the British ambassador in Ankara, Turkey, during World War II, also spied for the Geman Abwehr, to whom he gave hundreds of pilfered secret documents. In return, the Germans paid him 300,000 British pounds—in counterfeit notes, he discovered to his chagrin.

∾

"What enables a wise sovereign or good general to strike and to conquer and to achieve things beyond the reach of normal men is foreknowledge. Foreknowledge comes only through spies. Nothing is of more importance to the state than the quality of its spies. It is ten thousand times cheaper to pay the best spies lavishly than even a tiny army poorly."

—Sun Tzu, in *The Art of War.*

∾

In a report issued in October 2010, the U.S. Office of Management and Budget stated that the government spent $80.1 billion on intelligence activities in the just-ended fiscal year, about 12 percent of the nation's $664 billion defense budget.

No breakdown was given as to how much money was spent on individual components of the intelligence community, but the lion's share is believed to be on such tech-heavy activities as the National Security Agency and the National Reconnaissance Office. Only twice before have Intel expenditures been disclosed—$26 billion in 1997 and $28.7 billion in 1998.

E

EARS ONLY

Information so sensitive it is not committed to paper. CIA occasionally briefs Congressional committees on this basis to guard against leaks, witting or otherwise, that could harm an ongoing operation. Ears Only is not a formal classification.

EDIBLE PAPER

Paper, used for writing messages, that is water soluble and that can be swallowed by an intelligence agent during an emergency. The dissolution is slow, and at one stage the paper assumes "the consistency of the plastic dentists use to fit false teeth," in the words of CIA veteran William Hood.

ELECTRONIC DECEPTION

According to the Defense Department's Dictionary of Military and Associated Terms, electronic deception is "the deliberate radiation, reradiation, alteration, suppression absorption, enhancement or reflection of electromagnetic energy in a manner intended to convey misleading information and to deny valid information to an enemy or to electronic-dependent weapons. Among the types of electronic deception are:

"Manipulative electronic deception. Actions to eliminate revealing or convey misleading telltale indicators that may be used by hostile forces;

"Simulative electronic deception. Actions to represent friendly notional or actual capabilities to mislead hostiles forces.

"Imitative electronic deception: The introduction of electromagnetic energy into enemy systems that imitates enemy emissions."

ELICITATION

Obtaining information from an individual or a group in a manner that conceals the true intent of the conversation. For instance, after I returned from a reportorial trip to Cuba in 1964, a Treasury Department intelligence officer asked for the loan of prints of any photographs I had taken. He expressed curiosity "about general conditions there." Grease pencil markings on the photos when they were returned tipped his true interest: the manufacturer of late-model buses and trucks that had been shipped into Cuba in contravention of the U.S. ban on exports to the Communist island. An officer will often conduct an hour-long interview for the sole purpose of asking a single question to which he needs an answer: "By the way, when the tour bus took you out to Veradero Beach, did you follow the coastal road, or did it go inland for a ways?" The officer does not say flatly, "We understand the Soviets helped the Cubans install surface-to-air missiles outside Havana." The casual American tourist would know only whether the suspected area is now off-limits.

ELINT

Acronym for "electronic intelligence," or the interception of electronic signals from radar, missiles, and the like.

ELSUR INDEX (Electronic Surveillance)

An FBI index containing the names of all persons overheard, even incidentally, on both court-ordered and warrantless electronic surveillances. The ELSUR Index also includes information on the initial date of the monitoring and the name of the target of the surveillance.

ENCIPHER

To convert a plain text message into unintelligible form by the use of a cipher system.

ENCRYPT

To convert a plain text message into unintelligible form by means of a cryptosystem; this term also covers the meaning of "encipher" and "encode."

ESSENTIAL ELEMENTS OF INFORMATION (EEIs)

A military intelligence term for the most urgently required intelligence data. Depending upon the level of command, EEIs can be momentous or mundane. A theater air commander wishes to know what anti-aircraft fire can be expected over a target area. A platoon commander will ask whether a given field is cleared of snipers. The term itself is often forgotten in the hurry of battle; a commander, however, makes known what he desires now and what can wait for tomorrow.

ESTABLISHED SOURCE

The FBI term for a person who has been previously used as an informant by the Bureau. Use of this designation implies that the established source is reliable.

ESTABLISHING BONA FIDES

The use of recognition signals that enables agents unknown to one another to meet and establish contact. (*See* RECOGNITION SIGNALS.) The usual device is the ostentatious display of a certain newspaper or magazine. A CIA legend features an officer who owned a beagle hound that he loved to use instead of a periodical to establish his bona fides. He cabled another station that he would be arriving, and that the greeter should look for the hound. "LOOK FORWARD TO MEETING YOUR BONO FIDO," came the reply.

EXECUTIVE ACTION

An euphemism for assassination. The term was used in some CIA documents obtained by the Church Committee to describe a program aimed at overthrowing certain foreign leaders, by assassination if necessary. No executive action assassination ever occurred, as the committee stated in its final report to the Senate. The British Intelligence Services, through MI5 director Sir Dick White, forbade assassination as an instrument of clandestine policy in 1956. A similar order to American intelligence was issued after disclosures that, at Presidential directive, CIA had tried to kill Cuba's Fidel Castro and had been involved in plots against Patrice Lumumba of the Congo.

EXFILTRATION

Smuggling an agent out of an unfriendly country.

EXPENSES

Opening gambit to entrap an intelligence target into working for an intelligence agency. Typically, the recruiting agent asks for an unclassified directory or public document, then insists on paying the person "for your trouble." After several such "favors," the agent asks that the person "sign a receipt for my records, so that I can be reimbursed for expenses." Once the person signs, he is hooked.

EXPLOITATION

The process of obtaining information from any source and taking full advantage of it for strategic or tactical purposes. Exploitation can be public and direct. For instance, when CIA obtained the text of Soviet Premier Khrushchev's scathing attack on Josef Stalin at a party conference in 1956, there was brisk internal debate over what use to make of the information. The decision was to give the document to *The New York Times,* which (as anticipated) published the full text. The impact upon world Communism was staggering; CIA's hand was not publicly revealed, although generally suspected. A cruder attempt at exploitation was the FBI's sub rosa circulation of tape recordings of the Rev. Martin Luther King, Jr., at sexual play. The damage to King's image as a civil rights leader was transitory; the grubbiness of the operation tarnished the reputation of FBI director J. Edgar Hoover even after his death.

EXTERMINATORS

See BUG.

EXTERNAL COLLECTION PROGRAM

Periodic visits by security officers of the National Security Agency to bars, restaurants, and other establishments in the area around NSA headquarters at Fort Meade, Maryland. The visits were made to determine whether NSA employees, in their after-hours gathering, discussed classified information, and whether "agents of hostile intelligence services frequented these locations," according to the Church Committee's final report. The "program" also involved alerting bartenders and other employees to report suspicious conversations. This bar-hopping lasted from 1963 until 1967, when

NSA security men decided they "lacked the personnel to carry on such a program."

EYE CLUB, I CLUB

An informal liaison group, social in nature, of British intelligence officers who work for the established intelligence service, the military, and the Foreign Office.

F

FALSE CONFIRMATION

A delicate phase of a disinformation or deception operation intended to give credence to the item of information being passed to the other side. Typically, the false confirmation would come from a source not readily identifiable with the persons or agencies involved in the major phase of the operation.

An example: The CIA station in London receives a high-level KGB defector and decides he can be put to more efficient use if the USSR believes him to be dead. An ambulance makes a conspicuous sirens-blaring visit to a known CIA safe house and drives away with a person on a stretcher. Attendants at the hospital to which the defector is taken are led to believe that he arrived dead, victim of poisoning. A "body" is removed in a sealed casket. Shortly thereafter, the head of the station's counterintelligence section is relieved of duty and returned to assignment in the United States, and rumors are set afloat that he was disgraced because of his "mishandling" of the defector, who killed himself while in custody.

Now the kicker: An advisory memorandum is circulated to other Western intelligence agencies alerting them of a new method KGB agents have of concealing poison capsules on their persons, one unknown even to their superiors. The memorandum disclaims any knowledge of how widespread such use might be, but notes that KGB officers keep it secret even from their superiors so that they have the option of committing suicide if they fall into disfavor. The memorandum also states that a KGB person might use the capsule if he has a change of heart during the midst of a defection. Once this memorandum is learned of by the KGB it confirms more effectively than any previous information the death of the defector that CIA has alive.

Credibility, of course, is the key factor. The operative rule is to let the "false confirmation" come to light through efforts of the other side, so that it is not a patent plant.

FALSE FLAG

Recruiting an agent or an informer through the guise of telling him the actual work will be done for another country or interest. False flagging is used when the potential recruit would not likely accept a direct approach from the country desiring his services. Harry Rositzke, long a Soviet specialist for CIA, cites an example: "In 1950 two American Jewish counterintelligence officers were recruited in Vienna by a Soviet intelligence officer masquerading as an Israeli." The FBI has encountered several instances in which KGB agents managed to pass themselves off as highly conservative Americans when recruiting right-wing government employees as informants. The pitch was that they should report on the workings of their agency "to help my patriotic organization to be sure the Commies aren't infiltrating our institutions." As former CIA officer David Atlee Phillips has written, "Today there are unsuspecting zealots around the world who are managed and paid as spies; they sell their countries' secrets believing all the while they are helping 'the good guys.'"

FALSE NAMES

From long experience, I have learned that active officers in CIA's Clandestine Services are not necessarily who they say they are, when it comes to names. A field operative will be known to his informants by an alias. He will use a pseudonym to sign cables to headquarters, and a made-up name for his informants (a cryptonym). (*See* WORK NAMES.)

FAMILY JEWELS

The self-admitted list of transgressions of the CIA charter compiled by its officials in 1973, following revelations that Watergate figures E. Howard Hunt and G. Gordon Liddy had used Agency facilities in some of their illegal activities. James Schlesinger, the then-DCI, on May 9, 1973, ordered "all the senior operating officials of this Agency to report to me immediately on any activities now going on, or that have gone on in the past, which might be construed to be outside the legislative charter of this Agency." Working the resultant reports, CIA's Office of the Inspector General compiled 693 pages of "potential flap activities," including the bugging of newsmen in hopes of tracing leaks of classified materials, Operation CHAOS against the anti-war movement, experiments with mind control drugs, and a mail-intercept program—some 300 items in all. To the lasting dismay of many Agency veterans, Schlesinger's successor, William Colby, a few months later yielded to political and public pressure and surrendered the list to the Rockefeller Commission, the first of several bodies to probe CIA over the next few years. By handing over the family jewels—a euphemism for testicles—Colby was said to have helped in the emasculation of the Agency that he had served for decades.

The "family jewels" list is available on CIA's home page.

FARM, THE
See CAMP PEARY.

FEDERAL SECURITY SERVICE (FSB)
The agency that replaced the KGB when the latter collapsed, along with the Soviet Union, in late 1991. Known as the FSB for its Russian name, *Federalnaya Sluzhba Bezopasnosli.* The FSB later split into numerous parts. See KGB (p. 115) for a discussion of its evolution.

FEEDBACK AGENT
A hostile agent planted within a rival intelligence organization who informs his superiors of the success or lack thereof of its own counterespionage operations. Also known as a "penetration agent," for having penetrated a rival service.

FERRET SEARCHES
Surprise "inspections" by agents of CIA's Office of Security. These officers are authorized to search even the personal homes or apartments of station chiefs to ensure that no security procedures are being violated (such as bringing classified material home for use in a non-secure area). Ferret searches are also used when an agency employee is suspected of illicit activity. Many are done with such discretion that the target does not realize that his lodgings have been "tossed" (searched). The privacy invasion means that ferret searches and the men who conduct them are not loved by their colleagues.

FCI

In the FBI, the office devoted to Foreign Counterintelligence, long considered a poor career path.

FIELD INFORMATION REPORTS (FIRs)

The basic reporting form of a CIA operative or contract employee working in the field. These are submitted directly to the CIA station, initialed by the station chief or his deputy, and sent by diplomatic pouch to Langley. Urgent FIRs are upgraded and sent by secure wireless.

FIFTH COLUMN

Term denoting subversives willing to work for the enemy within their own country. Although given wide popular use during World War II, "fifth column" is now considered archaic; the modern CIA and FBI version is "agents of influence."

In his play *The Fifth Column,* Ernest Hemingway wrote, "Oh, they always shoot from the windows at night during the bombardment. The fifth column people. The people who fight us from inside the city."

Attorney General Robert Jackson in 1940 defined the fifth column as "that portion of our population which is ready to give assistance or encouragement in any form to invading or opposing ideologies."

President Roosevelt recognized the danger of a fifth column in America in a memorandum dated May 21, 1940, to Attorney General Francis Biddle authorizing wiretapping in "grave matters involving the defense of the nation." As Roosevelt wrote, "It is...well known that certain other nations have been engaged in the organization of propaganda of so-called 'fifth-column' in other countries and in preparation for sabotage, as well as in actual sabotage. It is too late to do anything about it after sabotage, assassinations and 'fifth column' activities are completed."

FIREFLY

A chemical that spontaneously ignites—after a bit—when mixed with gasoline. OSS developed Firefly and used it to great effect during World War II on German trucks and tanks. Latter-day variants of Firefly are still to be found in CIA and other arsenals of unconventional weaponry. Although the compound is simple, its exact composition is best left undescribed.

FIX

A CIA term, of Cold War origin, that refers to a person who is to be compromised or blackmailed so that he will do the Agency's bidding. As intelligence historian Donald McCormick notes, "Those seeking out the possibilities of employing such tactics talk of a 'low-key' fix or an OK fix; the latter is actual blackmail."

FLAP POTENTIAL

The risk of embarrassment to an intelligence agency stemming from disclosure of an illegal or questionable activity, or of the defection of an agent. The agency's first impulse is concealment of the mishap (the British, for instance, delayed for days before confirming the 1951 defection of the spies Maclean and Burgess). Former CIA officer Miles Copeland states that the "frantic inquiries intelligence agencies used to make when leaks were suspected are now a thing of the past." By Copeland's testimony, the mode now is the "quiet flap," in which investigations are conducted with extreme discretion, so as not to alert other persons involved that they are suspect The quiet approach also means that persons caught red-handed are often permitted to go free (although in unemployed fashion) rather than make a public appearance in court to answer criminal charges.

Another type of flap potential situation concerned numerous illegal CIA and FBI surveillance and mail-opening operations of the 1950s and 1960s. The FBI under Director J. Edgar Hoover had a direct rule of thumb in handling flaps, potential or otherwise: "Don't embarrass the Bureau." But CIA's James J. Angleton, the counterintelligence chief, suggested that CIA develop a cover story for the mail intercepts to the effect that the project involved "certain research work on foreign mail..." Another Agency official stated that, if there should be an accidental compromise, the "Office of Security would utilize its official cover to explain any difficulties..." This official noted that "high level police contacts with the New York Police Department are enjoyed, which would preclude any uncontrolled inquiry in the event police action was indicated."

If any citizens griped about lost mail, they should be referred to the Post Office. If a disgruntled CIA employee revealed the intercept program, the charge could "be answered by complete denial of the activity."

FLAPS AND SEALS

A mail-opening course taught by the CIA's Technical Services Division beginning in the early 1950s as part of HT-LINGUAL. The basic method was simple. Glue on envelopes was softened by steam from a kettle. Carefully wielding a narrow stick, the agent pried open the envelope and took out the letter. One agent who took the flaps and seals course told the Church Committee that "you could do it with your own teapot at home." Skilled interceptors could open an envelope in five to fifteen seconds.

Ever conscious of technology, Technical Services Division in the 1960s developed a sort of "steam oven" designed to open one hundred letters simultaneously. But the dissolved glue often hardened before letters could be extricated; there was also an occasional mix-up of letters and envelopes, so that a citizen in Murmansk received a message intended for someone else's aunt in Kiev. So the HT-LINGUAL agents returned to their trusted kettle-and-stick method.

The FBI, not to be outdone by its intelligence rival, later developed an opening process said to require only a second or two for a single letter (contrasted with the five to fifteen seconds for CIA). But one CIA man familiar with the FBI method termed it "sloppy ... they'd have ink running all over the page." (*See* CHAMFERING.)

FLASH-ALIAS DOCUMENTS

See BACKSTOPPING.

FLOATER

A person used for a one-time or occasional intelligence job; low-level and, often as not, unwitting. For instance, MI5 might recruit a Charing Cross call girl to accompany a foreign diplomat on his evening rounds, simply to ascertain where he goes and to whom he talks.

FLOATING CONTACT

A surveillance subject who suddenly gets into a passing car or taxi. When this occurs, the surveillance team goes into an "all-skate"—the deployment of as many cars as are available to keep up the chase.

FLUTTER

The polygraph test administered to information-sensitive officers of the American intelligence community, both at the time of their recruitment and then on or close to the annual anniversary of their employment. Subjects are asked such questions as whether they have stolen money, engaged in homosexual or other offbeat sexual conduct, committed adultery, or compromised secrets. Although the accuracy of a polygraph is widely debated, its use is a key tool of the security offices of CIA, NSA, DIA, and other intelligence agencies.

FOODSTUFF

See CHICKEN FEED.

FORCED INTERROGATION

KGB questioning in which the severity of the subject's treatment was decided by the men wielding the truncheons; essentially, they could do anything they wished, physically or psychologically, to achieve the desired results. The subject, between sessions, was kept in a lighted, windowless cell; the interrogations were scheduled in no discernible time pattern, so that he quickly lost any concept of time. Food (and not very much of it) was also served at random times. Once the prisoner was disoriented and realized he had no chance of freedom, he generally did what the interrogators wished. The Soviets honed these techniques in preparing for Stalin's purge trials of the 1930s; they were later augmented by the use of drugs.

FORT HOLABIRD

The long-time site of the Army Intelligence School, on the eastern outskirts of Baltimore. "The Bird" was also headquarters of the Army Intelligence Command during the frostier days of the Cold War. Originally an Army locomotive repair depot, and a holding compound for German POWs during World War II, Holabird was the training ground for a generation of CIC and Field Operations Intelligence (FOI) operatives.

Many of the latter, in the 1950s, were Eastern Europeans of fierce anti-Communist bent who spoke scant English and who were allowed off the Bird only under controlled circumstances. They did occasional considerable damage to saloons along Dundalk Avenue. They then went away to Eastern Europe on covert missions.

CIC trainees undertook either the "A Course," for analysts, or the "B Course," for field agents. Mostly recent college graduates, they had the good sense to keep away from the FOI areas. Holabird also housed the Central Records Facility, the repository for every intelligence report ever received by the United States Army. Persons assigned there slaved as file clerks, their tedium broken by the fact that they had ready access to a section entitled "Perversions, Sexual—US ARMY Ex-CONUS," which featured depositions by and photographs of persons caught in awfully awkward circumstances.

Fort Huachuca, Arizona, is now the headquarters of U.S. Army intelligence and most of the activities formerly pursued at Fort Holabird. The training ground of uncountable hundreds of military spooks is now an industrial park being developed by the city of Baltimore. The only government function surviving is a Justice Department safe house for important (and vulnerable) witnesses in criminal trials. The safe house was once the main classroom building of the Army Intelligence School.

FRENCH ROOM

The conference room of the director of central intelligence, so named for reasons no one remembers.

FRIEND

A person persuaded to influence a foreign government, or some segment thereof. His motives are almost unfailingly ideological (a term that extends to protecting the family fortune). Such a Friend is numbered among a CIA station's most valued assets, because his initial commitment means that he will be willing to perform late-hour odd jobs as well. (For instance, if a CIA officer in Rome needs a car and guide to drive to an obscure town at 2:00 A.M., the Friend is apt to oblige.)

FRIENDS
Operatives of British MI6, or Secret Intelligence Service During World War II, being a Friend was highly secret—so much so that when Heinrich Himmler of the Nazi SS gave a public speech disclosing the names of all the most important Friends, from their chief downward, the translated text was promptly classified "Most Secret." Fitzroy Maclean, himself a Friend before entering Parliament, noted that his socially aware colleagues composed their reports on "sheets of deep blue writing paper of the kind then affected by many society hostesses."

FSR (Foreign Service Reserve)
The rank the State Department insisted be given to CIA officials working abroad under diplomatic cover through the late 1960s. State refused to permit CIA people to be integrated into their family as Foreign Service Officers (or FSOs). Since the FSR designation was printed in the State Department *Biographical Register* and embassy directories, little imagination was required for outsiders to spot CIA officers. Such anti-CIA publications as *Counterspy* used the FSR label to identify hundreds of supposedly covert CIA operatives working under embassy cover during the early 1970s.

FUMIGATE
To use electronic counter-devices to locate and neutralize listening devices concealed in a room. Horst Schwirkmann, of the West German intelligence service—one of the best fumigators in the business in the 1950s and 1960s—paid dearly for a prank he played on the KGB in Moscow. During a routine fumigation, Schwirkmann playfully rigged a device that emitted a high-frequency sound in the bugs he had just discovered. The sound not only severely damaged the KGB's receivers but also caused much pain to technicians listening in at the time. Several days later a KGB man surreptitiously doused Schwirkmann's leg with mustard gas as he walked in a Moscow park. For two days Schwirkmann lingered on the brink of death. He survived but was disabled for weeks.

FUNKSPIEL

German for "radio game," which in World War II was the German equivalent of the British "Operation Double-Cross." During the war more than half the clandestine radio stations in occupied Europe—Soviet, British and others—came under control of German military counterintelligence or the Gestapo. In uncountable instances the Germans "persuaded" arrested foreign spies to continue transmissions to their headquarters, using messages composed by German intelligence. Agents dispatched from England parachuted to certain detention, and death. To the Abwehr, the change of loyalty by Allied agents was called *umdrehen*, or "turning around." (*See* OPERATION DOUBLE-CROSS.)

The most famed funkspiel operation mounted by the Germans was NORDPOL, with both the Dutch and the British as victims. For some eighteen months, arrested Dutch agents continued communications with bases in England; at one time, fourteen "Dutch" radio stations actually worked for the Germans. NORDPOL resulted in the arrests of more than sixty British and Dutch agents who parachuted onto the continent.

FUSAG

Abbreviation for First United States Army Group, the totally fictional "force" created by Allied intelligence in 1943–44 and passed off to the Axis as the intended invasion army. FUSAG was part of the elaborate panoply of disinformation operations intended to shield the exact time, place, and composition of the invasion.

Safe House Interlude Three

Morality and All That

"I don't care what the CIA does. All I want from them is twenty-four hours notice of a Soviet attack."

—General George C. Marshall, while
Secretary of Defense in 1951.

∾

"It is only the enlightened ruler and wise general who will use the higher intelligence of the army for the purposes of spying. Spies are the most important element in war because upon them depends an army's ability to move."

—Sun Tzu, *The Art of War.*

∾

"Nobody enters the world of secret operations as a lark."

—James McCargar, former officer of The Pond, writing
as Christopher Felix in *The Spy and His Masters.*

∾

"Like war, spying is a dirty business. Shed of its alleged glory, a soldier's job is to kill. Peel away the claptrap of espionage and the spy's job is to betray trust. The only justification a soldier or spy can have is the moral worth of the cause he represents."

—Former OSS/CIA officer William Hood, in *The Mole.*

∾

"Good lord, man, if you're going to do things like that, then for Heaven's sake do them. Hard, and with everything you've got. No halfway measures in that sort of thing."

—Comment of a British intelligence officer to
an American counterpart on the off-again/on-again
nature of the Bay of Pigs operation.

∾

"The CIA is amoral. It was authorized by Congress to be so. It was paid to be."

—Edward Korry, former ambassador to Chile, in a letter to The Church Committee.

G

G'S, THE

FBI term for teams of surveillance specialists—government employees, but not FBI agents—who on the surface appear to be ordinary citizens, and thus are hard to spot when they are at work. G's range from mothers pushing baby-strollers to smooching college students to Joe Six-Pack construction workers.

G-FIVE

The Gulfstream V jet, the aircraft of choice for CIA travel abroad. It can carry twelve passengers halfway around the world without refueling.

GAS-GUN

A KGB assassination device that was capable of firing a burst of poison into the face of the intended victim. One version widely used in Western Europe in the 1950s consisted of a tube some seven inches long and slightly larger than a man's finger, with a firing pin and trigger at one end. The tube consisted of three sections. The trigger, when pulled, caused the firing pin to ignite a powder charge in the center section, which in turn crushed a glass phial in the third. The glass phial contained five cc. of hydrocyanide, which would vaporize upon contact with the air. According to the European intelligence expert Louis Edmund Hagen, When "held about two feet from a person's face, it would kill instantly, no trace being left on the victim. By swallowing a pill containing an antidote (amyl nitrate) beforehand, and by inhaling the vapour of another antidote released by crushing a glass phial immediately after the weapon had been fired, the operator of the gun could avoid being affected by his own poison."

Two persons killed by this sinister device were anti-Communist Ukrainian Nationalists in West Germany—Lev Rebet, editor of an exile newspaper in Munich, considered a prime enemy of the USSR and the KGB, and Stephan Bandera, head of the Organization of the Ukrainian Nationalist Revolution, or OUNR. Both were murdered by Bogdan Stashinsky, a Ukrainian forced into KGB service after committing a petty crime while a university student. As a reward for these murders, committed in 1957 and 1959, Stashinsky received the Order of the Red Banner from Andrew Shelepin, director of the KGB. Conscience eventually overcame Stashinsky; he defected and, after persuasion, convinced West German security authorities of his role in the killings. He was sent to prison for eight years, the judge stating, "The sentence pronounced by this court is not intended to destroy the accused. It is to help him atone."

GEHLEN ORGANIZATION

The German intelligence apparatus, seized intact by the American CIC in 1945 and put to work for the West. Its commander, General Reinhard Gehlen, ran Hitler's military espionage in Russia during World War II. Captured, Gehlen turned over his mammoth files and network of spies to the United States, and he ultimately became chief of the West German intelligence agency, the *BnD*, working directly under CIA. Pragmatism outweighed revulsion in the instance of Gehlen—he had never joined the Nazi Party—and he gave Western agencies invaluable aid in the immediate postwar years.

Hectored by a leftist Congressman about the Gehlen connection, as related to me by a person who worked in the White House at the time, President Truman retorted, "Well, we've also worked with another Hitler collaborator, a man *you* admire." Who? The congressman queried. "Joe Stalin," Truman replied. "Remember, he signed on with Hitler in 1939. This Gehlen fellow, I don't care if he fucks goats. If he helps us, we'll use him."

GEOINT (GEOSPATIAL INTELLIGENCE)

A relatively new spyspeak term, defined by the National Geospatial-Intelligence Agency as "the use and analysis of geospatial information to assess geographically referenced activities on earth....everything can see or know about the earth...GEOINT provides valuable information about the activities of our adversaries that may help shape foreign policy."

GETTING ONE FOOT INTO THE ORGANIZATION

The first toehold a prospective double agent gains in a rival intelligence agency. Most frequently, the double agent agrees to sell inconsequential information for money, which at once establishes his bona fides and which "obligates" him to the agency making the payment. A common opening ploy for Army Counterintelligence Corps agents in West Germany in the 1950s was to offer Communist agents a phone book for the U.S. headquarters command in Stuttgart, classified "For Official Use Only." The information contained therein was worthless, but the transactions permitted CIC to pass off numerous persons as "doubles."

GHETTO INFORMANT PROGRAM

A special FBI program to elicit intelligence on the black community, especially in urban areas, during 1967–73. Attorney General Ramsey Clark initiated the program in a letter to FBI Director J. Edgar Hoover in September 1967, citing a "widespread belief that there is more organized activity in the riots than we presently know about...[W]e must make certain that every attempt is being made to get all information bearing upon these problems...and... to determine the identity of the people and interests involved..." The FBI, in implementing Ramsey Clark's order, defined a ghetto informant as "an individual who lives or works in a ghetto area and has access to information regarding the racial situation and racial activities in the area which he furnished to the Bureau on a confidential basis." As examples, the FBI cited "the proprietor of a candy store or barbershop" in an urban ghetto area. The first GIs were passive listening posts; later, the Bureau encouraged them to undertake specific assignments, such as to survey bookstores specializing in black publications to determine "if militant extremist literature is available therein."

GHOSTS

Detainees whose existence the United States military and intelligence officers refuse to confirm to outsiders; term came into usage during early years of the "rendition" program.

GO-AWAY

A signal given by an agent that it would be unwise to make a prearranged contact in a public place. A go-away is included in the basic instructions to the agent and the person with whom he should make contact. The go-away can take many forms. In the passive sense, the party suspecting surveillance lets his hands dangle free as he walks past his contact. In the active sense, the party thrusts his hands into his pockets. (The variations are as many as one can imagine.) Active-passive signals shift on odd-even days of the month, thus requiring alertness by both parties.

GO PRIVATE

To break away from the intelligence community, usually with stolen funds, and attempt to establish a new life elsewhere under a different identity. CIA has an elaborate job-placement service for employees who wish to work elsewhere. So, too, do the British services. But the KGB and its affiliated organizations tended to send "retirees" to Siberia, or worse. Hence the word that a KGB official had decided to go private sent pulses of excitement through the relevant CIA station.

GO TO GROUND

To disappear, to go into hiding. An agent who suspects he is under surveillance, or other suspicion, seemingly drops off the face of the earth. Having a suspect go to ground, and not being able to retrieve him readily, can put a counterespionage agent's career in severe jeopardy. If the suspect reappears, he is said to have "surfaced."

GRADUATED

A Soviet mole who succeeds in moving from one job to a more sensitive position—for instance, from an American newspaper position into the State Department.

GRANNY

A non-Agency employee. (*See* OBSERVATION POSTS.)

GRAYMAIL

The threat by a defendant in an intelligence-related prosecution to disclose classified information in open court. His intent is to dissuade the government from pressing criminal charges. Several times in the early 1970s, graymail threats caused the United States government to abandon prosecutions of persons with intelligence backgrounds. In response, Congress passed the "graymail act"— formally, the Classified Information Procedures Act—which spells out pretrial procedures that a defendant must follow if he intends to attempt to use classified material in the trial. The trial judge first must review the evidence in secret and decide whether it is in fact germane to the case. The first defendant to invoke the graymail procedures under the act was the rogue American intelligence officer Edwin P. Wilson, who hired himself out as a terrorist trainer for the nefarious dictator Muamar Quaddafi of Libya. Five separate federal judges listened to Wilson's "evidence" that he actually worked for U.S. intelligence while in Libya, and each rejected him. Wilson served a multi-decade federal prison term.

Graymail is an old and recurring problem. In the 1950s, an officer in the CIA station in Rome was found to be padding receipts he obtained from his informants and pocketing the extra money. Confronted, he fled all the way to Mexico before being induced to surrender. But as William Colby, then in the Rome station, lamented, "CIA and the Justice Department concluded that he could not be prosecuted without exposing his entire operation and the Italian recipients, and destroying them among their associates." The agent resigned in disgrace but was not punished in court.

GRAY MAN, THE

The intelligence community's term for the perfect operator, "so inconspicuous that he can never catch the waiter's eye in a restaurant," in the words of former director of central intelligence William Colby. Short, frail, and bespectacled, Colby felt that his "deliberate cultivation" of the gray man image helped make him a successful spy during his years in the field.

An officer who has a nondescript appearance. As writers Tom Clancy and Grant Blackwood put it in their 2010 thriller, *Dead or Alive*, "The best spooks know how to fade into the background: how they walk, how they dress, how they talk. You pass them on the street and you never notice them." William Colby, who capped his long career as director of central intelligence, was the epitome of "the Gray Man." My wife for several years rode the same bus with the retired Colby along Que Street NW in Georgetown. She was amused that a person who was once one of the more powerful figures in the Western world went unnoticed as he sat alone and read his newspaper.

GRAY PROPAGANDA

Statements or publications where the source is nonattributed or deliberately confusing. For some two decades Radio Free Europe (RFE) purported to be an independent, privately financed broadcast apparatus directed against the Soviet Bloc. RFE even ran public service ads (i.e., donated by the publication) in major American periodicals asking for donations to continue its crusade. In fact, the bulk of RFE's money—and the sum of its policy direction—came from CIA. The cover was thin and fooled few discerning persons, either American or Soviet.

In 1961, I heard a high RFE official plead for contributions from a group of Philadelphia business executives at a Union League luncheon. A tycoon arose and asked, "Why can't the United States government support your program? God knows but we pay enough taxes." The RFE official replied, "The government contribution is substantial, but we want your participation anyway." I was at the luncheon as a reporter, and I knew from some earlier experiences the source of the "government contributions" the RFE official mentioned. For mischief, I approached him after the luncheon and asked, "What percent of your budget does CIA meet now, eighty or ninety?" He flushed, stammered, demanded my name and organization, and within the hour had telephoned at least three news executives at my paper. As I told an inquiring RFE—read, CIA—security officer later, my sole purpose was to impress upon this turkey the fact that covert operations are more easily kept private if one does not gabble about them before luncheon groups with news reporters present. The security officer agreed.

GREAT GAME, THE

Century Anglo-Russian rivalry in Asia Minor, the key prizes at stake being India, Persia and Afghanistan. Although "Great Game" was put into popular usage by the 1901 novel, *Kim,* by Rudyard Kipling, it was coined by British Lieutenant Arthur Connolly in 1834 in a best-selling monologue, *Journey to the North of India*, in which he argued that the Russians could attack the north-west frontier if they were supported by the Persians and Afghans.

GRINDER

A debriefing room used to interrogate defectors. CIA maintains numerous such facilities within one hundred miles of the Washington area. Soviet defectors who have "gone through the grinder" report they were housed and fed in an adjacent room and given no idea as to their whereabouts (CIA preferred to keep such locales secret from KGB to avoid attempts to kill defectors). The grinding process requires the subject to repeat his story over and over again, in minute detail, while tape recorders turn. What he says is double-checked against verifiable information. As many as six months can be required to prove a defector's bona fides. The strain is mental rather than physical, but no KGB defector has anything nice to say about his stay in the grinder.

GRU (Glavnoe Razvedyvatelnoe Upravlenie)

The chief intelligence directorate of the Soviet General Staff— i.e., the Soviet military intelligence group. For foreign intelligence, GRU far surpassed KGB, both in money and manpower—and quite probably in accomplishments. Its alumni include Richard Sorge, who spied in Tokyo under cover as a pro-Nazi German journalist just before World War II, and the atomic spies who hastened along Soviet nuclear development.

GRU was headquartered in an anonymous two-story stone building near the old Khodinsk field at Moscow's Central Airport. Perhaps appropriately, all windows face inward toward a courtyard. No one, not even a ranking official, is permitted to carry a briefcase into the building, and leashed ferocious watchdogs roam the premises. GRU was identified only as "Military Department 44388"; the letters GRU (and their meaning) were unknown to the ordinary Soviet. GRU's main spy school on Militia Street in Moscow, a pleasant building with Georgian columns and an iron lattice fence is simply "Military Department 35576."

GRU's foreign spying was done primarily through its military

attaches abroad, supplemented by the industrial espionage operations of its Military-Industrial Commission, or VPK by its Russian
initials. The VPK's annual "requirements book" is said to number
at least six hundred pages, chiefly running to electronics and space
equipment sought in the West. Its budget for such acquisitions was
said to have been bottomless.

GRU and KGB were unfriendly rivals; they worked in tandem
only under duress. GRU maintained its own communications system from foreign embassies to Moscow, and GRU agents had their
own *rezident* (although in smaller embassies economy dictated closer
cooperation). Such Soviet enterprises as Aeroflot, the USSR airline,
provide cover. At one time in the late 1970s, nine of eleven Aeroflot
employees in the United States were GRU operatives, according to
FBI sources.

GRU runs its own assassination squads abroad. Neither service
can kill the other's agents—with sanction. (*See* KGB.)

GUERRILLAS

"An organized band of individuals in enemy-held territory,
indefinite as to number, which conducts against the enemy irregular operations, including those of a military or quasi-military
nature."—OSS definition. (*See* RESISTANCE GROUP.)

GUIDANCE

"The general direction of an intelligence effort, particularly in
the area of collection," according to the Church Committee.

GUOJIAANQUAN BU

The Ministry of State Security (MSS) of the People's Republic
of China, with offices in tbe West Garden Section of Beijing, near
the Summer Palace. Its leaders have boasted of having "hundreds
of thousands" of sources world-wide. In the US, major targets are
high-tech companies in the Silicon Valley.

H

HANDLING AGENT

The FBI agent responsible for directing the undercover activities of an informant. According to the FBI Manual, the handling agent "should not only collect information, but direct the informant, be aware of his activities, and maintain such a close relationship that he knows the informant's attitude towards the Bureau." The handling agent is also responsible for having the informant submit a written report, or else sign transcriptions of his oral reports. A limited exception to this rule exists for extremist informants who may submit oral reports in cases of imminent violence.

HARD TARGETS

The closed and secret societies of the old Soviet Union, the People's Republic of China, and their satellites, as contrasted to the "soft" targets of neutral and allied nations. Hard targeting became the primary emphasis of CIA intelligence gathering in the early 1970s, for several reasons. Too much money was being spent on useless information (such as internal struggles in the French Communist Party). Agents in the field tended to concentrate on easy-to-obtain information, rather than going "into the guts of the enemy." Hard targeting was a prime accomplishment of Richard Helms, the then-DCI.

HARMONICA BUG

A minute transistorized transmitter that can be placed inside the mouth-piece of a telephone handset. One version is in a permanent listening mode so that any conversations in the room can be monitored and transmitted to a listening post nearby. Another (the most commonly used) is activated only when the phone is being employed for a conversation. Mossad has yet another version that contains a small charge of *plastique* explosive. After the subject has been exploited to Mossad's satisfaction, an electronic impulse makes the harmonica bug explode, to the fatal discomfort of whomever happens to be using the telephone at the time.

HEAD OF STATION (HOS)

The officer in command of a British Secret Intelligence Service (SIS, or MI6) installation in a foreign country; equivalent to a CIA chief of station (COS).

HEAD OFFICE

The headquarters, in Pullach, West Germany, of the Gehlen Organization, that nation's long-time supreme intelligence organization. Pullach was officially secret for years, although well known to the KGB through the evil offices of double agent Heinze Felfe, who worked a decade for both Gehlen and KGB. Felfe's photographs and physical descriptions gave KGB perhaps a more intimate knowledge of Pullach than that of the building engineer.

HEAVY MOB, HEAVY SQUAD

Officers of girth and muscle who the CIA uses in situations where brute strength is more important than finesse; i.e., when a defector had to be brought through an airport, and the KGB is apt to try a kidnap or a killing. The FBI version is the heavy squad. Men of the heavy mob also do bodyguard duty for the DCI and other top Agency officers.

HEDDY

A simulated aerial bomb that duplicates the noise of a falling bomb, intended to create confusion and fear in the target city. The Heddy, weighing only about two ounces, was an OSS creation for World War II. A delayed fuse activates several seconds after the Heddy is dropped from an airplane. The device produces a whistling sound for $2\frac{1}{2}$ to $3\frac{1}{2}$ seconds, after which the explosive charge detonates, producing a sound similar to that of a large firecracker. OSS used the Heddy to clear areas into which it intended to parachute agents. A secondary use was to harass factory sites to disrupt war production.

HEEL-LIFT

A CIA gadget that causes the wearer to walk with a slight limp—a thick leather pad that is inserted into one shoe. A wadded-up handkerchief will suffice in an emergency. The changed gait, along with other disguise techniques, is intended to change the wearer's appearance.

HOLIDAY ESPIONAGE

Odd-job missions performed by intelligence agents during the course of casual trips away from their home station. The "vacation"—often legitimate—provides the cover story for the travel. For instance, Colonel Stig Wennerstrom, the Swedish traitor, spied for the Soviets while on vacation trips to Wiesbaden, West Germany, and Spain. In the words of Swedish journalist H. K. Ronblom, who wrote the definitive book on the Wennerstrom case, "A few weeks' holiday association with people from whom it was possible to extract a little information was practically risk-free." One specific mission performed by Wennerstrom during his holiday spying was to ascertain the state of U.S. military alert during the 1958 Lebanon crisis. Wennerstrom visited an American air force officer stationed in West Germany with whom he was friendly and wheedled from him the fact that the United States was alerting paratroopers for possible deployment in Lebanon.

In reality, no intelligence officer is ever fully on holiday, for the professional is constantly alert for information of intelligence value—even bus and subway schedules and local maps.

HOMOINTERN

Slang for The Apostles, the Oxford University club which spawned such traitors as the homosexuals Guy Burgess and Anthony Blunt, as well as Kim Pbilby and Donald Maclean. A ploy on the term Comintern, or Communist International.

HONEY TRAP

Sexual entrapment for intelligence purposes, usually to put a target into a compromising situation so that he or she can be blackmailed. According to the British intelligence expert Robert Moss, the Cuban DGI once gave press credentials to classy Havana hookers and set up a call-girl operation targeted at UN officials. But the operation had to be aborted hastily when the Cubans realized the whores' principal clients were Soviets. (*See* SEXPIONAGE.)

HOSPITAL

KGB euphemism for a prison to which an agent was sent. (*See* DOCTOR.)

HOT ZONE

An area subject to intense security measures or admission restrictions. Field agents are schooled to avoid such areas.

HT-LINGUAL

Cover name for a CIA mail-intercept project that lasted more than 20 years and involved the opening of some 215,000 letters to and from the Soviet Union that were read and photographed by agents in a special facility in New York. (HT-LINGUAL was the term used by CIA's Counterespionage Staff; the Office of Security, also involved in the operation, used the code-name SR-POINTER.)

HT-LINGUAL started with a request by CIA's Soviet Division (SR) in early 1952—supported by other ranking agency officials—that Soviet mail be scanned, and that the names and addresses of correspondents be recorded by hand. The intent was fivefold; according to a CIA memorandum of July 1, 1952:

- Furnish much live ammunition for psychological warfare;
- produce subjects, who if proven loyal to the United States, might be good agent material because of their contacts within the Soviet Union;
- offer documentary material for reproduction and subsequent use by our own agents;
- produce intelligence information when read in the light of other known factors and events; and
- create a channel for sending communications to American agents inside the Soviet Union.

Although the original HT-LINGUAL project involved only the recording of exteriors of envelopes, CIA counterintelligence chief

James J. Angleton noted that some mail was opened by agents "swiping a letter, processing it at night, and returning it the next day." At Angleton's behest, Richard Helms, then the director of CIA clandestine services (Operations), approved expanding HT-LINGUAL in 1955 to include systematic opening. Postal officials assigned CIA a "secure" room at LaGuardia Airport where mail could be opened and photographed. Selected letters were also screened for secret writing and microdots; CIA even developed techniques for opening mail sealed with "the more difficult and sophisticated adhesives."

In later assessments, HT-LINGUAL's contribution to intelligence was disputed. Although HT-LINGUAL produced many "operational leads," few of these were converted into actual operations. The SR (Soviet Union) Division of CIA found some occasional items of interest; but other parts of the Clandestine Services, on the other hand, downgraded HT-LINGUAL's value, and the Office of Security found its product to be "of very little value... meager..."

HT-LINGUAL eventually led to a jurisdictional squabble between CIA and the FBI. In the mid-1950s, the FBI arrested the Soviet master spy Rudolph Abel, and also learned of the existence of three other ranking agents. Yet the bureau was stymied in trying to find the link between these agents and their controls. On January 10, 1958, an allied nation's counterintelligence agency (most likely the Gehlen Organization of West Germany) told the FBI of a specific address in the Soviet Union used as a mail drop for agents abroad. When the FBI tried to institute a watch program for Soviet mail, it stumbled headlong into HT-LINGUAL. After a brisk bureaucratic tussle, CIA retained control of the intercept program, with the FBI receiving reports on the requested targets. (*See* MAIL COVER.)

HUFF DUFF

Communications jargon for High Frequency Direction Finding (HF/DF).

Safe House Interlude Four

The Philby Follies

Three of the most famed—and effective—spies in history worked in the upper echelons of the British government: H. R. "Kim" Philby and Guy Burgess of the Secret Intelligence Service, and Donald Maclean of the Foreign Office, who spied for the Soviets for more than a decade.

Just before Burgess, a brash homosexual, was detailed to Washington in 1950, a friend cautioned him on his behavior: "Don't be aggressively left-wing. Don't get involved in race relations. And, if you can, avoid homosexual incidents."

Burgess replied, "In other words, Hector, you mean I shouldn't make a pass at Paul Robeson?" [The African-American singer was both homosexual and a communist.]

~

"Donald's a sweetie!"
> —Lord Inverchapel, British ambassador to the U.S., commenting on Maclean shortly before he fled to Moscow with Burgess, his homosexual lover.

~

"I have no reason to conclude that Mr. Philby has at any time betrayed the interests of this country or to identify him with the so-called 'Third Man,' if indeed there was one."
> —British Foreign Secretary Harold MacMillan, defending Philby in Parliament November 7, 1953, just after Burgess and MacLean fled, amidst speculation that a third person was involved in their spying. SIS sacked Philby, and over the next decade built a case that had him on the brink of arrest. He scooted off to Moscow.

~

"Oh, that's bad news! Very bad news! You know, you should never catch a spy. Discover him and then control him, but never catch him. A spy causes far more trouble when he's caught.... Unhappily, you can't bury him [an arrested spy] out of sight, as keepers do with foxes."

—MacMillan, as prime minister, commenting on the arrest of a Soviet spy in 1962.

I

IA

FBI term for an "informational asset."

IDENTIFIERS

Soviet term for an informant who could identify persons of intelligence interest or of suspicious ideology. SMERSH made wide use of identifiers in screening Russian repatriates who, for one reason or another, had been outside the USSR during World War II. Stalin insisted that each of these five to six million expatriates be returned to the USSR, voluntarily or otherwise. The word of the identifier often determined whether they went to the Gulag, to the gallows, or to a civilian life.

ILLEGAL

An intelligence agent who operates in a target country without the benefit of official status. He lives under an assumed or created identity, and has minimal or no contact with his nation's overt representatives.

If CIA has ever succeeded in planting an illegal inside the Soviet Union, no such case has ever been publicized. The Soviets, however, have taken advantage of the open American society to run literally scores of illegals into the United States—the most notable being Rudolph Ivanovich Abel, a colonel in KGB, who lived undetected in New York for eight years. (After arrest he was traded for U-2 pilot Francis Gary Powers.)

Normal overseas tours for KGB illegals were for seven years, the amount of time required to meld into the target nation and be of operational value. Even though the illegal might have had a wife and family in the USSR, his only contact was via an occasional microdot letter smuggled to him with his "official" communiques. The illegal was often supplied with a nominal "wife" who is also trained in covert activities and who performed such support functions as radio operator; these pairings also provided both parties with a sexual outlet, thereby enabling them to avoid romantic entanglements that might endanger their missions. A firm KGB rule required an illegal to be married before he leaves the USSR on his first mission, and a start on a family was vigorously encouraged. The concern of KGB was not familial, however: the spymasters know the existence of a wife and child—as hostages, literally—was a degree of insurance against defection. At least one defector has told Western intelligence that his first "vacation" after seven years in the field was extended for several months until his KGB superiors were satisfied that his wife was pregnant.

ILLNESS

KGB euphemism for an agent who had been arrested. (*See* DOCTOR.)

IMINT

Imagery intelligence, derived from photos taken from space, from either reconnaissance aircraft or satellites. According to Keith Hall, one-time director of the National Reconnaissance Office (NRO) "Imint made possible arms limitations agreements with the former USSR."

INDICATOR ORGANIZATION

A group deemed typical of others working toward a common political or philosophical goal. When assets are limited, an intelligence agency will single out a particular organization for intensive coverage, on the theory that its activities will reflect those of similarly oriented groups. Given the lock-step workings of Communist-dominated front groups in, say, the anti-nuclear movement, close scrutiny of a single organization tells the FBI what it needs to know.

INDISPENSABLES

Former Nazi intelligence and counterintelligence experts taken into the Gehlen Organization of West Germany in the late 1940s and early 1950s. Ironically, much of their work was against the extreme right (the political grouping from which they had come) rather than the Communists. The indispensables also worked for Dr. Otto John, the controversial head of the *BJV (Bundesamtfür Verfassungsschutz)*, or Federal Office for the Protection of the Constitution, charged with keeping both left and right extremists away from the government and out of key organizations in labor, the press, and private associations. John mysteriously disappeared into East Germany in the 1950s, the announced victim of a kidnapping. Such, too, was the story he told on his return to the West a year later. In fact, John had worked as a Communist agent for years, and he was carefully isolated from any further significant work in intelligence.

INFILTRATION

The placing of an agent in a target area within hostile territory or within a targeted organization. The FBI effectively used infiltration to gain intelligence on Fascist and Communist groups beginning in the late 1930s. The bureau, at Presidential direction, used the same technique in the 1960s in trying to confirm foreign financing of extreme anti-war groups. The Congressional outcry was so shrill that the practice was abandoned; the stricture extends even to infiltration of avowed terrorist groups.

INFORMANT

A person who wittingly or unwittingly gives information of intelligence value to an agent or the service for which he works. There are two broad types of informants: those an intelligence agency first recruits and then inserts into the target group or country; and those who are already in place and who are "turned" (recruited) as informants. Such persons are the backbone of any intelligence or law enforcement organization; consequently agents spend a considerable portion of time in their recruitment and care.

The FBI further categorizes its informants: "Subversive" informants are those used to investigate "activities aimed at overthrowing, destroying or undermining the Government of the United States or any of its political subdivisions by illegal means." Those in the other category, "extremist" informants, have their mandate extended to include investigation of activities "denying the rights of individuals under the constitution." In FBI practice, "extremist" investigations are concerned with extremist groups—the Ku Klux

Klan and the Black Panther Party, as well as a variety of terrorist organizations devoted to "guerrilla warfare."

An intelligence organization also faces the constant risk that an informant will overstep himself and become involved personally in an illegal activity—and even that a zealous handling agent will assist him. Robert Hardy managed to infiltrate a group of anti-war activists in Philadelphia in 1970 who planned to break into the draft board office in neighboring Camden, New Jersey. Hardy told the Church Committee that he supplied essential directions and support:

> Everything they learned about breaking into a building or climbing a wall or cutting glass or destroying lockers, I taught them. I got sample equipment, type of windows that we would go through, I... taught them how to cut the glass, how to drill holes in the glass so you cannot hear it, and stuff like that, and the FBI supplied me with the equipment needed. The stuff I did not have, the [FBI] got off their own agents.

The line is often blurred between what an intelligence agency terms an "informant" and what the targeted group calls the detested "informer." Under the latter definition, the informant-informer has a somewhat odious role in history, even from the viewpoint of the people who used him. As the nineteenth-century British constitutional scholar Sir Thomas May wrote, "Men may be without restraints upon their liberty; they may pass to and fro at pleasure: but if their steps are tracked by spies and informers, their words noted down for crimination, their associates watched as conspirators—who shall say that they are free?"

Informers are so reviled in Ireland that contemporary citizens often shun descendants of persons who betrayed their countrymen to the British two or three centuries previously. When historian Helen Landreth consulted records for her book *The Pursuit of Robert Emmet,* she had to sign an agreement not to disclose names of informers she might find in government archives dating to 1803. The stated reason: to avoid retaliation against their descendants.

INNERE STADT

The international sector—Fifth District—of Vienna during the postwar years of occupation by the United States, French, British, and Soviets. Administrative responsibility and policing of the *Innere Stadt* rotated on a monthly basis. KGB regarded the *Innere Stadt* as a sort of espionage free-fire zone where normal spying ground rules did not apply. CIA personnel tended to avoid the *Innere Stadt* unless urgent business required a cautious visit there. Many of KGB's more brutal assassination and kidnapping operations were staged in the *Innere Stadt*.

INSIDE MAN

A CIA case officer who works out of a United States embassy abroad with State Department cover. (*See* LIGHT COVER; OUT-SIDE MAN.)

INSPIRE

To deceive a detected enemy agent into accepting false information and reporting it as truth to his superiors. An agent so deceived is said to be "inspired." Because he is unaware of the "inspiration," he is not the same as a "doubled" agent.

INSURGENCY

A condition resulting from a revolt or insurrection against an established government that falls short of civil war.

INTELLIGENCE

"The product resulting from the collection, evaluation, analysis, integration, and interpretation of all available information that concerns one or more aspects of foreign nations or of areas of operation that is immediately or potentially significant for planning." Such is the definition cited in the *Dictionary of United States Military Terms for Joint Usage*, published by the Departments of Army, Navy, and Air Force. Former CIA executive Sherman Kent calls intelligence "the kind of knowledge our state must possess regarding other states in order to assure itself that its cause will not suffer nor its undertakings fail because its statesmen and soldiers plan and act in ignorance."

"Intelligence" can be subdivided into a multiplicity of subcategories:

- *Strategic intelligence* is that "required for the formation of policy and military plans and operations at the national and international level."
- *Tactical intelligence* is working-level information about the day-to-day activities of an adversary, particularly in a military context.
- *Combat intelligence* is information for immediate battlefield use.
- *Operational intelligence* is the information required to conduct clandestine espionage missions in a target country.

IN THE NET

A person who had performed an espionage assignment for the KGB, thereby making himself vulnerable to blackmail; witting or not, he was then "owned" by KGB.

INVISIBLE GROUP

Thugs recruited from East German prisons by the East German State Security Service (SSD) and used for strong-arm jobs both by SSD and KGB. Missions ranged from murder to kidnappings and beatings of anti-Communists in West Berlin. The invisible group grabbed or killed scores of prominent anti-Communists during the 1950s; by the computation of West German intelligence, there were 255 abductions and 340 attempted abductions in West Berlin alone during the 1950s. Apolitical for the most part, the invisible group were offered reduced sentences or outright freedom for their efforts. In actuality, after the first mission, they either accepted an "invitation" to become full-time agents or were themselves assassinated.

ISOLATION

Early CIA cryptonym—or cover name—for the Agency's training facility at Camp Peary, Virginia, on the narrow neck of land between the James and York rivers near Williamsburg, Virginia. In its first years, the purpose of Camp Peary was a fairly well-guarded secret, hence a trainee sent there was said to be in isolation.

INTELLIGENCE CYCLE

The steps by which information is assembled, converted into intelligence, and made available to consumers. The cycle is composed of four steps: (1) *direction:* the determination of intelligence requirements, preparation of a collection plan, tasking of collection agencies, and a continuous check on the productivity of these agencies; (2) *collection:* the exploitation of information sources and the delivery of the collected information to the proper intelligence processing unit for use in the production of intelligence; (3) *processing:* the steps whereby information becomes intelligence through evaluation, analysis, integration, and interpretation; and (4) *dissemination:* the distribution of information or intelligence products in oral, written, or graphic form to departmental and agency intelligence consumers. This formidable definition comes from the Church Committee.

At the working level, the intelligence cycle is more succinctly stated, "Get it [information] and get it out."

INTELLIGENCE DATABASE

All holdings of intelligence data and finished intelligence products at a given department or agency.

IVORY, THE

According to legend, a small ivory plaque that the British monarch gives to his or her chief of the Secret Service as a token of office; it also supposedly ensures swift access in times of emergency.

JARKING

A term from the British Special Air Services, or SAS, the UK's chief special forces organization. It means the planting of miniature transmitters inside weapons that are apt to fall into the hands of terrorists. According to "Andy McNabb," pen name of a former SAS officer, in his 1995 book, *Immediate Action,* "The idea was that the devices would be activated when the weapon was picked up and the terrorists' movements could then be monitored. The US Special Forces used a similar gadget during the Vietnam War, planting tracking devices into arms that were air-dropped into areas controlled by the Viet Minh or the National Liberation Front."

JEDBURGH TEAM, JEDS

The basic intelligence team that entered occupied Europe during World War II, usually by parachute. The usual composition of each team was an American OSS officer, a British SOE agent, and a member of the French Resistance. At their peak some ninety Jedburgh teams operated in France, coordinating the efforts of resistance groups of thirty to fifty members each. The Jeds disrupted German defenses after the Normandy invasion, blowing up bridges and rail lines and ambushing enemy convoys. The Jeds also operated in Scandinavia.

The teams took their name from their quarters during training—Jedburgh, a royal burgh on the Jed River in the Scots border country of Roxburghshire. According to intelligence historian Anthony Cave Brown, the burgh was "famous for its abbey and infamous for 'Jeddart Justice,' in which a man was hung first and tried afterwards." Among American Jeds was Major William E. Colby, who in 1974 became director of central intelligence.

JETRO

Acronym for the Japanese External Trade Organization, a government-run international commercial intelligence service whose coverage rivals that of the CIA. JETRO maintains offices in forty-nine countries, including five in the United States; it is concerned mainly with markets and potential U.S. exporters to Japan. JETRO specialists give special attention to computers and other electronic gear that can be pirated and produced at a lower cost in Japan.

JOCK STRAP MEDAL

A decoration awarded to a clandestine operative of CIA. These medals are retained in Agency headquarters until the agent retires, and sometimes forever, if security warrants. The CIA joke is that such medals can be worn "only on your jock strap," since they must be concealed.

JOINT REPORTS AND RESEARCH UNIT

Cover name for the CIA station in the United States embassy, Grosvenor Square, London; some functions are done by another cover office, the Political Liaison Section.

Safe House Interlude Five

Perils of the Spy Trade

"I know very well what loneliness is. From the age of ten, for the last twenty-nine years, I have only spent ten years among my own people. I didn't want this and I didn't seek it.... I will soon be thirty-nine. Is there much left?

—Letter from Soviet spy "Gordon Lonsdale" to his wife and children, written a few hours before his arrest in January 1961. The KGB snatched up "Lonsdale" at age 11 and gave him the identity of a child who had been born in Canada and taken to Finland at an early age, where he died. As Conon Trohmovich Molody, he was sent to Canada to live with an aunt who posed as his mother. At age 16, he returned to the USSR for espionage training, and thence to Canada, where he established a Canadian identity. He worked as a KGB agent both in the U.S. and in Great Britain. A defector led to his downfall. He was sentenced to 25 years in prison and freed in a spy-swap.

∽

"Anxiety is the occupational disease of espionage."

—William Hood, formerly of OSS/CIA, in his memoir, *The Mole.*

∽

"It tells on one to go on so long leading a double life, one side of which is normal existence and the other a secret existence in which there is not a single person with whom one can talk. I do not believe this counts for so terribly much if it lasts perhaps for a few months or a year, but when it goes on for something like ten years it begins to have a tremendous psychological significance if one cannot in some way tell someone about it or speak openly to someone."

—Air Force Colonel Stig Wennerstrom, the Swedish traitor, in his interrogation statement. He spied for the Germans during World War II, then switched his loyalties to the Soviet Union.

K

K

Vernacular used by Westerners who were living in Moscow for an agent (or agents) of the KGB, e.g., "The Ks are following us tonight."

KATSA

Israeli Mossad term for a case officer.

KEEPING BOOKS

The process of keeping rosters of unfriendly intelligence agents operating in one's territory. This is a major chore of the counterespionage sections of CIA stations abroad. CIA routinely compiled a biography of every Soviet diplomat posted abroad (as did KGB of each American diplomat) and Agency counterintelligence specialists were confident of their ability to identify the vast majority of KGB agents working under diplomatic cover.

KEGEBESHNIKI

In-house term by which officers of KGB describe themselves; a contraction of the Russian words in the agency's title.

KEY

Soviet intelligence term for a means or method of persuading a person to work as an agent or informant. In postwar Austria, for instance, the Soviets concentrated on Austrian civilians working in low-level jobs for the American military establishment—cleaners, secretaries, translators, typists, etc. According to the defector A. I. Romanov, "A particularly popular 'key' was to promise an individual that any of his relatives who were prisoners in the USSR would be found and released as quickly as possible.... Another way was to obtain work with the Western allies for persons who were known to have pro-Communist views."

KEY INTELLIGENCE REQUIREMENT (KIQ)
Topics of particular interest to national policymakers, as defined by the director of central intelligence. KIQs are analogous to the military's EEIs (essential elements of information).

KGB *(Komitet Gosudarstvennoe Bezopasnosti)*
During the era of the USSR, the intelligence collective known as the Committee for State Security, which MI5, the British counter-intelligence service, called "the biggest spy machine for the gathering of secret information which the world has ever seen."

Although the KGB later operated under other names, its primary functions remained unchanged, even though spread amongst several components. Its first post-Soviet designation was as the Federal Security Bureau, or FSB for its Russian language initials. Specialists in Russian intelligence more or less agree that the terms "KGB" and "FSB" are more or less interchangeable, hence I intend to treat them as a continuing entity. Orwellian in scope, the KGB touched the life of virtually every inhabitant of the USSR. In addition to foreign intelligence functions, KGB ran the internal Soviet police, the censorship system, immigration, and the prisons; it also monitored education, the church, labor, and other organizations.

The longtime headquarters were in an ornate, rococo building on a square near the Kremlin named for Felix Dzerzhinsky, the founder of the original USSR security organ that evolved into the KGB. Other Moscow buildings handle overflow: administrative offices in Machovaya Ulitza, and the First Chief Directorate, which handles activities outside the USSR, in a half-moon-shaped building on the ring road around Moscow. (See below for descriptions of post-Soviet offices.) The KGB called itself "The Sword and Shield" of the Communist Party.

Soviet intelligence has a dual nature. Its influence abroad, according to David J. Dallin, constituted "an arm of foreign and military policy, and as such it is comparable to analogous agencies of other powers. It is, however, also part and parcel of the international Communist movement, and in this it is a unique intelligence system." Foreign communists must play both roles. The first statutes of the Communist International, written by Lenin in 1919 (the "twenty-one conditions for admittance"), required that

"Communists *everywhere* [emphasis added] are obliged to create a parallel underground apparatus which should help the party to fulfill its duty towards the revolution." [*See* COMINTERN.]

KGB was a lineal descendant of the first Soviet security organization, the *Cheka* (or *Ve Cheka)*, founded in 1917. The word comes from the tongue-twisting full Russian title, *Vse-Rossiyskaya Chrezvychaynaya Komissiya Po Borbe S Kontrrevolitisiey I Sabotazhem*, meaning the All-Russian Extraordinary Commission for Combating Counterrevolution and Sabotage. Because of local *Chekas*, the all-Russian or central organization was sometimes called the *Ve Cheka* to distinguish it from the subordinate groups.

Since *Cheka*, Soviet security and intelligence has been known by a succession of names, due to reorganizations and political changes. They are:

- 1922–23: *GPU*, for *Gosudarstvennoe Politicheskoe Upravlenie*, or State Political Administration.
- 1923–34: *OGPU*, for *Obedinennoe Gosudarstvennoe Politicheskoe Upravlenye*, or Unified State Political Administration.
- 1934–38: *NKVD*, for *Narodnyi Komissariat Vnuirennikh Del*, or People's Commissariat for Internal Affairs.
- 1938–46: *NKGB-NK VD*, the former an acronym for *Narodnyi Komissariat Gosudarstvennoe Bezopasnosti* (despite the split of police and security functions, the organization still answered to a single boss, Lavrenti Beria).
- 1946–53: *MVD-MGB*, for the previous agencies, now elevated to ministry level, the *Ministerstvb Gosudarstvennoe Bezospasnosti*, for state security; and the *Ministerstvo Vnuirennikh Del* for internal affairs.
- 1954–1991: *KGB*. Disbanded by President Mikhail Gorbachev on December 3, 1991.
- January 2, 1992–December 21, 1993. President Boris Yeltsin designates the former KGB as the Federal Counterintelligence Service (FSK, for *Federalnaya Sluzhba Kontrrazvedk*).
- December 1993–present: *FSB*, or Federal Security Service, for its Rusisan initials *Federalnaya Sluzhba Bezopasnosti*, even though some functions were removed from central control and vested in other agencies. The major change was that foreign

intelligence operations were put into a new agency known as the Foreign Intelligence Service, or SVR (for its Russian language initials, *Slzzhva Vneshney Razvedki.*

Recommemded reading: The best—and as of this writing the only—detailed study of the newly-shaped Russian security services is *The New Nobility: The Restoration of Russia's Security State and the Enduring Legacy of the KGB,* by Andrei Soldatov and Irina Borogan, two incredibly brave Russian journalists who literally put their lives at risk in doing the book. It was published by Public Affairs in 2010.

KGB AND FSB LEADERS

Felix Dzerzhinsky, the founder of the security police group that became KGB, was a Pole who spent twenty years in the anti-Czarist underground, fighting the *Okhrana,* the royalist secret police. Neither side treated prisoners nicely, and the experience convinced Dzerzhinsky that running a police state was not a job for the squeamish. In a rare press interview in June 1917, shortly after the Soviets came to power, "Iron Felix" laid down the operating principles that guided KGB for many decades:

> We stand for organized terror.... Terror is the absolute necessity during times of revolution—The Cheka [the organization that eventually became the KGB] is obliged to defend the revolution and conquer the enemy even if its sword does by chance sometimes fall upon the heads of the innocent.

Despite his reputation for cruelty (he dropped in on tortures with a spectator's enthusiasm), Dzerzhinsky was known to members of his service as "our father." He died in his sleep in 1926.

Vyacheslav Menzhinsky, also a Pole, was a more rational man than Dzerzhinsky, and it was under his auspices that Russian intelligence began fruitful operations abroad. He developed the *Comintern* (the Communist International), an umbrella group that wed Communist parties throughout the world to the USSR, both for political and intelligence purposes. But he fell afoul of Stalin's paranoia, and in 1934 he was poisoned.

Genrikh Yagoda, by most accounts, was the man who administered the poison. Another Pole, he eagerly ran the earliest of Stalin's purges. But in 1937 he was accused of "softness" and put into the dock, where he "admitted" not only that he killed Menzhinsky but also that he was a "foreign agent." Yagoda was taken to the basement of the Lubyanka prison and shot.

Nikolai Yezhof, Yagoda's successor, stood only five feet tall, and he deserved his *sotto voce* nickname, "The Bloody Dwarf." In two brisk years, Yezhof (at Stalin's direction) purged not only the Soviet army—killing 90 percent of the general officers and 80 percent of the colonels—but also his own intelligence service. Yezhof was known for impatience; if a prisoner would not talk he would smash a chair, take a jagged fragment, and (with assistance) ram it up the man's rectum. Stalin approvingly called Yezhof "Our Mailed Fist" and "Our Blackberry," both puns on his name in the Russian language. The *"Yezovchina"*—the Russian term for his reign—rivaled in brutality the worst years of Ivan the Terrible. But he did establish two precedents. He was the first Russian to head Stalin's secret police, and he was the first director to leave the office alive. In 1938 Yezhov was sent off to the position of "Commissar for Inland Waters," and he disappeared from public view. There is scholarly speculation, but no evidence, that Stalin eventually had him shot.

Lavrenty Beria, a Georgian, was Stalin's last and most trusted thug. He took command of the police apparatus in 1938 and controlled it tightly for fifteen years, until his patron's death. Under Beria the NKVD (the then-name for KGB) became veritably a state within a state, managing vast portions of Soviet industry and answering only to Stalin. A squat, beady-eyed sadist, Beria liked to spend slow evenings in the torture chambers of the Lubyanka, the KGB prison where events tended to be hard-core. (For some of Beria tenure, separate officers headed the MGB and NKVD, but insofar as state security was concerned, Beria was the dominant figure.)

Beria's sexual appetite focused on teen-aged girls. He is said to have kept an eye out for targets as his car carried him through the streets of Moscow. If he saw someone who appealed to him, he would order his driver to seize the woman and take her to his quarters.

The British journalist Edward Crankshaw, who reported from Moscow during World War II, described Beria in words that became the arch-description of the Soviet spy boss: "...shortish, bald, thick-necked, the face pallid in the Kremlin manner, the nose a little like a duck's bill, but sharp, the mouth tight and thin, the manner gentle and coldly, abstractedly benign—the whole effect of that pedantic aloofness which makes people think of scholars when they should really think of fanatics of the most dangerous kind."

When Stalin died in March 1953, Beria joined the rush to seize the dictator's crown. Such was not to be. His own colleagues distrusted putting such a hoodlum at the head of state. CIA, also wary of a Beria succession, floated a story that he actually had been on the American payroll for years. In any event, in June 1953 Beria was lured to a Kremlin meeting, where fellow Politburo members seized him, and he was subsequently shot. (News of the death was not reported until December 1953, when *Pravda* called him a "foreign agent.")

Sergei Kruglov, who headed the Kremlin security force when Stalin died, had the reputation of a murderer; he was said to have shot personally many of the Red Army officers condemned during the purge trials of the 1930s. Kruglov ran security for the Yalta, Teheran, and Potsdam conferences of the wartime Big Three (Roosevelt, Churchill, and Stalin); for these services, he was made an Honorary Knight of the British Empire and was given the Legion of Merit by the U.S. government, surely the only foreign spymaster ever to wear such awards. After Beria's death, Kruglov ran both the Ministry of the Interior and the Ministry of State Security. But two years later, the Politburo decided no single man should run the entire security apparatus. So, in 1954, Kruglov was made Minister of the Interior only.

Ivan Aleksandrovich Serov, who became Secretary of State Security, was an unrepentant Stalinist and also a Beria deputy; that he continued in power was taken as evidence that the new Kremlin leadership did not yet dare challenge KGB as an institution. Serov's power base was his friendship with Premier Nikita Khrushchev, with whom he had first worked closely in 1938 in the Ukraine. Serov properly blooded himself in the secret police by directing the murder of scores of thousands of civilians in the Baltic states during World War II.

A busy man socially, Serov in his prime was well known to

Westerners in Moscow—although some thought it amusing that he continued to wear the thick-soled shoes that lesser KGB thugs consider part of their uniform. Oleg Penkovsky, who had frequent contact with Serov while working simultaneously for CIA and GRU, described him as "not the most brilliant of men. He knows how to interrogate people, imprison them, and shoot them." When Serov accompanied Khrushchev to London in 1955, the press denounced him as a "butcher, odious thug and grinning gunman." The criticism so outraged Serov that he stormed back to Moscow.

But Serov thrived on brute force. He personally led the KGB goon squad that broke into a Budapest banquet hall the night of November 3, 1956, and hauled a delegation of Hungarian officials away from a supposed "state dinner." Hungarian Defense Minister Pal Maleter, who had run the recent uprising in his country and then been lured to Moscow on a pretext, was among those arrested; he was shot. Serov fell from power in 1959 with disclosure that a longtime KGB official, Pyotr Popov, had worked as a CIA mole.

Aleksandr N. Shelepin, the next KGB boss, was only forty years of age when he assumed power in 1959 after a career in the *Komosol* the Communist youth organization, and as a leader in what passes for Soviet "labor organizations." Shelepin stands as the only intelligence chief in recent history to publicly acclaim an assassin. The honoree was Bogdan Stashinsky, who murdered two exile dissidents in Western Europe in 1957 and 1959. After the second killing, Shelepin summoned Stashinsky to KGB headquarters and—in the name of the Presidium of the Supreme Soviet, as the Politburo was then known—awarded him the Order of the Red Banner. Shelepin left KGB in 1961 to run the Soviet labor confederation. But he remained such a powerful figure that in August 1964, he was called upon by dissidents in the Politburo (notably Leonid Brezhnez) to direct the coup d'etat that drove Nikita Khrushchev from power. But he soon fell into disfavor with Brezhnev (who apparently sensed him as a rival for power) and was stripped of all party posts.

Vladimir Semichastny was also young when he took the helm, only forty-three, and he was scarcely known even within the USSR bureaucracy. Some analysts have suggested Khrushchev wished just such a nondescript man running KGB during his consolidation of power in the USSR. Semichastny attracted public attention only once. When Boris Pasternak won the Nobel Prize for literature, Semichastny called him a "pig." Pasternak smiled. But Semichastny, with his policeman's dogged dedication to files, did embarrass his service and his country—and Khrushchev—in his bungled handling of the case of Frederick Baaghoorn, a Yale professor. Because Baaghoorn had served in the State Department during the war, KGB drones convinced themselves he must be a spy when he came to the USSR on a research trip. They arrested him on trumped-up charges at the Metropole Hotel in 1963 and then tried to trade him for a low-level Amtorg chauffeur caught spying in New York. President Kennedy made a personal issue of the case, and Khrushchev had to free Baaghoorn. Semichastny lasted another four years, but quietly out of sight.

Yuri Vladimirovich Andropov was the KGB chief best known to the West because he ultimately became Soviet premier. He also enjoyed perhaps the best press of any chief ever. A thin man with scholarly demeanor, Andropov certainly appeared more benign than the scowling Beria. Further, he was not a professional KGB man. He spent his career as a bureaucrat and diplomat before taking charge of KGB in 1967. But he earned his bloody spurs: In 1956, for instance, as ambassador to Budapest, Andropov worked with Serov in betraying supposed "allies" to grisly deaths.

Thus Andropov adjusted well to the cynical realities of KGB-dom. He pioneered the use of "psychiatric" treatment of dissidents; he slammed the door on Jews trying to flee a nation that did not want them; he was surrogate paymaster to uncountable international terrorists who did KGB's bidding. But when Andropov succeeded Leonid Brezhnev as premier in late 1982, these cruelties had to be explained away.

Cleansing a KGB director to make him fit as chief of state is on its face an impossible task; even the most cursory of glances spots the thousands of crushed lives left in Andropov's wake. Nonetheless, KGB disinformation worked to scrub the blood off Andropov's sword. The naive American press helped. The *Washington Post*, one of the more gullible accomplices, called Andropov a "well-educated and enlightened man—even a closet liberal—despite the stigma... as head of the KGB." One former CIA officer commented, "Calling

Andropov a 'closet liberal' is akin to calling Jack the Ripper an 'alley liberal' because that's where he killed his victims."

Vitaly V. Fedorchuk, Andropov's successor, held office only seven months—from May through December 1982—before moving on to the more sensitive job of Minister of Internal Affairs. Fedorchuk is one of the rare KGB chiefs to have done intelligence work abroad. A native of the Ukraine, Fedorchuk served in the Red Army during the war, then was assigned to East Germany as head of KGB's "Directorate of Special Departments." This unit bore responsibility for peacetime kidnappings, killings, and sabotage. His mettle proved, Fedorchuk returned to his native Ukraine as KGB regional chief in 1970, at a time of swelling nationalist unrest. In the words of Soviet expert Adrian Karatnycky, "In 1972, he orchestrated the most severe wave of political arrests and repressions to have occurred anywhere in the USSR in the post-Stalin era." Fedorchuk purged Ukraine party boss Petro Shelest and thousands of his adherents; KGB became the *de facto* government of the Ukraine. At the end of the decade, Karatnycky has written that Ukrainian political prisoners accounted for "over 40 percent of the Soviet Union's known political prisoners; nearly two-and-a-half times the proportion of Ukrainians in the Soviet population." Fedorchuk effectively scotched any idea of Polish labor dissidents finding support in the Western U.S.S.R.

Viktor M. Chebrikov, a metallurgist by training, a career KGB-nik by trade, had the fortune to be close both to Brezhnev (he is from Denpropetrovsk, where Brezhnev once was party boss) and to Andropov. His first major KGB post, in 1967, was personnel chief; a year later, he became one of six deputy directors. Chebrikov kept a low profile; when CIA analysts scurried for information about their new adversary, they found only twelve lines about him in the official USSR government yearbook.

Vladimir Kryuchkov, the last head of the KGB, made a serious error in political judgment in 1991 when he led a coup attempt against President Mikhail Gorbachev. He was faced down by Boris Yeltsin, an icon of the nascent democratic movement who had been elected president of the Russian republic earlier in the year. In the aftermath, Yeltsin handled the KGB gingerly. He decided the only way to curb its power was to split it into smaller independent agencies. He was reluctant to disband the KGB entirely. But on August 23, 1991, hundreds of Muscovites stormed Lubyanka Square and overturned the monument to Felix Dzerzhinsky, Lenin's first security chief. The KGB era reached an end.

The fact that its leaders historically lacked any hands-on experience in real espionage has not deterred KGB from aggressively challenging the West, through disinformation, active measures, support of terrorists and thefts of technological and other intelligence. The conclusion of Western analysts was that KGB was so institutionalized as an apparatus at this stage that a change of leadership did not affect its ongoing foreign operations. The director is significant only in terms of internal Soviet and party politics; he remains a security policeman first and foremost, hence the KGB's power.

Kh. V. (Khranif vechno)

Russian words for "to be kept in perpetuity." Intelligence files to be so maintained bear the *Kh. V.* stamp. But the words are rarely spoken directly by insiders. They prefer the obtuse words, *"Khristos voskresye,"* an Eastern greeting exchanged by Orthodox Christians after a church service. When spoken by one Soviet intelligence officer to another, the words had no religious meaning; however, their first letters, *Kh. v.,* "signaled that the files being discussed were to be retained permanently."

KING GEORGE'S CAVALRY

A British term meaning, in effect, when all other efforts fail, buy what you need ("Send in King George's Cavalry").

KINTEX

During the communist years, the official export/import agency of the Bulgarian government. In reality, according to defector testimony, the directors were ranking members of the Bulgarian intelligence services, and its wares included weapons for terrorists and drugs.

KNUCKLE DRAGGER

A paramilitary soldier working for CIA. The term began as a derogatory one—that the "paras" (usually military men detached to

Agency duty) were "such apes that their knuckles drag the ground when they walk." But one can now use the word to a "para" without expecting a punch in the mouth.

KONTORA GRUBYKH BANDITOV

Russian for "Office of Crude Bandits," a play on KGB's real title, *Komitet Gosudarstvennoy Bezopasnosti*, or "Committee for State Security." This was an inside joke among KGB officers and would not be heard from the Soviet man-in-the-street. KGB had no illusions about the nature of its work and discuss it with cynicism—among themselves, but not with outsiders.

KREMLIN KOMMANDANT (KK)

A KGB section that was answerable only to the head of the Soviet Union—a personal inspectorate of "spies who watch the spies." Agents assigned to the KK must swear an oath of allegiance to the Politboro. The KK supervises Kremlin security as well.

L

"L" PILL

The so-called "suicide capsule" carried by British and American agents during World War II, a lethal dose of cyanide encased in glass. Concealed in a false tooth, the "L" pill could be worked free by the agent's tongue; a sharp bite was required to break the glass, with death following quickly. If the agent accidentally swallowed the pill—say, during his sleep—it would pass through his body unbroken and harmless. Persons liable to capture who knew of such top secret plans as the Normandy invasion were fitted with an "L" pill.

LEAGUE OF FREE JURISTS

A lawyer-oriented group founded in West Germany in the late 1940s to wage political warfare against the puppet East German government, and to facilitate escapes from behind the Iron Curtain. UJF (the initials for its German name) was supported, but not controlled, by CIA. Its greatest strength was advice on how East Germans could avoid—if not circumvent entirely—new Communist laws restricting the economy. UJF kept a close watch on misconduct of East German lawyers and police, with the stated aim of justice once Communism was overthrown. With the detente of the 1960s, UJF ceased to be a significant force.

LEAK

The deliberate or accidental disclosure of classified information. In the current Washington sense, the former is most often the reason: officials in government leak secrets in order to advance their programs or damage those of bureaucratic rivals.

In the intelligence context, a leak is apt to come from a loose-tongued person who cannot resist bragging about the importance of his work, often after being encouraged by Eros, ego, or John Barleycorn. The existence of such blabbermouths means that low-level counterintelligence functionaries spend an inordinate amount of time hanging around bars and restaurants near sensitive installations, listening for persons who should know better than to talk about their work in front of strangers.

Despite the understandable human thirst for "inside" information, wary Washington officials occasionally shut themselves off from disclosures of classified material for fear they might inadvertently leak it. For instance, in 1961, the director of central intelligence, Allen Dulles, tried to brief Postmaster General J. Edward Day on CIA mail intercept programs, prefacing his remarks with the comment that "he wanted to tell me something very secret." Do I have to know about it? Day asked. "No," replied Dulles. Whereupon Day stated, "My experience is that where there is something that is very secret, it is likely to leak out, and anybody that knew about it is likely to be suspected of having been part of leaking it, so I would rather not know anything about it."

The word "leak" put a new term into the American political lexicon in the early 1970s. Irked by disclosures of several sensitive items (notably the American bombings of Vietcong installations in Cambodia), the Nixon White House created a special unit to try to contain the leaks. E. Howard Hunt, the former CIA officer in charge of the office, promptly termed his operation "The Plumbers."

Leaks can carry truly grave consequences. In May 1961 Attorney General Robert Kennedy encountered Hugh Sidey of *Time-Life* at a cocktail party. According to Kennedy biographer Evan Thomas, the President's brother said, "Hugh, do you have anyone in Cuba? Big things are about to happen. Better get someone there." The ill-fated Bay of Pigs invasion was mounted three days later. The operation had already been compromised elsewhere (chiefly by talkative Cubans) but that the nation's ranking law-enforcement official would make such a statement to a journalist illustrates the scope of the practice—and the odds against anyone being prosecuted. As DCI George Tenet told a congressional hearing on May 5, 1997, "We file crimes reports with the Attorney General every week about leaks, and we're never successful in litigating one."

LEGAL

An intelligence officer who works abroad with no attempt to conceal his nationality. But his actual work usually is by no means legal under laws of his host country. The legal is attached to the embassy or to another open activity of his government. But his cover job shrouds his true mission. KGB legals made up the bulk of any embassy staff in Western countries. Even when expelled for "activities incompatible with diplomatic status," these spies are never acknowledged as intelligence officers. The official position of the United States government is that the State Department has "an unyielding policy against the issuance of false passports or, indeed, their use by official or unofficial personnel under any circumstances." Such was written, supposedly with a straight face, by long-time CIA officer Kermit Roosevelt in his 1979 book, *Countercoup*. Roosevelt's statement does not jibe with my first-hand knowledge of the use of American passports abroad.

A legal who uses diplomatic cover has immunity from arrest. His true identity is presumed to be known by the other side. An "open" legal will not be directly involved in espionage himself—common sense says he will be under surveillance—but he will keep in frequent contact with the ranking resident clandestine agent. As British journalist Stephen Stewart has described the legal, "His function is to effect exchanges, to receive warnings from the host country about the activities of his resident, and generally to help undo the cumbersome tangles which any espionage service leaves in its wake."

The Soviets enhance their number of legals through use of the United Nations and other international organizations. Although sworn to work as international civil servants rather than in the interest of the USSR, the Soviets do no such thing. Arkady N. Shevchenko, Undersecretary of the UN until he defected in 1978, has written, "It is probably no exaggeration to count over half of the more than seven hundred Soviets in New York City as either full-time spies or co-opts under KGB or GRU orders or influence." In the political section of the Soviet Mission to the UN itself, at one time no less than twenty-one of twenty-eight "diplomats" worked either for KGB or GRU, Shevchenko stated.

LEGAT

Cable abbreviation for "legal attache," the not-so-secret title used by FBI agents assigned to American embassies abroad. Legats (pronounced "lee-gat") first appeared in Latin America just before

World War II, when FBI Director J. Edgar Hoover sought to build a bureaucratic fence to keep out the archrival Office of Strategic Services. As matters worked out the FBI, and not the OSS, had counterintelligence responsibility in Latin America for the duration of the war. Hoover thereafter began implanting his legats in embassies worldwide. Their prime function today is liaison between local law enforcement agencies and their American counterparts. In some instances the legat might even be a non-FBI person; in Spain, for instance, the Drug Enforcement Agency has at times held the position. Legats are often pestered by traveling American businessmen in pursuit of advice on local legal matters. These persons are politely shunted to a commercial attache.

LEGEND

The elaborate (if bogus), "biography" that an intelligence agency prepares for an officer who is to be dispatched abroad with an assumed identity. The depth and verifiability of the legend depends upon the sensitivity of the mission. The legend disguises the agent's true background and gives him a plausible reason for living in the new country. The KGB historically used Russians disguised as Canadians born of emigre parents, who then moved to the United States.

LEGITIMATE

CIA word for an outsider—a businessman or a journalist—who is exactly what he purports to be, and not living under a cover story. ("Oh, he's legitimate.") A legitimate is unwittingly useful to a CIA station because he can occupy the attention of surveillance teams that might otherwise be pestering actual officers. For mischief, an embassy political officer might dine publicly with a legitimate to further the conception that the visitor is an intelligence officer, thereby stimulating interest in his movements. This raises certain risks, the least of which is that the legitimate might have trouble obtaining a visa when next he tries to enter the country.

LETTER-DROP

A location where an agent can leave a secret communication to be retrieved by his control, or by another agent. A good letter-drop must have contradictory features. It should be in a busy enough area that a stroller is not conspicuous. Yet it also should be secure enough that the message does not fall into the wrong hands. Further, security demands that some time lapse between the deposit of a message in the letter-drop and its retrieval. The sorts of drops used by Western and rival intelligence agencies during the past decades form an endless list: from loose stones in fences in Central Park in New York to radiators in Moscow apartment foyers to toilet tanks in the United States Capitol.

The person who leaves a message in a drop so indicates by a visible signal posted elsewhere—a chalk mark on a wall, a thumb-tack on a park bench, even a piece of adhesive tape on a particular post in the esplanade on F Street Northwest behind the National Press Building in Washington (a KGB signal for several months in the late 1960s). The retrieval agent does not go to the drop until the signal tells him that it is "loaded."

According to Soviet expert William Hood, formerly of CIA, public telephone booths were favored drops for KGB. (*See* DEAD DROP BOX.)

LIGHT COVER

The use of diplomatic credentials by a CIA officer stationed abroad. Such an agent identifies himself as an "American official" or "embassy staff" without elaboration. Most officers with light cover at the outset make their true positions known only to local security officials with whom they have contact. But word eventually gets around to most everyone else of substance in the capital. In Soviet Bloc countries an officer under light cover was considered the lightning rod who attracted potential defectors who needed access to CIA in a hurry. He is also the accepted contact in the event that the agency of the "host" country desires to discuss professional ground rules about the conduct of agents.

LIGHTNING BOLT *(blyskawica)*

Vernacular among Polish intelligence attaches and code clerks for a top priority message.

LINECROSSERS

Army military intelligence term for low-level agents who are sent behind enemy lines in a combat situation. These persons are particularly valuable when the area they enter is part of their homeland, occupied by enemy troops. The U.S. Army's Counterintelligence Corps made wide use of linecrossers during the Korean War. So, too, did CIA, which managed to infiltrate South Korean linecrossers into the big Soviet naval base at Vladivostok. (*See* BORDER CROSSERS.)

LITERARY SPOOKS

Despite the desired secrecy of espionage and good intelligence work, the spy trade has long attracted men of letters, both journalists and more serious writers. Many kept quiet about their activities; others did not, and built literary careers upon their clandestine experiences. The most famous "quiet spy" was Daniel Defoe, author of *Robinson Crusoe* and many other works, who worked extensively on covert missions for the British Crown, yet wrote not a word about his activities. Undoubtedly there are others of more recent vintage, and perhaps history ultimately will reveal them.

Intelligence services of all nations recruit journalists as either full-time agents or casual informants, for obvious reasons. Journalists have easy access to important officials who do not always guard their tongues when speaking to a newsman, and, of course, the nature of their work provides an excellent cover for clandestine activities. Chapman Pincher, the veteran British writer and espionage specialist, records that Soviet intelligence was particularly anxious to recruit journalists during the 1930s. Similarly, many prominent intelligence figures worked as newsmen before turning to spying for their own countries. Roger Hollis, wartime head of MI5, worked in China during the 1920s as a stringer for the *South China Times* and then for the *Peking Times;* oddly, both papers were anti-British at the time. Kim Philby worked as a correspondent for *The Times* of London before joining MI6; simultaneously with his newspaper duties, he worked as a Soviet agent. After his exposure, he worked as a correspondent for *The Economist* and the *Observer* in the 1960s, based in Beirut.

Richard Helms's first job, after graduating from Williams

College in 1935, was as a United Press correspondent in Europe; a minor coup was an interview with Hitler. Helms was to become director of central intelligence three decades later.

LITERARY CHUTZPAH

In 1929 the Soviet writer N. G. Smirnov published a novel, *The Diary of a Spy*, the central character of which was a cold-blooded and ruthless but most successful British spy named Edward Kent. Victor Sukulov, a Red Army officer and intelligence trainee, was so smitten with the book—and the glamorous Englishman—that he adopted "Kent" as his legend name. When he began to rise through intelligence ranks, wiser persons counseled that the name attracted undue attention, and he was persuaded to abandon it. Sukulov's choice, in retrospect, makes about as much sense as an MI5 fledgling insisting on being called James Bond.

THE BOND MYSTIQUE, PRO AND CON

Ian Fleming, a former officer of the British Secret Intelligence Service, wrote several competent but modestly received spy books about James Bond, Agent 007, during the late 1950s. Soon after his election, President Kennedy mentioned that Fleming was his favorite "escape reading" author, an unsolicited accolade that made Fleming a very rich man. But despite his popularity with Kennedy, James Bond was considered with disdain by intelligence professionals, chiefly because of his reliance upon whiz-bang gadgetry. The British agent Greville Wynne, while being transported by the KGB from Hungary to the USSR via a military aircraft, decided that escape was impossible. But he mused, "I suppose that James Bond would have spat from his mouth a gas capsule (concealed in his molar) which would have overcome everyone but himself and would then have leapt to safety with a parachute concealed up his backside. But I regret that the British Intelligence Service lags behind Bond in ingenuity."

The name for Fleming's fictional agent came when the writer, a devoted bird watcher, saw a book, *Birds of the West Indies*, by a Philadelphia ornithologist named James Bond. As Fleming later wrote to Bond's wife, "It struck me that this brief, unromantic, Anglo-Saxon and yet very masculine name was just what I needed.... In return,

I can only offer you or James Bond unlimited use of the name Ian Fleming for any purposes you may think fit. Perhaps one day your husband will discover a particularly horrible species of bird which he would like to christen in an insulting fashion by calling it Ian Fleming."

Somerset Maugham, an SIS agent in Geneva during World War I, perhaps prefigured Bond's high-life spying in his novel *Ashenden*, about a British agent. As one of Maugham's agents poured himself a snifter of brandy, he remarked, "In my youth, I was always taught that you should take a woman by the waist and a bottle by the neck."

GHOST WRITERS IN THE SPIES

Once an intelligence agency debriefs a defector, it often exacts further value from him by encouraging the writing of a "memoir." Such accounts contain much useful and accurate material; nonetheless, they must be read with caution, and the foreknowledge that ultimate editorial control is wielded by an intelligence agency. Kim Philby did double duty for the KGB after fleeing to Moscow. First came his own *My Silent War,* chockful of both misinformation and outright mischief (unfounded slurs against former SIS colleagues, chiefly). Philby persuaded his old friend Graham Greene to write a foreword for the book; despite the prestige lent by Greene's name, *My Silent War* was dismissed by serious readers as silly propaganda. Yuri Andropov, then head of KGB, "encouraged" Philby also to help fellow spy Gordon Lonsdale write his memoir, *Spy: Twenty Years of Secret Service.*

The West has its own ghostwriters. *Handbook for Spies,* ostensibly by the defected Soviet agent Alexander Foote, actually was written by MI5 officer Courtney Young, case officer for the turned agent. Young carefully peppered the book with disinformation to mislead the Soviets as to exactly what Foote had told MI5 about Russian intelligence.

SPOOKONYMS

For varied reasons, many persons who write about espionage do so under pen names. Herewith a sampling of some of the more prominent:

E. Howard Hunt, former CIA officer	Robert Dietrich, John Baxter, Gordon Davis, David St. John
Edward Spiro, former Czech resistance fighter	E. H. Coolridge
James McCargar, former officer in the Pond [*See* POND]	Christopher Felix
Rupert Allason	Nigel West
Donald McCormick	Richard Deacon
Andre Leon Brouillard	Pierre Nord
Richard Henry Michael Clayton	William Haggard
David John Moore Cromwell	John le Carre
John Creasy	J. J. Marric, Michael Halliday, Gordon Ashe, Anthony Morton, Norman Deane, Jeremy York, among undisclosed others, for a total 562 books.
John Innes Mcintosh Stewart	Michael Innes
Kingsley Amis	Robert Markham
Alistair Maclean	Ian Stuart
Robert Ludlum	Jonathan Rider, Michael Shepard

LITMUS TEST

A counterintelligence trick intended to put false information before a suspected informer or agent and to monitor the results. For instance, the suspect might be told that a prospective Soviet defector intends to meet an agent at a certain location at a set time. Surveillance teams flood the area (discreetly) to see if any KGB agents show up to monitor the meeting. Another variation is to give false information to a suspect and then see if it showed up in unfriendly hands or is mentioned in radio traffic from the local Soviet embassy.

LITTLE AMERICA

A facility that exists only in the fertile minods of spy fiction writers. The usual description is of a Soviet intelligence training school near Winnitz, in the Ukraine—literally a replica of a small American city, complete with drug and department stores and a snack bar. Only English is spoken by the trainees and their instructors; the currency and newspapers are American. The purpose of Little America is to acquaint agents with the minutiae of everyday life in the United States. Trainees spent up to five years in Little America before their dispatch to the United States.

Such, anyway, is the frequently told story. William Hood, who spent some four decades as an intelligence officer, specializing in Soviet matters, says the idea of a "Little America" is a "shop-worn myth."

LIVE LETTER BOXES

Subagents who wittingly or unwittingly pass messages to other persons. For instance, he or she might be asked to drop off a parcel at a specific address, or to post a letter from a distant city while traveling.

LIVE LETTER-DROPS (LLDs)

A low-level operative recruited to receive letters and forward them to a case officer. According to long-time CIA agent William Hood, persons who seldom travel and who receive so little mail that they are unlikely to confuse personal letters with spy correspondence are the best LLDs. Traffic is slow—perhaps as little as one letter every year or two—so the case officer will sometimes mail "dummy letters" to ensure that the drop is operative.

LIVE TAP

A telephone tap that is monitored by a listener, rather than being recorded for later study. Live taps are used sparingly, given their high manpower cost. An example: The FBI suspects that a Czech spy is about to leave the United States, and it wishes to stay informed of his airline reservations. Thus an agent will put a tap on his home telephone and listen to all conversations, so that arrest teams can be ready.

LOCK STUDIES

A special course for FBI agents chosen for "black bag jobs"; essentially, instruction in how to pick locks and open safes. The courses were conducted at the bureau laboratory in Washington. (*See* DAME.)

LOG SUMMARIES

The notes an FBI wiretap team compiles during a shift of listening to telephone conversations. The calls themselves are tape-recorded. The listening agent adds "supplementary notes" concerning the identities of the speaking parties and the subject of the conversation, if unclear from the tape. But because of the lack of specific instructions, the Church Committee noted, "the summaries tended to be over-inclusive rather than under-inclusive; the supervising agent noted, for instance, that any information obtained about the subject's sex life or drug use would usually be included in the log summaries."

LONDON CAGE

A rather rough interrogation center the British set up at 6-7 Kensington Palace Gardens, London, for the questioning of major Nazi criminals after World War II. Key figures of the Abwehr, or German military intelligence service, were processed through London Cage. The camp was directed by Lieutenant Colonel Alexander Patterson Scotland, a native of South West Africa who joined the German Army to protest British colonialism (the British and the Germans contested control of his homeland), then in disgust went to British intelligence. His background made Scotland a formidable adversary.

LONG MARCH THROUGH THE INSTITUTIONS, THE

Soviet intelligence's attempt to infiltrate and influence the British "establishment," beginning in the early 1930s by planting long-term "moles" in such places as the Foreign Office and other Whitehall departments, media centers such as *The Times* and the British Broadcasting Corporation, the unions, and apparently even the Church of England. Michael Straight, an American who was recruited as a Soviet agent while at Cambridge, used the term in his 1960s confession to the FBI. Just how far the Soviets got on their "long march" is still a subject of heated debate in British intelligence circles. British intelligence writer Chapman Pincher first brought the term to public notice.

LONG VIEW PUBLISHING COMPANY, INC.

Now defunct publishing arm of the Communist Party, U.S.A. once based at 239 West 23rd Street, New York (also the CPUSA national office). Long View published such Communist periodicals as the *Daily World*, successor to the *Daily Worker*, and *Voz del Pueblo*, a "workers' paper" in Spanish. Anything with the Long View imprimatur was slavishly subservient to the Moscow line. A curious citizen who sent one dollar to Long View for a trial subscription to the *Daily World* might receive the five-times weekly newspaper for years on end. Journalistic nonsense, the paper was nonetheless valuable in that it announces Soviet disinformation themes in more or less literate English.

LOOT, THE

Information obtained through an intelligence operation. (From the French gangster term, *"le grisbi."*)

LUBYANKA

The prison section of KGB headquarters at 2 Dzerzhinsky Square, two blocks from the Kremlin. In pre-revolutionary Russia, Lubyanka was the name of the entire complex of buildings. The square was dominated by two insurance companies, "Russia" and "Anchor." A single Soviet insurance company succeeded them, known by the acronym *Gosstrakh*, from the words *gosudarstvennoye* and *strakhovanive*. The first word means "state"; the second, "insurance." But in Russian, the word *strakh*, the last syllable of the acronym, means "terror." So, in Russian jest, the complex has gone from "state insurance" to "state terror."

Uncountable thousands of persons have been imprisoned and executed in Lubyanka, including at least three deposed chiefs of the secret police. From the testimony of the few prisoners who came out of Lubyanka in condition to tell their stories, the first exposure to the brutal, grim prison is a shock, regardless of what they *thought* they knew of conditions there. Greville Wynne, the British businessman who was a major Western contact with Oleg Penkovsky, remembered an "elevator within an elevator," into which he was squeezed in a standing position, his face pressed against a small peephole. The elevator descent—"down, down, down"—lasted "probably less than a minute, but it seemed like an eternity. That slow sinking journey was the end of my life—"

Safe House Interlude Six

Wit Saves Necks

In 1980, a CIA officer flew into Tehran to establish contact with six American diplomats who had taken refuge in the Canadian embassy after their own embassy was seized by radical Iranians. Fluent in Farsi, and knowledgeable about Iranian society and customs, the officer traveled on a West German passport, with backup documentation showing that he was German. After a week, the officer escorted the Americans to Mehread Airport; they also carried bogus passports that CIA technicians had fashioned in Tehran, and prepared to board an international flight.

A suspicious immigration inspector spotted a flaw in the West German passport. "Why," he asked, "does your passport show only the middle initial 'H'? All the West German passports I have seen always include the full middle name.

The entire party froze. Americans traveling with false documents during the Khomeni reign faced arrest and a possible show trial and execution.

The CIA officer stared down at the floor in feigned embarrassment. "Yes," he said, "you are correct. Most passports do have the full name. But I must confess to you. You will notice that my date of birth is 1935." He hesitated, as if unwilling to continue. "I am ashamed of my middle name. You see, it is 'Hitler.'"

The Iranian relented, and the party flew to safety within the hour—shaken but safe, saved by the quick wit of the CIA officer.

M

MAD (Militarischer Abschirmdienst)

West German military counterintelligence, the "Military Screening Service." Comparable in function to the U.S. Army's CIC, charged with protecting the West German armed forces *(Bundeswehr)* from espionage and subversive activities.

MAIL COVER

A request to the U.S. Postal Service, by an intelligence or law enforcement agency, to examine the exterior of mail addressed to or from a particular individual or organization. The mail itself is not opened. The person or organization is not made aware of the cover.

MAKE

When a person under intelligence surveillance identifies his followers, he "makes" them. An identified surveillant is "made."

MAKING A PASS

The physical handing of a message to a courier or agent.

MAIN ENEMY

A widely used translation of the Russian term *glavnyy protivnik,* which can also be read as "main opponent" or "main adversary." By whatever translation, the *glavnyy protivnik* of KGB was the United States. But in GRU usage, oddly, the translation takes another twist: to *probable* enemy. When a Western interrogator is talking with a captured spy, and is uncertain which of the services he owes loyalty to, whether the spy uses "main enemy" or "probable enemy" can be significant.

MAYDAY BOOK

A detailed book listing the exact procedures to be followed in the event an agent in the field suspects that he is about to be arrested.

The Mayday Book—a term borrowed from the airlines and shipping—is available to a duty officer at all times, and persons who could be responsible for extricating the agent from danger must be reachable by telephone at any hour. The agent activates the emergency procedures by speaking a coded phrase over the telephone. He is instructed to dial a telephone number that is used for no other purpose (one can imagine a panicked agent receiving a busy signal) and that is tested at least once daily to ensure that it is in working order.

MEASLES
A killing done so discreetly that death appears to stem from natural causes. KGB poison needles were a prime source of "measles" during the early Cold War years.

MEMUNEH
Title given the head of Mossad, the Israeli intelligence service, who by law cannot be named publicly during his service.

MERCURY LOADS
Pistol slugs containing a dot of mercury, which causes a drastic increase in penetration of and damage to the target. A tool of a professional assassin. A mercury load will enable .22-caliber long-rifle round to gouge a huge chunk out of concrete—or to destroy much of a victim's head.

MFS (Ministerium fur Staatssicherheit)
The East German Ministry for State Security, run by KGB. According to two KGB defectors, the *MfS* is "Russian through the top three layers," although East Germans appear in the nominal hierarchy. Because of their low esteem, *MfS* officers are known as "eminently purchasable" by Western agencies. But they are seldom "purchased," because, as one former CIA officer states, "They carry K-Mart goods, nothing of value." (He referred to the cut-rate American discount house, and he meant that the *MfS* defectors to date were not worth the processing effort.)

MI5

Historical and widely-used name for the BRITISH SECURITY SERVICE. Great Britain's internal security organization, responsible for counter-espionage and counterintelligence within the United Kingdom (*See* BRITISH SECURITY SERVICE.)

MI6

Great Britain's overseas intelligence organization, formally known as the "Secret Intelligence Service," or SIS. It is roughly comparable in function to America's CIA.

SIS was formally established only in 1910, but the British had centuries of intelligence experience on an ad hoc basis. According to the British academician Keith Jeffrey, who published an authorized history of MI6 in 2010, since its founding in 1782 the Foreign Office "assembled networks of spies when the country was particularly threatened," obtaining funding from parliament through the "Secret Service Vote" which permitted the diplomatic community to have deniability for naughty work done on its behalf. Members of the diplomatic and consular services were "expressly barred" from intelligence work, and Whitehall sniffed that only the "lowest classes" of locals were liked to be recruited as sources. In due course, MI6 officers were permitted to operate from embassies under the guise of "passport control officers."

SIS worked closely with the OSS during World War II, and much of its tradecraft was adopted by the CIA. But, as many "old boys" are fond of saying, "The Brits taught us everything that *we* know, but certainly not everything that **they** know."

Once the world's premier intelligence service, MI6 has declined along with the rest of the British Empire. In the opinion of many professionals, its only accomplishment in recent decades was to provide a background for the James Bond espionage novels. MI6's main offices are in Century House, Number 100 Westminster Bridge Road, London—with a Mobil Oil gasoline station occupying the ground floor.

MI6's headquarters at Vauxhall Cross on the River Thames draw a bit of friendly ridicule by being dubbed "Leggoland" or "Babylon" because of its chunky, baroque architecture.

MICE

CIA acronym used to summarize the four most common motives for the defection of a KGB functionary: Money, Ideology, Compromise, and Ego.

MICRODOT

A German technical development that put British intelligence into a tizzy the first days of World War II. A document was photographed through a camera, similar to a *reversed* high-powered microscope, onto a special film that had virtually no grain. The result was a *micropunkf,* a small, shiny full-stop negative from which could be read, through a microscope used in the ordinary way, the text of an entire document. Ewen Montagu of British intelligence said the microdot process, when discovered, "was terrifying to our security people." The dot could be pasted over any period in a book or a newspaper or letter, almost impossible to detect by casual observation. Given the flood of mail that went through Allied censorship stations, the possibilities for espionage use of the dots were endless. Fortunately for the Allies, the Germans' use of the microdots was limited by their inability to supply field agents with the necessary cameras.

MICROPUNKT

German for microdot. (*See* MICRODOT.)

MIGHTY WURLITZER

A CIA program in which stories were planted in either controlled or friendly publications outside the United States and then reprinted elsewhere, with the aim of either discrediting the Soviet Union or calling attention to an incident the United States wished to publicize. For instance, a writer on a British newspaper would be given a true summary of a problem in Soviet agriculture. The printing of the story in his newspaper gave it further legitimacy, and it could then be circulated by such aboveboard agencies as the United States Information Service. USIS officers could simply hand the printed item to local editors and say, "This is what the *Times* of London said last week; you might find it of interest."

Frank Wisner, one of America's more renowned operatives of the postwar period, is credited for originating—and naming—the Mighty Wurlitzer. Signs of the Wurlitzer's continued existence are visible to close readers of the foreign press, but CIA people no longer boast about it, even *sotto voce*. (*See* COMEBACK.)

MIKETEL

An ordinary telephone that has been converted (clandestinely) into an open microphone capable of intercepting all conversations within hearing range—even when the telephone is not in use. A minute transmitter is planted in the mouthpiece of the telephone. A remote beeper signal, transmitted by a conventional telephone call, activates the transmitters (but without making the phone itself ring). The transmitter is powered by the current within the telephone system; hence no battery or other external power source is required. The person doing the bugging simply listens on the telephone to the conversation in the vicinity of the wired phone, or attaches a tape recorder so that he may review what is said at his leisure. One company advertised its version of the miketel as a "Coast-to-Coast Room Bug Transmitter." Another called the device the "Tele-Ear," and cautioned in its ads:

WARNING!
THE TELE-EAR IS NOT A "BUG"!

Because the very nature of this fantastic device makes it possible to monitor areas without observance, we must point out that federal law permits the use of the TELE-EAR *ONLY* as a burglar alarm.

It is illegal to use the TELE-EAR to surreptitiously monitor the conversations of parties that are unaware of its presence!

MINIMAX FIRE EXTINGUISHER COMPANY

Cover name for the London office of the Secret Intelligence Service in Broadway Buildings, 54 Broadway, opposite the St. James's Park Underground Station, during the first months of World War II. Later the brass plaque with the Minimax name was supplemented by another sign, "Government Communications Department." (Today the old SIS offices are occupied by the legal and public health divisions of the Thames Water Authority.)

MISCHIEF, INCORPORATED
Left-wing British euphemism for "MI," the formal designation for Great Britain's two major intelligence services, MI5 and MI6.

MOBILE BRIGADES, MOBILE GROUPS
The special units used by Soviet intelligence for executions of "state enemies" abroad. According to one-time Soviet agent Alexander Orlov, "The decision to perform an 'execution' abroad, a rather risky affair, was up to Stalin personally....It was too dangerous to operate through local agents, who might 'deviate' later and start to talk." Hence the use of what Orlov called mobile brigades.

MOLE
A high-level penetration agent who can give the innermost secrets of an intelligence service to its enemy. The most famed mole in espionage history was H. A. R. "Kim" Philby, who rose to the top of British counterintelligence while working as a Soviet agent. (For more on moles and the term's origin, see the Introduction.)

MODI'IN
Israel's military intelligence service.

MONEY—Cost of Intelligence
Between the two World Wars, agencies as the British Secret Intelligence Service scrambled to stay afloat financially. In 1935, as the European political crisis worsened, Admiral Sir Hugh Sinclair, then the director, lamented that his budget "only equals that spent every year on the *maintenance* (not the cost) of one of H. M.'s destroyers in Home Waters."

The U.S. intelligence community has been remarkably close-mouthed on its expenditures over the years. In October 2010, the agency said that during the fiscal year that just ended, it spent $80.1 billion—up from $25.8 billion and $28.7 billion, respectively, in 1997 and 1998, the only two previous years for which the information was made public. The figure is for the entire community, no breakout figures were made public about how the money was allocated. Past reliable estimates are that CIA's share is far less than such technological-depending activities as NSA and the National Reconnaissance Office.

MONGOOSE, OPERATION

The actions that President John F. Kennedy directed CIA to undertake in November 1961 "to help Cuba overthrow the Communist regime." MONGOOSE eventually included such actions as simple intelligence and propaganda operations; sabotage of factories and bombings of power lines; spreading nonlethal chemicals in sugar fields to sicken cane cutters; and plots to murder Premier Fidel Castro. Although CIA was to receive public and Congressional criticism for MONGOOSE, the prime mover was President Kennedy; CIA acted on his direct orders.

MOONLIGHT EXTRADITION

The extralegal deportation of a person sought for intelligence or law enforcement purposes. He is arrested by police of a friendly state and delivered across a border without the bother of judicial procedures. A good example: in 1949, Soviet atomic spy Morton Sobell, alerted of his impending arrest, fled to Mexico in expectation of taking a freighter to Eastern Europe. But Mexican police working with the FBI grabbed him in a Gulf Coast city and drove him nonstop to the Texas border, where he was handed over to American authorities without benefit of formal extradition. Since Sobell had entered Mexico under a false name, he had no appellate recourse.

MOONSHINE

An electronic device, circa World War II, used to amplify and return the pulses of German radar and thus simulate large numbers of approaching ships or aircraft.

MORALE OPERATIONS

A branch of the OSS that had perhaps the broadest mandate for creative mischief in the history of warfare. As stated in an OSS authorization manual, these operations encompassed "all measures of subversion other than physical used to create confusion and diversion, and to undermine the morale and the political unity of the enemy through any means, operating within or purporting to operate within enemy countries and enemy-occupied or controlled countries, and from bases within other areas, including neutral areas, where action or counteraction may be effective against the enemy."

Morale Operations' objectives were "to incite and spread dissension, confusion and disorder; to promote subversive activities against his [the enemy's] government by encouraging underground groups, and to depress the morale of his people...to discredit collaborationists, to encourage and assist in the promotion of resistance and revolt against Axis control by the people of these territories, and to raise their morale and will to resist." The techniques authorized included "agent provocateurs, bribery, blackmail, rumors, forgery, false pamphlets, leaflets and graphics, and 'freedom stations' masquerading as the voice of groups resistant within enemy and enemy occupied countries when used for subversive deception."

MOSSAD

The Israeli intelligence agency responsibile for gathering and analyzing information abroad, and for taking active measures against foes of the Israeli state. Formally, "The Institution for Intelligence and Special Assignments." In Hebrew, the formal name has two variants: *Mossad le Aliyah Beth,* and *ha-Mossad le-Modiin ule-Meyuhadim.*

Founded in 1951, Mossad reports directly to the prime minister, with only cursory oversight by the Knesset, the national legislature. Given extraordinarily free rein by Israeli public opinion, Mossad's eye-for-an-eye retaliations against such enemies as the Palestine Liberation Organization make it a much-feared organization. Intelligence experts put Mossad at the top rank of the world's agencies, on a par with CIA and KGB.

Mossad is a lineal descendant of a cluster of intelligence and security forces that date to pre-independence days. The major ancestors are the *Shai,* the intelligence division of *Haganah,* the underground army created by Jewish settlers in Palestine; the *Shin Beth,* responsible for internal security; and *Aliyah Beth,* which helped homeless Jews get into the then-British mandate. The Foreign Ministry (after 1948) had its own intelligence section for liaison with allied agencies, and there was a police intelligence unit as well.

In 1951, Prime Minister Ben Gurion reorganized the sprawling structure. *Aliyah Beth* and police intelligence remained intact. Two other groups emerged. *Aman* took responsibility for military intelligence, in close alignment with the armed forces. The new agency, *Mossad,* took on the broad range of duties that its title, "special assignments," would suggest.

Mossad's central office is on Oliphant Street in the Talbieh section of Jerusalem.

MOTHERHOOD
See AGENT OF INFLUENCE.

MOUCHARD
Double agent, in French.

MOVEMENTS ANALYSIS
Term for a constant surveillance of the daily travels of officials of a Soviet embassy and its satellite offices, such as other Bloc embassies, trade missions, the Aeroflot airline, the TASS news agency, and the like. By close and prolonged study of these movements, counterintelligence agents pinpointed which officials do legitimate diplomatic business, and which seem to be engaged in spying. James Bennett, a counterespionage specialist for the Royal Canadian Mounted Police, developed movements analysis as a means of keeping tabs on Soviet diplomats in Ottawa. A variation of the system is now used by all other Western intelligence agencies. Movements analysis gave MI5 the evidence that was used as the justification for expelling 105 Soviets from Britain in 1971. MI5 had more than 300 persons on its list; only the most flagrant were thrown out of the country.

The Soviets now counter movements analysis by dispatching non-intelligence personnel on rounds that parallel those of actual agents—the aim being to occupy and confuse Western counterintelligence people.

MUGBOOK
A photographic album or file maintained in CIA stations that contains the picture and brief biographical sketch of hostile intelligence officers operating in the area. New agents were expected to

spend hours studying the mugbook so that they could spot KGB or other unfriendly operatives at a glance. This knowledge is useful when an agent needs to know whether he is under surveillance. Friendly police and intelligence agencies help keep the mugbooks current by providing photographs of diplomatic personnel who go through customs control at international airports.

MUSIC BOX
A radio transmitter (KGB).

MUSICIAN
KGB term for a radio operator.

MYTHS ABOUT THE SPY TRADE
• That the FBI cut back on wiretaps temporarily each year before Director J. Edgar Hoover's appearance before the House Appropriations Committee. If asked about the number of bugs in operation, Hoover could give a deceptively low figure. Not so. The Church Committee found no significant blips in the number of taps before, during, or after Hoover's testimony during the five-year period. In 1970, for instance: on February 5, the Bureau maintained 39 wiretaps; when Hoover testified on March 5, there were 36 taps; on April 7, there were 37 taps.

• That Mata Hari never exposed her breasts while dancing (although she was liberal in affording audiences views of other anatomical regions) because her first husband, Randolph MacLeod, a British army officer, had bitten off her breasts in a jealous rage before leaving her. (He was suspicious of her from the outset, having made her acquaintance through a blind matrimonial ad.) In fact, Ms. Hari performed frequently in the buff, and the French autopsy report after her execution showed no such deformity.

• That Mata Hari was a woman of exotic Indian heritage who first danced in the nude at age twelve in a religious ceremony. Actually, she was born Margaretha Zelle, daughter of a Dutch shopkeeper. Her first husband, MacLeod, took her to India soon after they wed; whatever she knew of Indian customs came from that brief sojourn.

• That the British Secret Intelligence Service selects cover names for agents from the 1914 London telephone directory. "A chestnut of a story heard by every schoolboy in the United Kingdom, but not true at all," deposes a veteran of the SIS who once worked with such matters.

N

NASHI

Russian word for "ours," meaning in KGB slang an agent or collaborator. In an attempt to neutralize defectors and anti-Communist nationalists, the KGB tried in the 1950s and 1960s to spread the impression that anyone who spoke native Russian was *nashi*. The ploy did not succeed.(*See* SVOI.)

NATIONAL ALLIANCE OF RUSSIAN SOLIDARITY (NTS)

An anti-Communist Russian exile group formed in Yugoslavia in postczarist days. CIA took control of the willing NTS in the late 1940s and used its members for a host of espionage and line-crossing missions. Persons recruited from within NTS trained at a camp in Badwiesse, Upper Bavaria; and also at the U.S. Army's Intelligence School, Fort Holabird, Maryland; the Special Warfare School, Fort Bragg, North Carolina; and at CIA's Camp Peary near Williamsburg, Virginia.

NTS's goal was to proselytize liberal Russian exiles and to overthrow Communism in the USSR and replace it with a democratic parliamentary system. Leaders carefully screened members; they scorned the royalist philosophies of White Russians, and they would admit no person above thirty-five years of age. The German-born intelligence expert Louis Hagen (a British resident after 1936) compared its politics to the right wing of the British Labor Party, or to the left wings of the American Democratic and Republican parties.

NATIONAL CLANDESTINE SERVICE

Office under the Director of National Intelligence that supplanted the CIA's Operations Directorate in the label-shuffling that was part of the post-9/11 "reform" of the intelligence community.

NATIONAL COUNTERTERRORISM CENTER

Created by Presidential order in August 2004, the center implements a key recommendation of the 9/11 Commission: "Breaking the older mold of national government organizations, the NCTC should be a center for joint operational planning and joint intelligence, staffed by personnel from the various agencies." It comes under the jurisdiction of the Office of the Director of National Intelligence (ODNI). Its formal mission statement: "Lead our nation's effort to combat terrorism at home and abroad by analyzing the threat, sharing that information with our partners, and integrating all instruments of national power to ensure unity of effort." The staff of more than 500 persons (as of January 2011) is drawn from more than 16 departments and agencies, the bulk of them from CIA and the FBI.

NCTC is at a Northern Virginia site known as "Liberty Crossing," the exact address of which is the proverbial "undisclosed location." Although the massive buildings and their electronic clusters are clearly visible from several public roads, the media have tacitly agreed not to publicize the specific location. (When I inquired whether I should include the location in this book, a friend who is assigned there said, "Do that, and I am going to give you a good butt-kicking. Why make things easier for the bad guys?" Hence I am keeping my mouth shut.)

NATIONAL INTELLIGENCE AUTHORITY (NIA)

An executive council created by President Truman on January 22, 1946, to exert authority over the simultaneously created Central Intelligence Group (CIG). NIA was a predecessor to the National Security Council. Now defunct. (*See* CENTRAL INTELLIGENCE GROUP.)

NATIONAL INTELLIGENCE DAILY

A Washington newspaper that has perhaps the most tightly controlled circulation (sixty copies)—and most authoritative information—of any in the world. Published by CIA, the NID presents Agency daily reports in newspaper format, with brief summaries at the head of each story for the hurried reader. William Colby instituted the format soon after becoming director of central intelligence in 1974, to "emphasize the more important items and to offer the recipient the choice between a quick headline summary and reading in depth." (Colby first broached the newspaper idea while a junior officer in Stockholm in the early 1950s; the then-DCI, Allen Dulles, rejected the proposal. When Colby "suggested" the newspaper again, he was DCI. Publication began promptly.)

NATIONAL INTELLIGENCE ESTIMATE (NIE)

An estimate of the capabilities, vulnerabilities, and probable courses of action of foreign nations—friendly, enemy, and neutral. Although issued under the signature of the director of central intelligence, an NIE represents the composite view of the intelligence community. Individual agencies can express their dissent from consensus opinion through footnotes or addenda. In addition to national and regional studies, the intelligence community also produces periodical "Estimates of the World Situation." By custom, "Copy Number One" goes onto the desk of the President of the United States.

NATIONAL RECONNAISSANCE OFFICE (NRO)

The United States government agency responsible for managing satellite reconnaissance programs for the entire intelligence community. Although assigned to the United States Air Force for cover purposes (under the Under Secretary of the Air Force and the Office of Space Systems), NRO in fact is run by the National Reconnaissance Executive Committee, which is chaired by the director of central intelligence. President Eisenhower created NRO in 1960 as an outgrowth of the U-2 plane incident to give better management to the space and aerial reconnaissance program. NRO's existence was accidentally revealed to the public by a Senate committee in 1973, which listed it among the intelligence agencies that should make their budgets public. The Department of Defense annual report says only that NRO is charged with "the collection of specialized foreign intelligence through reconnaissance programs."

For its first decades, NRO was located in Room 4C-956 of the Pentagon. In the 1980s, it moved to the Virginia suburbs, near Dulles International Airport, and occupies three spectacular office buildings that bring to mind the architectural splendor of Brasilia. It and the NSA command the lion's shares of the national intelligence budget, dwarfing CIA and FBI.

NATIONAL RESETTLEMENT PROGRAM

The CIA's equivalent of the Justice Department's Witness Protection Program, for defectors and their families, rather than vulnerable witnesses in criminal prosecutions.

NATIONAL SECURITY AGENCY (NSA)

The agency responsible for the security of United States communications and for breaking the codes and ciphers used by other nations. President Truman created NSA by executive order on October 24, 1952; its predecessor was the Armed Forces Security Agency. NSA's existence was not officially acknowledged until 1957, although it occupies a conspicuously large building on the Fort Meade military reservation, easily visible from the Baltimore-Washington Parkway. NSA is arguably the most secretive agency in the American intelligence community. Wags say its initials stand for "No Such Agency."

NATIONAL SECURITY COUNCIL INTELLIGENCE DIRECTIVE (NSCID, or NEE-SID)

The formal order by which the National Security Council directs CIA or another intelligence agency to carry out an assigned mission. NSCIDs tend to be general, with the objective shrouded in euphemistic language. The nuts and bolts are defined more specifically in a follow-up paper called the "Director of Central Intelligence Directive," or DCID ("dee-cid").

The NSC (for a nonexistent example) might talk about the hostile attitude of the government of Jamaica and suggest "exploratory measures" to bring about a friendly successor. The DCID would go into the specifics of how to finance opposition parties, and the adverse propaganda that could persuade Jamaicans to change governments. Put side by side, no direct connection could be made between the NSCID and the DCID. Unless, of course, one understood the implications of the NSCID. (*See* DIRECTOR OF CENTRAL INTELLIGENCE DIRECTIVE.)

NATIONAL SECURITY LETTER

Letters which the FBI, the CIA, or other agencies send to companies when seeking information on terrorist or espionage investigations; permitted under post 9/11 legislation. Recipients are not required to respond, but persons involved in NSLs state that compliance is "surprisingly high."

NATIONAL VOICE OF IRAN (NVOI)

A clandestine radio station that broadcast into Iran from Soviet Azerbaijan beginning 1959, representing itself as the voice of unidentified "progressive" elements of the Iranian people. NVOI's purpose was to promote Soviet policies in Iran, and to spread anti-U.S. propaganda. During the seizure of the U.S. embassy in 1979–80, NVOI praised the "struggling young people...[who] proved to the world the conspiracies and intrigues of U.S. officials against Iran." Formally, the Soviet government disavowed any knowledge of or connection with NVOI.

NAVAJO CODE TALKERS

Native American Navajo Indians who served as radio communicators with the Marine Corps during World War II. Battlefield conditions do not permit the use of ciphers, so the Marines were temporarily stymied in developing a secure means of radio talk. Phillip Johnston, an engineer and son of Navajo missionary parents, suggested Navajo radiomen, noting that their verbal forms and tonal characteristics would be totally incomprehensible to the Japanese. He was correct and the Navajo Code Talkers contributed mightily to the Marine victory at Guadalcanal.

NEIGHBOR

A KGB term for another Soviet intelligence agency operating in the same country, or the same embassy. Under the Soviet system, no single "chief" controled all intelligence operations in a country; the KGB had its own operations, as did the GRU, the trade ministry, and other agencies.

"NEVER BE A CAREY"

Irish imprecation against becoming an informer or traitor. The nineteenth-century informer James Carey told the British the identity of one-time comrades who assassinated many high officials in Ireland. (*See* INFORMANT.)

NEVER SAY ANYTHING

Play on the initials of the ultra hush-hush National Security Agency, which, outsiders maintain, does not acknowledge, even to itself, the fact of its existence.

NINHYDRINE, NIN

A color reagent that is an internal security agent's favored friend. The reddish-black powder is lightly sprinkled on files where unauthorized hands are thought to be prowling. These hands almost immediately turn vivid violet when the ninhydrine—"nin," in spyspeak—reacts with the amino acid in the skin. Three days are required for the color to fade, and washing only makes it worse. Because it is easily visible to the eye, nin is useful for catching the village-idiot type of spy.

NKO

Need to know, as in "This report should be distributed on an NKO basis."

NO-TRAVEL LIST

A roster of CIA clandestine officers who have been "burned"— i.e., become known to the adversary—and hence are restricted to headquarters assignments.

NOFODIS

"No foreign dissemination"—a subcategory of classification that means a document must not be circulated outside the United States government. The nofodis designation can be used either to protect a particularly sensitive source of information or to conceal U.S. interest in an event elsewhere in the world.

NOISE

A mass of information that hindsight analysis proves to be useless or irrelevant, but that cannot be readily sorted through by the contemporary analyst or decision-maker. Roberta Wohlstetter, who wrote the landmark study on Pearl Harbor (*Pearl Harbor: Warning and Decision*), coined the term, concluding that "we failed to anticipate [the attack] not for want of the relevant materials, but because of a plethora of irrelevant ones." The creation of diversionary noise is an intelligence agency's role in any sizable military operation—e.g., the deceptions employed before the June 1944 invasion of Europe during World War II.

NONDISCERNIBLE MICROBIO INOCULATOR

The tongue-twisting term that DCI William Colby used, to describe a dart gun for firing lethal toxins, in an appearance before the Church Committee. Although the gun was never used and Colby volunteered the fact of its existence, the Church Committee brandished it during public hearings as an example of the perfidious weapons in CIA's arsenal. Colby's embarrassment was alleviated by his special counsel, Mitchell Rogovin. When a committee staff member dropped the gun on a table in front of Colby, Rogovin hastily scooped it up and handed it to Senator Frank Church. Hence Colby was not photographed with the "nondiscernible microbioinoculator" in hand. Many persons in CIA, active and retired, felt Colby was grandstanding, showing off unused tradecraft to curry favor with the Committee.

NOT-TO-CONTACT LIST

An FBI file on reporters and newspapers that had been critical either of the bureau or of director J. Edgar Hoover. Persons or organizations on this list received a brushoff when they sought information from the bureau. The bureau ran name-checks (i.e., a review of its computerized files) on reporters before extending them any cooperation on a story. If anything in the reporter's personal or professional life was suspect, he would be ignored.

NOT WITTING

A person not cognizant of the existence of a classified project, although he might be involved in it as part of his normal course of business. Such a person can also be called "unwitting." (*See* WITTING.)

NOTIONAL

A British coinage of World War II vintage has come to have diverse meanings. Originally, "notional" described the multi-level deceptions the British used against the Germans, and referred, in particular, to the misinformation fed back to Berlin after German agents had been captured and neutralized. The aim was to give the Germans imaginary but credible information that would convince them their agent was energetically active. For instance, according to Ewen Montague of the disinformation directorate, "a double agent notionally went to Bristol and notionally saw a ship (which may or may not have been there)." But the ship sighting was reported as gospel truth.

In current usage, notional has taken on expanded meaning. In positive intelligence, notionals are fictitious, private commercial companies that exist solely on paper, as the ostensible employer of intelligence personnel, or as the ostensible sponsor of activities in support of clandestine operations. In this context, notional can be applied to many of the "proprietary" companies the CIA has created to mask its covert activities.

To the FBI, however, a notional is a splinter group set up (by the bureau itself) to draw away membership from a target organization, thereby disrupting or destroying it. During its COINTELPRO project, the FBI ran three separate types of notional organizations:

• An organization whose members are all bureau informants. In one scheme, the FBI created an all-informant branch of a Communist group in a southern city. The initial purpose was to cause the Communist Party USA the expense of sending organizers to the area to work with the ostensibly friendly club and financing the travel of its members to national functions. The ultimate goal of members was to begin to deviate from the CPUSA line and be expelled from the main organization, so they "could claim to be the victim of a Stalinist-type purge."

• A notional organization with some unsuspecting (non-informant) members, intended to drain strength from the target group. For instance, in one southern city the FBI set up a Klan organization to attract members from the United Klans of America and managed to grow to a strength of some 250 persons.

• A wholly fictitious organization, with no actual members, used solely to mail letters or pamphlets attacking the target group. To use another example from the FBI COINTELPRO project, "The Committee for Expansion of Socialist Thought in America" for years attacked the CPUSA from the position of the "Marxist right." The "committee" consisted of one FBI agent, a letterhead, and a post office box mailing address.

Numerous CIA notionals, created to counter Communist organizations in Western Europe during the Cold War years, remain active and unrevealed. An informal rule of thumb is that CIA has its own counterpart to any front group that the Communists and their fellow-travelers manage to devise.

NOVATOR

KGB term, an acronym of the Russian words *novye*, for new, and *torit*, to flatten. It referred to a newly recruited agent abroad: a *novalor* was newly flattened and owned by KGB.

N.R.A.

"Nothing Recorded Against." British term for findings of no adverse information when a person is subjected to a security investigation.

NUGGET

British term for bait to be offered a potential defector—a woman, money, political asylum, or a piece of information.

NUMBER CRUNCHERS

The massive computers used by the National Security Agency to break encrypted messages plucked from the sky by electronic intelligence sources.

NURSEMAID

KGB officers who accompanied Soviet delegations or touring groups that traveled abroad. They were alert for any evidence of errant behavior or dangerous associations with foreigners. If the nursemaid (*nyanki* in Russian) saw anything out of the ordinary, the suspect Russian was shipped home immediately. The *nyanki* took no chances: if he permitted a Soviet citizen to defect, he faced a sentence to a labor camp in Siberia or even, in rare cases, execution for treason.

Safe House Interlude Seven

Spying Soviet Style

"Espionage is one of the basic means used by capitalist nations in their fight among themselves, and in particular in their fight against the USSR. Foreign intelligence agencies began to send their spies into Soviet Russia immediately after its emergence. Foreign espionage in our country is closely tied up with diversionist and wrecking activities and is aimed at the undermining of Soviet military and industrial might."

—Soviet Political Dictionary, 1940.

∾

"Espionage is needed by those who prepare for attack, for aggression. The Soviet State is deeply dedicated to the causes of peace and does not intend to attack anyone. There it has no intention of engaging in espionage."

—Soviet Premier Nikita Khruschev, speaking to the chairman of the Japanese Communist Party in 1962.

O

OBSERVATION POST (OP)

An apartment or office that overlooked a target of intelligence interest, such as the rear of a Soviet embassy or the entrance to the Cuban Mission to the United Nations in New York. CIA regularly uses non-Agency employees ("grannies") to live in OPs; CIA pays the bulk of the rent. In return, Agency technicians and photographers use the OP to take photographs of persons entering or leaving the target building and to monitor room microphones and sophisticated directional listening equipment. The grannies frequently are retired couples, hence the name.

OFFICE OF STRATEGIC SERVICES (OSS)

The United States' dominant intelligence agency during World War II. Formally created by President Roosevelt in June 1942 (after months of shadow existence), OSS gathered strategic and economic intelligence; conducted espionage, sabotage, and paramilitary operations; coordinated and supplied underground resistance movements; and made general mischief against the Axis. OSS was run by Major General William Donovan, a Medal of Honor winner in World War I, and a lawyer with a lifelong interest in intelligence matters—so much so, in fact, that the FBI's J. Edgar Hoover and the military intelligence establishment considered "Wild Bill" a sworn enemy. Hoover succeeded in keeping OSS out of South America, and General Douglas MacArthur would not permit it to operate in his Pacific Theater. But given a free hand elsewhere, OSS flourished. President Truman curtly abolished the agency on October 1, 1945, bowing to ill-defined fears that a "super-intelligence service" might arise in postwar America. OSS was reborn a few years later, in somewhat modified form, as the Central Intelligence Agency.

OFFSET ARRANGEMENTS

A system that prevents deep-cover CIA employees from becoming rich through their cover jobs. Any income earned from these jobs, or from cover businesses, is "offset" against the employee's CIA salary. Any money earned in excess of the salary eventually goes to the U.S. Treasury. The bottom line is that the officer receives only his government salary. (Also called "offset money.")

OH SO SOCIAL (OSS)

Derogatory term for the wartime Office of Strategic Services, based upon the fact that much of its hierarchy was drawn from graduates of Ivy League schools and socially proper New York law and brokerage firms. (Ironically, the OSS director, General Donovan, was the son of an Irish-American railroad worker, born in a waterfront district in Buffalo, New York, light years distant from the Social Register.) Derision aside, the "tea cup spies" were useful because much high-level political and economic intelligence could be gleaned from drawing room talks with princes and industrialists. At its zenith, OSS ranks contained such a medley of personnel— ranging from American academics to European emigre fighters to downright thugs and safecrackers—that the Oh So Social label was not taken seriously by anyone who knew the organization.

OLD CROWS

Electronic warfare specialists who use radio and radar receivers to monitor radar, navigation, and communications transmitters, and to jam transmissions on occasion. Term dates to World War II when electronic warfare first came into use. Operators of the equipment were known originally as "ravens" after the British code word for the electronic countermeasures program. Americans working in the program gradually changed the term to "crow." And, as the contingent aged, the name evolved to "old crows." In 1964 a group of the specialists formed a fraternal/professional organization known as the "Association of Old Crows," composed in equal parts of persons who work in the government and the private sector. Understandably, the Old Crows have a close relationship with the Department of Defense and the National Security Agency. The group has offices in Alexandria, Virginia.

ONE-SHOT

An informant who thinks he can make a one-time deal with an intelligence agency, exchanging an item of singularly important information for a large amount of money. Such seldom happens. In the words of former CIA case officer William Hood, "Grasping greenhorns have about as much chance of swinging a deal like this as the average football fan would have of surviving more than a few minutes in a Super Bowl game."

ON THE GROUND

To place a new or prospective agent under light surveillance is to see what he or she looks like "on the ground." CIA routine procedure in the 1960s was to conduct a loose surveillance of any "walk-in" who volunteered information, to determine whether he was controlled by a rival agency. U.S. tradecraft is for such a recruit to break any contact with discernible intelligence agencies before making his overture to the opposition. The Soviets—through the 1960s, at least—were not as careful.

ONE-TIME PAD

A code system that relies upon the sender and the receiver having identical copies of "pads," usually some 50 pages, each covered with lines of letters or figures chosen at random. The person sending the coded message uses letters or numbers from one of the pages; the receiver, who is told the page being used that day, consults his copy of the pad to decipher the message. Since each page is different, the code is unbreakable. The risk is that a field agent will have to discard his pads in an emergency, thereby losing his ability for clandestine communication with his control. The German Foreign Office initiated the use of one-time pads in the early 1920s. The Germans used pads of 50 numbered sheets, each legal-sized, containing 48 five-digit groups distributed in eight lines of six groups each. "Each 240 digits were random, and no sheet duplicated any other," writes code expert David Kahn. "For the first time in history, the official communications of a government were absolutely secure against the prying eyes of others." Oddly, although the fundamentals of the system were developed—and patented—by an American, Gilbert S.

Vernam, the United States military did not adopt it until the eve of World War II.

OPEN TEXT

Message sent in uncoded form. An intelligence agent operating in unfriendly territory routinely encodes the most innocuous of dispatches.

OPERATIONAL CLIMATE

The gist of the political, economic, and cultural situation in a given country that is the target of intelligence efforts—a situation that, for better or worse, facilitates intelligence activity in the country of the opponent. The most important (and obvious) requisites are one's freedom to stay anywhere in the country without reporting to the police, to select one's profession freely, and the absence of one's need to carry official identification and show it upon demand. Soviet Bloc intelligence services also listed these other criteria for possible espionage:

- The strength, capability, professionalism, technical equipment, and effort expended by the opponent's intelligence and counterintelligence services;
- The attitude of the individual citizen toward his own country—patriotism, pride in being a citizen, and the willingness, in case of need, to lay down one's life;
- The patriotism of those individuals who are the principal targets of intelligence efforts—cultural, political, and economic circles;
- The coexistence of various ethnic groups of citizens and their ability to mutually tolerate each other or the disputes between them;
- The amount of crime in the country;
- The professionalism of the police apparatus, its technical equipment level, and the average rate of uncovered and punished crimes;
- The level of education of the average citizen and his general political outlook;
- The attitude of the average citizen toward intelligence and

counterintelligence officers. (According to defector Josef Frolik, "The Czechoslovak Intelligence Service, along with the intelligence services of the other Communist countries, have a professional respect for the intelligence agencies of the United States. This point results in the fact that the overall agent environment [in the United States] is evaluated as being very negative with respect to the Communist intelligence services.")

Agent Environment is the Soviet Bloc services' term for what CIA calls "operational climate."

OPERATIONAL INTELLIGENCE

In CIA usage, the information necessary to identify potential agents, their tastes, their attitudes, and people with access to them and through whom American intelligence could work. CIA's William Colby felt that operational intelligence often became "an end unto itself." Much energy was expended on learning inside information on Communist embassies and how they worked internally, and in finding local citizens who had contacts with the Communist diplomats and who would find even more information. According to Colby, too often these persons proved to be in minor positions and to possess minor information. A contrary view, expressed by a CIA official with long experience in Western Europe, goes as follows: "Get your foot in the door, and keep it there, and eventually you'll come up with significant information." This official expresses what is known as the "Fuller Brush Man" approach to intelligence: "You gotta' make housecalls to make sales, and you gotta' make housecalls to get intelligence."

OPERATION SECURITY (OPSEC)

The methodology of concealing an operation from detection by the adversary. Originally a military term, now one that is widely used in the intel community.

OPERATIONAL USE

Using a person, group, organization, or privileged information in a clandestine operation or in support of a clandestine activity.

OPERATIVE

See AGENT.

ORCHESTRA

In Abwehr (German military intelligence) usage during World War II, any espionage organization working against the Reich. Abwehr procedure was to subtitle "orchestras" according to their areas of operation ("Maritime Orchestra" or "Brussels Orchestra"). Hence when the Abwehr detected an "organization" reporting to Moscow, it became the famed *Rote Kappelle,* or "Red Orchestra," one of the more successful intelligence rings of World War II.

ORDER OF BATTLE (OB)

Information regarding the identity, strength, command structure, and disposition of personnel, units, and equipment of any military force. OB intelligence is usually compiled and maintained by the military services, which further breaks the information down into "Tables of Organization," or personnel strength, and "Tables of Equipment," or material. The OB enables a commander to know the strength and composition of forces facing him on the battlefield.

Changes in the OB can indicate strategic decisions. For instance, intelligence officers in General Douglas MacArthur's Far East Command in the spring of 1950 noticed that the North Korean People's Army (NKPA) was moving numerous tank units toward the 38th Parallel, the demarcation line between North and South Korea. MacArthur's intelligence chief, Major General Charles Willoughby, dismissed the OB shifts as insignificant. Several weeks later the tank units spearheaded the Communist invasion of South Korea. Five months later, MacArthur and Willoughby similarly ignored other OB intelligence suggesting Chinese Communist intervention in the Korean War. These two episodes support the axiom: "Intelligence is only as good as the people using it."

ORGANIZATIONAL COVER

The use of legitimate corporation offices abroad (as well as non-intelligence U.S. government agencies) as a cover for covert agents. The preferred procedure is for CIA to obtain the blessing of a senior corporate executive, although on occasion no one in the company will be witting of his true mission. Working under organizational cover is onerous because the agent usually must perform his corporate job for credibility purposes; thus only his evenings and weekends (and other odd moments) can be given to CIA. Further, his corporate salary goes into the U.S. Treasury, and he must live on his agency income (although he might draw extra expenses if his corporate job requires a high lifestyle).

The corporations that provide cover to CIA vary from year to year; obvious ones would be airlines, banks, hotel chains, and trading companies. Of the myriad U.S. agencies, only one is strictly off limits to CIA cover assignments: the Peace Corps. (*See also* COVER ORGANIZATIONS.)

OUTSIDE MAN

A CIA case officer who works abroad as an ostensible private citizen with no overt contacts with either the CIA station or the United States Embassy. (*See* DEEP COVER, INSIDE MAN.)

P

P.4

A super-secret branch of MI6, the British intelligence service, which "persuades" professionals such as attorneys, physicians, and accountants to pass along information concerning national security that they obtain from clients. P.4's very existence violates ethical standards of the relevant professional societies; thus it is an unacknowledged activity. CIA briefly considered such a section in the late 1950s, but rejected it on ethical grounds. The British felt no such constraint.

PACKED UP

Phrase describing an intelligence operation that is terminated, either because of failure or fear of exposure.

PALMER RAIDS

The mass arrests, on the night of January 2, 1920, of some 10,000 persons in 33 cities, all believed to be members of the Communist and Communist Labor Parties. The raids, by the FBI and immigration agents, were directed by Attorney General A. Mitchell Palmer, who feared the country faced anarchy and sedition. Acting under Senate pressure to move against "alien radicals," Palmer decided that the "very liberal" provisions of the Bill of Rights were expendable during the crisis and that in a time of emergency there were "no limits" on the power of the government "other than the extent of the emergency." Civil libertarians widely protested the illegality of the raids, and the detention of many of the persons arrested without bail or access to lawyers. Hundreds of those arrested were later deported as illegal aliens, including such Communist stalwarts as Emma Goldman.

Given that the Comintern had publicly called for the overthrow of "decadent capitslist governments," Palmer had ample reason to act. (*See* COMINTERN.)

PANEL SOURCES

FBI informants who are not involved in a group under investigation, but who will "attend its public gatherings on behalf of [the] FBI for intelligence purposes or as potential witnesses." Panel sources were first developed to act as witnesses in Smith Act trials of Communist Party members in the 1950s, when it was necessary to prove such simple facts as the existence of the CPUSA, the dates and places of public meetings held by the party, and similar matters. To avoid surfacing regular informants within the CPUSA to establish such facts, the FBI developed panel sources. Some of these panel sources were pressed into service involuntarily. During the 1960s, one of my reportorial colleagues was directed to attend a Communist meeting; when he returned, he was instructed to write not a news story, but a "memo for the FBI," summarizing what had happened. He protested—"I'm a newspaperman, not a spy"—but complied. Later the reporter was called to testify at a deportation proceeding involving one of the persons who had spoken at the meeting.

PAPAKHA

Russian word for "big hat," used by KGB underlings to denote officials of importance in their organization. The less-liked *papakhas* are called *zhopas* (literally, asses). A CIA recruiter who hears a target call his superior a *zhopa* knew that he was fishing in promising waters.

PAPER MERCHANT

An unscrupulous person who manufactures "intelligence reports" out of whole cloth and peddles them to one or more services. Such con men thrived in Western Europe in the late 1940s and early 1950s, to the acute embarrassment of both Western and Soviet Bloc agencies. Many sold the same bogus reports both to CIA and MI6. Given agencies' zealousness in protecting covert sources, such subterfuges could go undetected for months, with the similar reports (although coming from the same source) confirming one another.

One paper merchant who achieved singular success in World War II turned to fraud when he found purity of motive was not sufficient qualification for joining British intelligence. Felipe Fernandez, a left-wing Spanish journalist, volunteered his services to SIS in 1941 but was rejected because of Communist leanings. Undeterred, Fernandez sought out the Abwehr. The Germans hired Fernandez, and he took up quarters in Lisbon and flooded the Abwehr with elaborate reports, supposedly coming from a vast network he controlled in England. ARABEL (as the Abwehr called Fernandez) had as his only tools a fertile imagination and a guidebook to Britain. But the Germans bought his reports, whereupon he returned to SIS, documented his contacts, and was taken in as double agent GARBO. Through May 1945, when the European war ended, GARBO/ARABEL supplied the Germans with literally hundreds of bogus reports, receiving in return 20,000 pounds. The Germans gave Fernandez the Iron Cross; the British, the King's Medal for Service in the Cause of Freedom.

PARAMILITARY FORCES, PARAS

Units of soldiers not attached to the formal military services of any nation, even though they might resemble conventional armed forces in organization, equipment, training, or mission. Paras range from small training missions that work with local friendly soldiers to vast organizations such as the brigade of Cuban exiles that comprised the Bay of Pigs invasion force. CIA has traditionally served as the cover organization for American paramilitary forces, members of which are drawn from the armed service, mercenaries, and local armies. An American assigned to paramilitary duty with CIA "resigns" from his service, with the understanding that he can reenter without loss of rank or seniority upon completion of the mission.

During the 1960s and 1970s, CIA relied heavily upon foreign recruiting of so-called soldiers of fortune to support friendly governments and oppose Communist takeovers of emerging African nations. (So, too, did former colonial powers such as Belgium and France, which tried to maintain toe-holds in their former holdings.) Contrary to popular legend, CIA recruited through intermediaries, and *not* through the classified advertisements of such adventure magazines as *Soldier of Fortune.*

Another source of paras is soldiers caught on the losing side of a revolution or coup. For instance, CIA more or less openly supported Nicaraguan exiles opposing the leftist Sandinista government that took power in that Central American nation in the late 1970s. Working from bases on the Nicaraguan border, these paras conducted enough sabotage and espionage missions to keep the government on edge (CIA's intention being to dissuade the Sandinistas from military adventure and subversion elsewhere in Central America).

The free-booting life of a para is offset by the fact that, since he belongs to no organized military force and wears no recognized uniform, he is subject to being shot as a spy if captured.

PASSWORD
See RECOGNITION SIGNAL.

PATRICE LUMUMBA UNIVERSITY
A KGB-conducted school in Moscow for Third World youths, many of whom arrived in the USSR expecting to be trained as physicians, but instead were schooled in sabotage, bomb-making, and other terrorist tactics. The youths were kept segregated from the general Soviet population, to avoid undue exposure to the anti-black racism endemic in the USSR.

PENETRATION
The process by which an intelligence agent gains access to the organization and work of another intelligence service, unknown to the latter.

PERSONA NON GRATA (PNG-ed)
The diplomatic term for a person who is told to leave the host country because of unacceptable conduct. Since many spies operate under diplomatic cover and hence have immunity from arrest, they are "persona non grata-ed" when caught. (The verb form of the word, which might cause grief to a philologist, is nonetheless common among both diplomats and spooks.)

Many such cases never reach public view because the host country chooses not to make a major issue of the offense. One such instance was a Czech intelligence plot in 1958 to have an agent put atropine salt into shakers in a cafeteria of Radio Free Europe in Salzburg, Austria. (RFE was a major target of the Soviet and Bloc intelligence services.) Atropine can cause hallucinations and, in great enough quantities, even death. But the person given the assignment was a double who worked concurrently for CIA and exposed the plot. The Czech intelligence official responsible, Jaroslav Nemec, who had diplomatic immunity as a "vice consul," was PNG-ed out of the country—quickly but quietly.

Ph.D. INTELLIGENCE

A term of derision J. Edgar Hoover, the late director of the FBI, used to describe the academic-heavy Central Intelligence Agency. Hoover so detested the CIA and its "Ivy League" director, Richard Helms, that he severed all liaison with the Agency during his latter years.

PIG

KGB term for a traitor.

PIGEON

The target of a surveillance.

PIGGYBACKING

Relying upon a friendly intelligence agency to supply the fruits of a covert investigatory technique, such as the result of a wiretap or a bug. For years Western intelligence agencies piggybacked on one another throughout the world—the British providing information from its former protectorates in the Arab nations; the Americans watching Latin America and parts of Western Europe; the Israelis spying on Middle East nations. The exchange meant maximum coverage at minimal expense. Unfortunately, CIA's troubles of the mid-1970s caused several Western agencies, notably Israel's Mossad, to begin withholding previously shared information. Piggybacking has revived, to a large extent, since 1981.

PINKERTON

Agent of the Pinkerton Detective Agency, which served as the primary military intelligence arm of the U.S. Army during the Civil War and continued a close alliance with federal and local law enforcement agencies thereafter. During the late 1800s, the

Pinkerton Agency performed many of the functions now under the purview of the FBI. In the late 1800s, the Pinkertons became notorious as strikebreakers who beat up pickets and wrecked union halls. The name remains a dirty one in labor circles.

PISCINE, LA.
See SDECE.

PIT, THE
A basement area in CIA headquarters where classified documents are shredded, pulped, or burned (or combinations thereof). Through the 1970s, the residue was dumped into the Potomac, which flows a few hundred yards north of the building. Environmentalists complained of the pollution, so now CIA's destroyed secret papers are sold for landfill in West Virginia.

A secondary usage for "The Pit" refers to the round-the-clock operations centers that CIA divisions maintain to handle crisis situations. Because of the architectural style of the CIA building, these centers tend to be windowless rooms whose frenetic human activity overwhelms the capacity of the air-conditioning system.

PITCH
An attempt by an intelligence agency to recruit a person from the opposition.

PLANT
1. A listening or observation post used to provide a vantage point for watching a surveillance subject. An ongoing routine for an FBI field office is to establish "friendly relations" with the management of major hotels. Thus, if a surveillance subject suddenly rents a room and the bureau desires an adjoining room to use as a plant, any previous guest is quickly transferred elsewhere.

2. A person put into proximity to an investigative subject with the intention of exploiting a known or perceived weakness. When the FBI was trying to discredit the Rev. Martin Luther King, Jr., as a philanderer, for instance, an agent suggested "placing a good-looking female plant" in his office. Bearded about such a technique before the Church Committee, former FBI official

William Sullivan called it a "common practice among intelligence services all over the world. This is not an isolated phenomenon. This is a common practice—tough, dirty business. Whether we should be in it or not, that is for you folks [the Senators] to decide. We are in it... No holds were barred. We have used that technique against Soviet agents. They have used it against us." Sullivan, however, offered no defense for the campaign against Dr. King.

PLAYBACK

The reprinting, in another country, of false information that an intelligence agency managed to have published abroad. "Playback" is intended to give credibility to propaganda or disinformation campaigns. For instance, KGB will plant, in an Indian newspaper, a bogus story about American nuclear planning. When the story is picked up in Western Europe, it is attributed to "the authoritative Indian political daily *Southern Hindustani Bugle.*" (Also known as *blowback* or *domestic fallout.*)

PLAY MATERIAL

Accurate information deliberately given a rival intelligence agency as a means of establishing the credibility of an agent who is attempting an infiltration. Since play material often involves turning one's own operative over to the enemy, it is an especially ruthless technique. In the 1950s, for instance, the KGB wished to infiltrate an agent named Nikita Khorunzki into the CIA-run National Alliance of Russian Solidarity (NTS), which was running missions into the Soviet Union. Khorunzki sought out a known CIA agent and told him that a somewhat overblown blonde with gold teeth was, simultaneously, the girlfriend of a lieutenant in the Soviet Army Mission in Frankfurt and a Soviet army deserter named Vassily Graburov. Checking his index, the CIA man discovered that Graburov had offered himself to American intelligence as an informer on KGB affairs. Surveillance quickly revealed that he was using the frowzy blonde as a courier to maintain contact with the Soviet lieutenant. Graburov was exposed and arrested.

His bona fides now established, Khorunzki managed to secure a job as a teacher at the NTS espionage school at 53 Kaiser Friedrick

Promenade in Bad Homburg. He stayed there—at unrevealed cost to NTS and CIA—for several years before being found out and sent to jail for fourteen years. Trial testimony suggested that he revealed details of specific NTS missions, as well as giving to KGB the names of NTS family members still in the Soviet Union.

PLUMBING

The support structure that enables agents to operate in the field. "Plumbing" is an all-inclusive term that means agents have detailed maps and train and subway schedules, as well as safe houses, clandestine letter-drops, surveillance teams, and technicians who can bug houses or apartments, tap phones, do clandestine photography, and find a bottle of Scotch at four in the morning. Generally the plumbers in this infrastructure are unaware of their ultimate employer. When an agency is preparing for an operation, the preliminary logistics are called "putting in the plumbing."

PNUTS ("PEANUTS")

Possible Nuclear Test Site. A word heard among U.S. Air Force intelligence officers.

POINT, THE

The Harvey Point Defense Testing Facility near Elizabeth City, North Carolina, training ground for operatives of the Special Activities Division. Originally created as a CIA paramilitary training facility, it is now in the domain of the National Clandestine Service. The regimen rivals—or surpasses—that of the SEAL training facility to the north. (*See* SPECIAL ACTIVITIES DIVISION.)

POSITIVE VETTING

British security procedure wherein persons with access to classified material must be questioned and their background and previous associations and activities investigated and verified. Despite repeated security scandals, the British did not institute such a system until the mid-1950s. The American version, the "background investigation," or "full-field investigation," dates to the early days of World War II.

PRELIMINARY INVESTIGATION

A first-phase FBI probe of a subject whose involvement in criminal, subversive, or extremist activities is questionable or unclear. It is undertaken to further define his involvement and to determine whether a statutory basis exists for a full investigation. According to the FBI Manual, a preliminary investigation is supposed to be confined to a review of public source documents, record checks, and "established sources" and informants. (*See also* ESTABLISHED SOURCE.)

PRETEXT INTERVIEW

A conversation in which the agent arranges to talk about one subject when he is really interested in a totally different matter. The relevant questions are casually interjected into the interview. A pretext interview can also be arranged for the sole purpose of gaining access to a house or office for an agent, who will then try to conceal a microphone or other listening device on the premises. Newspaper reporters and writers have been known to use the same subterfuge. (*See also* ELICITATION.)

PROBE MICROPHONE

A microphone that can be put into a wall and transmit conversations in the adjoining room. The installers must drill a hole to within a hair's-breadth of breaking the internal surface. In some FBI field offices, such a device is known as a "spike mike."

PROCESSING THE TAKE

Transcribing, translating, and analyzing the material gathered through telephone taps and room bugs. Processing scores of hours of such material is costly and difficult. Since the targets often have reason to suspect their conversations are being monitored, the material is considered "low-grade ore."

PROGRESSIVE JOURNALIST

See RABCOR.

PROPAGANDA

By OSS definition, the "deliberate direction or manipulation of information to secure a definite object. It is promotion masked as to its (1) origin or source; (2) interests involved; (3) methods employed; (4) intent; (5) content spread; and (6) results accrued to the target.... The contents of propaganda may range from absolute truth, through selection, distortion, half-truths to complete falsehood—what is appropriate in order to secure positive action."

PROPRIETARY COMPANY

An ostensibly private business firm or office created and operated by an intelligence agency, as a means of providing cover for secret operations. CIA runs two types of these companies. The "operating proprietaries" actually do business as private firms. They are incorporated where they are officed, they file the applicable state and federal tax returns, and they obtain the licenses necessary to a legitimate business operation. (They also have been known to earn substantial profits.)

There is also the "nonoperating proprietary," sometimes called a "notional." Consisting of a letterhead, a mailing address, and a phone number, this type is essentially a mail-drop business based in the office of a friendly (although non-CIA) law or business firm. The "notional" aspect gives a covert agent a visible means of support; for instance, if he claims to work for Sunshine Enterprises, Ltd., in Washington, such a company can be found in the phone book, and someone will answer the telephone when it rings, and respond to mail.

In at least two instances, CIA used proprietaries for operations that skirted violating the law prohibiting Agency domestic operations. One such proprietary was an ostensibly private security company in the Washington, D.C., metropolitan area, which was controlled by CIA's Office of Security and was used for operations where no government identification was permissible, or where other considerations required "deep cover." In 1967, the Office of Security used the firm to monitor anti-war and other dissident groups for evidence of any actions planned against CIA facilities. Targeted were the Women's Strike for Peace, the Washington Peace Center, the Congress on Racial Equality, and the Student Nonviolent Coordinating Committee. The surveillance was low-level and amateurish, with the proprietary company hiring construction workers, other blue-collars, and members of their families. These "agents" received no deep training, and their reports to CIA were mostly useless. But the program continued until 1970, under the code name MERRIMAC. CIA justified MERRIMAC as an exercise of its statutory right to protect its physical facilities.

Another borderline proprietary dealt with telegraphic intercepts. Inundated with scores of thousands of cables recorded on a new magnetic tape system, the National Security Agency in 1966 pleaded with CIA for administrative help. Due to the dubious legality of its SHAMROCK interception program—whereby NSA snatched up 150,000 international telegrams monthly—NSA wished the messages to be processed discreetly. CIA obliged by renting office space in lower Manhattan under the guise of a television tape processing company, designated LPMEDLEY. For the next seven years, NSA read purloined cables in comfort and privacy, thanks to the CIA proprietary company. The Church Committee strongly criticized both MERRIMAC and LPMEDLEY. (*See* NOTIONAL.)

PROTECTED INFORMATION

Information derived from clandestine sources. The fact that such information is known must often be concealed in order to protect the source.

PROTECTIVE SECURITY

British term that encompasses all measures taken to keep classified information out of unfriendly hands. Sir Martin Furnival Jones, while director of MI5, stated the formal dcefinition in these sentences:

"The body of regulations which regulate the behaviour, in relation to security information, of those who have access to it and... the selection of those who have access to it. It involves the processes of selection which are supposed to weed out those who may be unreliable and it embraces also their supervision once they have been taken on. It involves their education in security, in the things they should do and the things they should not do when they have charge of security information. It embraces an enormous range of rules for the handling of classified material....It embraces the physical measures taken for the protection of information, such as locks and safes, guards on buildings and pass systems. In support of counter-espionage the Director of the Protective Security Branch is very much concerned with it."

PROVAL

"Calamity," in Russian; in KGB circles, an operation that had gone horribly awry, with much embarrassment to all parties involved. In CIA, a person held responsible for such a disaster is retired (as happened to principal figures in the Bay of Pigs); in KGB, the culprit was either shot or transported to Siberia. Historically, the Soviets seemed less concerned about *provals* than did Western agencies, chiefly because they have the advantage of a closed society in which neither press nor politicians discuss failures, much less criticize them. (*See also* FLAP POTENTIAL.)

The worse *provals* in Soviet intelligence history occurred in the course of forty days in 1927: a police raid on the Soviet consulate in Peking, on April 6, which revealed incontrovertible evidence of spying; arrests in France four days later of numerous French Communists who admitted espionage; and finally, the breaking of a Soviet spy ring in London on May 12 that resulted in Britain severing diplomatic relations with the USSR. These *provals* were costly because the USSR at the time was trying to establish respectability in the world community.

PROVISIONAL OPERATION AUTHORITY

CIA term for giving a station permission to recruit a potential asset. Such persons must be "vetted" by headquarters before becoming a full-fledged agent.

PROVOCATION

Having an agent propose or agree to a nefarious deed on behalf of an opposition intelligence agency. Once the opposition agrees, the offensive agency has "moral justification" to proceed with its own dirty deeds. In 1963, for instance, CIA had numerous meetings with a high Cuban official, codenamed AMLASH, to discuss the assassination of Premier Fidel Castro. (AMLASH wanted a rifle with telescope; the CIA contact man gave him a fountain pen with a needle point and suggested he fill it with Black Leaf-40, a commercial poison.) There was much suspicion in CIA that Castro knew of

CIA plots to kill him and that AMLASH talked with CIA as part of a provocation scheme. By macabre irony, CIA official Desmond Fitzgerald and AMLASH had their last meeting on November 22, 1963. When Fitzgerald left the meeting, he learned of President Kennedy's murder. The juxtaposition of the AMLASH plot and the JFK killing suggested that Castro ordered Kennedy murdered as a retaliation—a suspicion that is unlikely ever to be proved or disproved to the satisfaction of doubters. The Church Committee spent months pursuing the theory with no success. (*See* AGENT PROVOCATEUR.)

PROVING IT OUT

Double-checking an agent's claimed veracity by attempting to verify easily provable portions of his reports. Haphazard, but a good method of catching an unimaginative cheat. For instance, if the agent claims to have obtained X information from Ambassador Y at an embassy reception, the control asks what Y was wearing, and what time the party broke up. The asking of the questions hints that the control knows what transpired at the party (and in fact he often does know). Fumbling answers suggest that a liar, not an agent, is at work.

PROVOCATION AGENT

An agent whose sole function is to provide false information for ulterior purposes. His story might be palpably false; nonetheless, it sows suspicion wherever received and must be either confirmed or disproved. KGB had been known to try to mask serious intelligence operations by "flooding" the West with provocation agents, each of whom carries bizarre stories that must be checked. KGB's hope was that Western counterintelligence will be so over-worked that serious agents can slip through the security nets.

PUTTING IN THE PLUMBING

Organizing the operational support facilities that are needed before any significant intelligence operation is set into motion— including safe houses, training facilities, covert paymasters, even office staff and typewriters.

Safe House Interlude Eight

So, Why Spy?

"Every kind of service, necessary to the public good, becomes honorable by being necessary."
>—Nathan Hale, America's first spy, 1776.

∾

"Spying is spying. You have to make up your mind that you are going to have an intelligence agency and protect it as such, and shut your eyes and take what is coming."
>—Senator John Stennis, chairman of the Senate
>Armed Services Committee, 1971.

Q

QUIET ONES

Homosexuals who were used by the KGB for entrapment of Westerners or other targets. Quiet ones could be either male or female. The Soviet Union treated homosexuals harshly; hence for them KGB missions were a means of survival, even if only temporary.

R

RABBLE ROUSER INDEX

FBI file used to target persons for its CONINTELPRO operation. As field agents were instructed by FBI headquarters, "The Index will consist of the names, identifying data, and background information of individuals who are known rabble rousers and who have demonstrated by their actions and their speeches that they have a propensity for fomenting racial disorder. It is desired that only individuals of prominence who are of national interest be included in this index. Particular consideration should be given to...those individuals in this category who travel extensively. The fact that an individual is on the Security Index or Reserve Index does not preclude his inclusion on the Rabble Rouser Index."

This guideline was issued in October 1967; a month later a further directive broadened coverage to include persons with a "propensity for fomenting" disorders affecting the "internal security," not just racial matters. Eventually the Rabble Rouser Index grew to cover a range of organizations from the Southern Christian Leadership Conference to the Black Panther Party, Ku Klux Klan, and Students for a Democratic Society.

RABCOR

Russian-language abbreviation for "worker-correspondent," a system of volunteer journalists that emerged during the first years of the Soviet regime. The *rabcors* were intended to replace the old "pro-capitalist, reactionary" journalists of the Czarist era; they were to write "progressive reports" on the status of Soviet society for *Pravda* and other party newspapers. In practice, the *rabcors* numbered more than three million and were a key element in the informer system that kept Soviet society subservient to Stalin. Little of what they wrote went into public print; their "stories" in fact were raw intelligence reports. So successful was the *rabcor* system that Soviet intelligence extended it to Western targets, with the emphasis on persons working in such strategic installations as military bases and telegraph offices. As has been noted by David J. Dallin, "The great advantage of the *rabcors* as a cover for espionage was their appearance of legality; there could be no objection to a worker writing to his newspaper about happenings in an industrial plant. Even a *rabcor* who broke the rule of secrecy and sent reports from a military establishment could honestly deny any link to foreign intelligence." In many instances the *rabcors* seemed honestly ignorant of their true mission.

According to the *Small Soviet Encyclopedia* (quoted by Dallin), The *Daily Worker* in New York claimed 800 *rabcors* in 1934; the British *Daily Worker*, 600. *L'Humanite*, the French Communist journal, had 1,200 *rabcors* in 1928 and 4,000 in 1934. The Soviets placed so much emphasis on the *rabcors* that Maria Ulianova, Lenin's sister, was designated chief spokesman for the movement, and published a book in 1928 entitled *The Rabcor Movement Abroad*.

The term *rabcor* has long disappeared from the Western intelligence vocabulary. The *rabcors* survive under the name "progressive journalists."

The existence of the *rabcor* network—and the true nature of the "correspondents" work—came to light during a French intelligence investigation in 1932. By turning a key French Communist overseer of *rabcor*, French agents revealed the extent of the espionage, and two Soviet agents directing the work were sent to prison. The court decried the fact that "French citizens and Communist militants... permitted themselves to be dragged into it by criminal propaganda of foreign origin."

RADIO SECURITY SERVICE (R.S.S.)

A World War II arm of the British MI5 responsible for detecting, monitoring, and locating clandestine transmitters. R.S.S. had offices on Hanslope Park in Buckinghamshire, about 35 miles from Oxford. Listening posts were scattered around Great Britain at strategic points; R.S.S. also benefited from some 1,500 amateur radio operators (called "Voluntary Interceptors") who worked from their homes. Transmissions of interest had to be transcribed by hand, as R.S.S. did not have sufficient recorders to give to each of the stations.

RATISSAGE

In French, literally, a rat hunt; World War II jargon for a counter-espionage manhunt.

RAVEN

A male KGB spy who was used in sexual entrapment operations. Ravens were chosen not for physical good looks, but for their ability to appeal to middle-aged women of influence who had learned not to expect the best—only attention and physical satisfaction.

The oft-repeated procedure is for the raven to make a casual contact with the target—at a cocktail party, at a museum, even on the street—and commence a low-key nonsexual approach. After the ultimate bedding comes the ultimate request for a "bit of help" on a newspaper article or other research. Hope and shame do the rest.

RAW

Research and Analysis Wing, India's external intelligence organization.

RAZVEDKA

The Russian word that translates literally as "true intelligence," defined by defected NKVD officer Alexander Orlov as that "procured by undercover agents and secret informants in defiance of the laws of a foreign country in which they operate."

READY FOR THE HIGH JUMP

KGB slang for an officer who feared that he was subject to assassination or dismissal from the service because of incompetence or internal political problems. An officer who deduced that he was "ready for the jump"—often signaled by an unexpected call for his return to Moscow—was apt to call the local CIA station and offer his services to the West.

RECOGNITION SIGNAL

A discreet but visible means of informing an unknown person—a control agent or cut-out—that you are the agent with whom he should make contact. For casual meets, the signal can be as innocuous as a specified magazine spread out on a bar or coffee table. The

more important the mission, the higher the degree of sophistication, with the requirement of signal and countersignal, response
and counterresponse. (By omitting the response, an apprehended
agent can alert the contact that something has gone wrong.)

In the autumn of 1945, Alan Nunn May, a British scientist who
had worked on nuclear projects in Canada, was ready to return to
Britain to continue his research—and his spying for the Soviet
Union. May, given the code name "Alek," received specific instructions on how to contact his new control agent:

1. Place.

    In front of the British Museum of London, on Great Russell
    Street, at the opposite side of the street, about Museum Street,
    from the side of Tottenham Court Road...Alek [May] walks
    from Tottenham Court Road, the contact man from the opposite
    side—Southampton Road.

2. Time.

    ...[I]t should be more expedient to carry out the meeting at
    20 o'clock [8 P.M.], if it should be convenient to Alek, as at 23
    o'clock, it is too dark. In case the meeting should not take place
    in October, the time and day will be repeated in the following
    months.

3. Identification signs.

    Alek will have under his left arm the newspaper *Times*, the
    contact man will have in his left hand the magazine *Picture Post*.

4. The password.

    The contact man: "What is the shortest way to the Strand?"
    Alek: "Well, come along, I am going that way."
    In the beginning of the business conversation, Alek says, "Best
    regards from Mikel."

The sentencing justice decried May's "crass conceit [and] wicked-
ness" in surrendering an important national secret and sent him to
prison for ten years. (May, an ideological spy, sold out his adopted
country for $700 cash and two bottles of whiskey.)

Recognition signals also can be bizarre. When atomic spy Klaus
Fuchs met a Soviet contact in New York in 1944, he was to stand on

a street corner with a tennis ball in his left hand. His contact would be wearing gloves and carrying a book with green binding and a pair of gloves. When he went to London the next year, Fuchs was instructed to stand outside the Momington Crescent underground station the first Saturday of each month, holding five books bound with string and supported by two fingers; in his other hand he was to hold two additional books.

The Soviets traditionally used such elaborate signals, as witness the instructions given KGB agent Alexander Foote when he was to meet a contact in Geneva:

> I was to be wearing a white scarf and to be holding in my right hand a leather belt. As the clock struck noon, I would be approached by a woman carrying a string shopping bag containing a green parcel, and holding an orange in her hand.
>
> One would have thought that this would have been sufficient to enable anyone to contact anyone, even an unknown, in the middle of a Swiss street. The woman would ask me, in English, where I had bought the belt; and I was to reply that I had bought it in an ironmonger's shop in Paris. Then I was to ask her where I could buy an orange like hers, and she was to say that I could have hers for an English penny.
>
> Hardly sparkling dialogue, but sufficient to ensure that the meeting was foolproof and an example of the usual thoroughness of my employers.

The verbal part of the recognition signal was known to the KGB as a *parel,* a pair or two pairs of sentences that must be recited in precise prearranged sequence. When circumstances are such that an agent cannot comfortably carry around tennis balls or an orange—an embassy party, say, or a meeting in a business office— the KGB procedure is to use a verbal signal. When the Swedish Colonel Stig Wennerstrom went to Washington as a Soviet spy in 1952, he carried a carefully arranged password. Someone from the Soviet embassy would say to him (in the course of normal diplomatic contact): "Nikolai Vasilovich asked to be remembered to you."

Wennerstrom was to reply: "Yes, I know him very well. We used to meet sometimes at Spiridonovka."

Wennerstrom heard the exchange from the Soviet air attache during a protocol meeting. The men were alone, and the Swede started discussing business, only to have the other man clasp a hand over his mouth and gesture wildly toward the ceiling. "No, no," the Russian's warning stare mimed, "The walls have ears."

REFERENTURA

A specially secured room in a Soviet or Soviet Bloc embassy for meetings of members of the *rezidentura* (see p. 188) and for safe-keeping files and other support materials. According to Josef Frolik, a Czech intelligence officer who defected in 1969, the *referentura* is kept secure by the embassy's "internal group," which also does the nuts-and-bolts clerical and logistical work necessary to any bureaucracy.

RENDITION

The seizure, by a law enforcement or intelligence agency, of a "person of interest" who is in another country, and transferring him elsewhere, either to his homeland, a "third-party nation," or to a detention facility such as the Guantanamo prison in Cuba. Renditions came into wide-use—and considerable controversy—during the war against terrorism. The term dates deep into history; for instance, Milton wrote of Charles I's capture and "rendition afterwards to the Scotch Army.; an 1860 encyclopedia noted the "renditions of fugitive slaves by the Northern states."

The first "rendition" case to reach the U.S. judicial system apparently took place in the 1880s and involved an accused Chicago embezzler and con man named Frederick Ker, who fled to Lima, Peru to avoid prosecution. His victims hired the Pinkerton Detective Agency to bring him back. The officer who went to Lima found that the country was temporarily occupied by Chile, so he found a Chilean army officer who helped him seize Ker and put him on a U.S. warship bound for Honolulu.

Once in the U.S., Ker claimed he had been kidnapped, and that normal extradition procedures should have been followed. The U.S. courts held that trial courts dealt only with the facts of the case, and that the mode by which a defendant was brought to trial was irrelevant. The U.S. Supreme Court upheld this position in *Ker vs. Illinois, 119 U.S. 436 1836.* Later SCOTUS rulings upheld the Ker doctrine.

Despite these rulings, such procedures were used sparingly in subsequent years, and generally involved seizures from third-world countries—or ones willing to turn a blind eye to the practice (the term "Mexican extradition" was widely employed when I was a newsman in Texas during the 1950s). In the 1980s, however, both CIA and FBI became uneasy with demands by President Reagan that accused terrorists be tracked down and brought to justice wherever they might be found, without regard to the legalities of the country where they found refuge. CIA was happy to take such persons out of circulation, but balked at being required to produce evidence in court, since the agency had no law enforcement jurisdiction.

In December 1996, following the hijacking of a cruise ship in the Middle East, and a futile attempt to persuade Italian authorities to seize the terrorists involved when they touched down near Rome, President Reagan issued National Security Decision Directive 207, which specifically authorized CIA to capture terrorists abroad and bring them to the U.S. for trial. (The text of the NSD has never been released.) William Webster, a former Federal judge serving as director of the FBI, issued a Justice Department order in June 1998 stating that "rendition" could be employed in instances where nations harboring terrorists did not have a functioning judicial system that would permit extradition to be employed.

In succeeding years, CIA and the FBI have conducted an unknown number of rendition operations around the world, with many of the detainees whisked away to Guantanamo or to "undisclosed locations"—i.e., nations willing to take custody of the prisoners.

Opposition has been furious and on-going from civil libertarians, but CIA officers involved in rendition operations insist that they have produced valuable intelligence.

RESISTANCE GROUP

OSS definition: "Individuals associated together in enemy-held territory to oppose the enemy by any and all means short of military operations, e.g., by sabotage, non-cooperation, etc." (*See also* GUERRILLAS.)

RENT-A-COPS
See SSD.

RETRACING THE ANALYSIS
A process of evaluating how an intelligence estimate went wrong. "The purpose is to discover who made what wrong assessments, based on what misleading information, from what sources now considered to be unreliable..." William Safire of *The New York Times* used this language in November 1984 in suggesting that CIA find out how it managed to miss Bulgarian involvement in the plot to murder Pope John Paul II.

REZIDENT, ILLEGAL
A Soviet agent, who lived abroad without official cover, usually with an assumed identity, responsible for controlling subordinate illegal agents who worked in his area. The illegal *rezident* has no contact with the Soviet embassy or any of its personnel, and he maintained his own communications with KGB Center. In terms of authority, the illegal *rezident* has the rank of the formal KGB *rezident*. But, if arrested, he cannot plead diplomatic immunity: he goes to jail. The most publicized illegal *rezident* ever bagged by the FBI—insofar as has been publicly disclosed, in any event—was Colonel Rudolph Abel of the KGB, apprehended in 1957.

REZIDENTURA
The KGB section of a Soviet embassy, the ranking officer of which was the *rezident*, who operated under diplomatic cover. The *rezident* was the equivalent of a CIA chief of station. Because a *rezident* must have senior status in KGB, his identity as an agent was usually known to Western agencies, and hence he did little actual spying while abroad. Some *rezidents* did roam the cocktail circuit, for hard drinking seemed a prevalent trait. In Washington, the identity of the *rezident* was protected by a peculiar professional courtesy of the American press.

Soon after the *Washington Post* ran stories in the late 1970s naming several CIA station chiefs, I suggested to a reporter there that he do an article about the then-KGB *rezident*. I even offered him a photograph of the *rezident* at play at a reception. "That isn't news," the *Post's* man stated.

In the larger embassies—Washington, Bonn, London, and Paris—the GRU (Soviet military intelligence) often ran a *rezidentura* separate from that of KGB. GRU's sphere of interest covered both strategic and tactical intelligence, and seldom did the work overlap. A Soviet agent concerned with collecting strategic information went where the trail took him, with little regard to bureaucratic boundaries. Agents and analysts assigned to a strategic *rezidentura* tended to be the best and brightest the Soviets have to offer. But persons in a tactical branch of a *rezidentura* were generally restricted to operations within the country to which they were assigned.

RIDING SHOTGUN

Sending a second agent to surveil (and safeguard) an intelligence officer who is to meet a contact under dangerous circumstances. The "first shotgun" is often deliberately visible, a sort of night-watchman deterrent. The "second shotgun," however, is prepared to do whatever is necessary to protect the agent.

RINGING THE GONG

The prediction, by a CIA station, of a revolution in the host country. Richard Helms, when director of central intelligence, frequently admonished his chiefs of station to "ring the gong"—to "sing out loudly"—when they felt a major disaster was in the offing, according to longtime clandestine services officer Howard P. Hart.

ROLLING UP A NET

Arresting members of an intelligence apparatus (net) after the initial detection of its existence.

ROMEO SPY

An officer of the KGB or its successor agency who targeted Western officials—both female and male—in the hope that bed-talk might produce useful information. (*See* SEXPIONAGE.)

ROOF

The role played by a KGB agent sent abroad in a covert capacity. In KGB jargon, the "legend" was the false biography given an agent by

Moscow Center; the "roof" is the role that the agent assumes openly when he is sent to a new place. (*See* LEGEND.)

RUN DOWN A CASE

The decision to halt an operation involving a double agent, usually because of suspicions that the other side has become aware of the deception.

RUMOR

A false but plausible story put into circulation with the aim of causing harm to one's adversary. A rumor is a technique of Morale Operations, but only as a secondary weapon. As stated in an OSS manual, "Rarely can they [rumors] by themselves change basic attitudes. Their function is to confirm suspicions and beliefs already latent; to give sense and direction to fears, resentments or hopes that have been built up by more materialistic causes; to tip the balance when public opinion is in a precarious state." The OSS, with its cupboard of psychologists and Madison Avenue admen turned operatives, created a recipe entitled "Properties of a Good Rumor":

A good rumor is one which will spread widely in a form close to that of the original story. Probably the main factor determining whether it catches on is the degree to which it is adapted for the state of mind of the audience. In addition, successful rumors embody most of the following qualities:

(1) *Plausibility.* A plausible rumor is tied to *some* known facts, yet is incapable of total verification. It may exaggerate, but it stops short of the incredible. It frequently appears as an "inside" story.

(2) *Simplicity.* A good rumor uses only one central idea as a core. Its basic message is simple and thus easy to remember.

(3) *Suitability to task.* To summarize opinions or attitudes which are already widely accepted, slogan-type rumors are best. ("England will fight to the last Frenchman.") To introduce "information" which will help build up *new* attitudes, however, narrative-type rumors are best (e.g., rumors which "prove" that Hitler is mentally ill).

(4) *Vividness.* Regardless of length or type, rumors which stimulate clear-cut mental pictures with *strong emotional content* are likely to be effective.

(5) *Suggestiveness.* The type of rumor which merely hints or suggests something instead of stating it is well adapted to spreading fear and doubt. The listener should always be allowed to formulate his own conclusions.

(6) *Concreteness.* The more concrete and precise a rumor, the less likely it is to become distorted in transmission.

OSS was so sophisticated in rumor-mongering that, by 1944, it put them into formal subcategories. Some examples:

THE CONFUSION RUMOR

Fear of inflation is the straightest and surest road to inflation. Working on this principle, OSS's Morale Operations floated three rumors:

- "The *Reichsdrucherei* [the German Mint] is printing large quantities of currency."
- "The value of the [German] mark in the black markets of Switzerland has dropped considerably."
- "Life insurance companies have asked the [German] government for extensive emergency loans. Because of the large number of deaths in the Reich, these companies are no longer solvent."

THE DECEPTION RUMOR

During the summer of 1944, marketplace rumors were started in Eastern Europe to the effect that the Germans were withdrawing German troops from the Crimea and leaving "all Romanians behind to be annihilated." Within days, women staged a demonstration outside the Bucharest home of their president, shouting, "Send our husbands home."

THE PERSONAL GOSSIP ATTACK RUMOR

OSS used many variations on the theme, "Where is Hitler?" OSS would state in its own broadcasts and through neutral press leaks that Hitler was expected to speak at such-and-such a Nazi anniversary observance. Such "commitments," of course, were solely of OSS's making. When Hitler did not appear, OSS would float reports of his "rumored death, disappearance, illness, psychotic condition, or flight from the country." The aim was to "sow doubt in the minds of the public and the *Wehrmacht,* and cast suspicions on the motives and integrity of the Nazi leadership." These rumors so unnerved the Nazis that on December 29, 1944, the German propaganda minister Goebbels claimed over Radio Berlin that he had "purposely planted rumors that Hitler was ill as part of a deep and far-flung scheme to lull the Allies into complacency and set them up for the winter offensive." Goebbels's attempt to deflate the rumors told OSS that they were effective.

THE HUMOROUS RUMOR

On June 16, 1943, OSS had its agents in occupied Europe float the quip, "Barbers in Holland are now charging five cents more for a shave, because German faces are longer these days." On August 25, 1943, feedback from the rumor was printed in the *Providence Journal:* "A Dutch underground newspaper reports that the barbers of Germany are now charging five cents extra each to shave Nazis because their faces are longer these days."

THE PIPE-DREAM RUMOR

These rumors promised a better life to Axis soldiers who left the war. One, aimed at Germans in North Africa, was that POWs captured in the Middle East lived lives of pleasant activity, and were used as chauffeurs for Allied generals. Several captured German airmen inquired about such assignments. They were disappointed.

THE BOGEYMAN RUMOR

Harking to a past war, British intelligence (with OSS help) broadcast that the German navy would be ordered to make a final suicidal attack against the British. Historical precedent gave credibility both to the rumor and its intended effect. World War I reports of such a happening caused a German navy mutiny. World War II ended before this particular rumor had any effect.

THE WEDGE-DRIVING RUMOR

These are nasty, for they exploit religious, racial, and other prejudices. Two of uncountable hundreds from OSS files:

- "At a dinner recently held at Karin Hall by Goering, beer was served in sacred vessels looted from churches in Northern Italy."
- "To save time and space, Himmler has ordered no distinctions be observed in cremations of Protestant and Catholic air-raid victims."

(*See* SIB.)

RUSSIAN INTELLIGENCE SERVICES (RIS)

The term used within CIA to denote the two major Soviet intelligence services, KGB and GRU. RIS began as a CIA acronym for Russian intelligence services in West Germany during the 1950s. It proved to be a local term that never "took" at Agency headquarters but was much used in the field. The more accurate designation would have been SIS, for "Soviet Intelligence Services," but the British pre-empted this label when MI6, the foreign intelligence service, became the Secret Intelligence Service. Courteously, CIA let the Brits have the initials SIS. (Secret Intelligence Service, in general usage, had about as much success as the attempt of New York City to rename Sixth Avenue "The Avenue of the Americas." In intelligence circles, one seldom hears anything of SIS or Secret Intelligence Service; the reference unfailingly is to MI6 or simply "Six." (*See* ORGANS.)

Safe House Interlude Nine

Spy Psyche

"The very qualities that form the character of a good intelligence agent—salesmanship, blarney, idealism, the ability to adopt a secondary personality and make it convincing, a touch of the rogue—are also those of the con man and the psychopath. Hence a dilemma of any society: Why do its own people turn against it? The psychotic will very readily take sides against his own country. He is as if commanded by Heaven to be a prop for any neighboring power which desires to swallow his fatherland. He hates the people around him, he hates his fellow countrymen, because he hates the real world."

—Rebecca West, Meaning of Treason.

∾

"How did this man get started as a traitor? He considered himself an idealist, which made him feel above the law, justifying means by ends. He became a Soviet agent through association with Red friends, through misguided idealism for the 'underdog.'"

—FBI Director J. Edgar Hoover, on
convicted atomic spy Harry Gold.

∾

"His character is perverted, often incalculable and frequently antisocial. Above all he tends to be devoid of guilt, indeed, may take a certain pride in his more bizarre achievements...The wartime Quisling was, in fact, more than half gosling: a weak, immature and childish character. The Quisling and the traitor have much in common with the school boy who speaks to the teacher whom he secretly hates, but whose attention he nevertheless covets."

—Dr. Richard Glovner, British psychiatrist
who testified at the trial of Dr. Klaus Fuchs,
who gave atomic secrets to the Soviets.

∾

"I just love officers. I've loved them all my life. There's nothing I like better than sleeping with them, without worrying about the money. And then I simply adore comparing the physiques and temperament of one race or nation with that of another."

—Mata Hari, executed by the French for alleged
spying for Germany during World War I, on
evidence that current historians of espionage consider
thin, even non-existent. She was a bit of a sleep-
around, but such was not a capital offense.

S

SAFE HOUSE

A house or apartment rented by a person with no discernible connection to an intelligence agency and used for clandestine meetings with agents and other contacts. The normal guise—both for CIA and KGB—was a small apartment hired by an out-of-town businessman who travels frequently and who needs a modest place for occasional overnights. The preferred location for CIA safe houses during the 1970s (and before) was in Washington, D.C., apartment buildings in the canyons of Connecticut and Massachusetts Avenues, and in suburban Northern Virginia.

One problem endemic to safe houses is the suspicious neighbors who mistake odd hours and sporadic traffic as evidence of smuggling, gambling, or vice operations. (A U.S. Army Counterintelligence Corps officer in Munich once put off an inquiring landlady by stating, yes, he indeed was a homosexual, and he *needed* the apartment; she raised the rent 50 marks but agreed to remain silent.) An agent can give a semblance of activity to a safe house by arranging for a constant flow of junk mail (clipping a postcard in *Fortune* that offers a hundred or more corporate annual reports) interspersed with an occasional personal letter.

During the late 1960s, custodians of one CIA safe house put it to frequent use with girlfriends, as a cost-effective alternative to motels in Northern Virginia. One of the girls, an Agency analyst, unthinkingly used the phone to call a parent long-distance. A fiscal clerk questioned the charge, made inquiries, and referred the matter to the Agency security office. A directive issued shortly thereafter warned that safe houses were to be used *only* for official business.

A prearranged safety signal—a drawn window blind, a flower pot on the balcony, the positioning of a vase in a window—tells whether there is any possible danger in the meeting.

For an officer working covertly abroad, a safe house serves as a refuge where he or she can spend some quiet time—reading, listening to music, whatever—and forget for a time the nerve-twanging business of spying. I have been told by several Clandestine Services officers that they expect two important things in a safe house: that both the bar and the library be amply stocked.

SAND HOG

An MI6 officer specializing in intelligence about petroleum; so named because much of their work is done in arid Middle East nations.

SCATTER MOVE

See COUNTERSURVEILLANCE.

SCHCHIT

A two-layered film developed by GRU that will "permit secret documents to be photographed at high exposure on top of innocuous snapshots," according to British intelligence expert Robert Moses. If the film happens to be processed by someone unwitting of its nature, only the holiday snapshots appear. (The word means "shield" in Russian.)

SCHPICK

Derogatory KGB term for a novice operative.

SDECE

Service de Documentation Exterieure et Contre-Espionage (pronounced "see-deck"), the French agency that performs both intelligence and counter-intelligence functions—often under rules of its own making. *SDECEs* reputation for ruthlessness makes it unpopular even with agencies of nations with which France is supposedly friendly. In the words of a retired American spook, *"SDECE* on an everyday basis makes Hoover's FBI look like an elementary school." Ideologically adaptable, *SDECE has* performed equally efficiently under left, center, and right-wing governments.

SDECEs offices on the Boulevard Mortier overlook the public swimming pool in the Pare des Tourelles, hence another nickname for the French service—*la piscine,* for "the swimming pool."

SDECE's name was changed by the Mitterand government to DGSE (*Direction Generale de la Securitie Exterieure*), but professionals still refer to it by the old name.

SECRET RESTRICTED DATA

Term used by the Department of Energy referring to information "revealing the theory of operation of the components of a thermonuclear or fission bomb."

SECRET VOTE

A stratagem employed by the British Foreign Office since its founding in the 1770s to provide "deniability" for its involvement in intelligence activities, especially those directed against friendly government. The sum required each year is approved by Parliament without explanation of how it is to be spent; such "oversight" as exists is by the prime minister and his staff. When the Secret Intelligence Service (MI6) was founded in 1909, a government committee said that through use of the Secret Vote for its financing, "our N[aval] and M[ilitary] attaches and Government ofiicals would not only be freed from the necessity of dealing with spies, but it would also be impossible to obtain direct evidence that we had any dealings with them as at all." [See also "deniability." (During its first decade, SIS was known as the Special Intelligence Service.

At the insistence of Commodore Sir Mansfield Cumming, the first MI6 director, officers' salaries paid with secret funds were "paid free of Income Tax.... It was undesirable that their names & connection with S. S. [Secret Service] should be known to anyone." According to Keith Jeffrey, who in 2010 published an authorized history of MI6 1910–1949, "This privilege, agreed to by the Foreign Office, was zealously guarded by the Service for decades to come."

For decades, CIA and other elements of the intelligence community had Congressional approval for concealing its spending in various military appropriations bills. The legislative turmoil of the 1970s led to the creation of intelligence committees in both branches of Congress who must approve spending.

SECURE TELEPHONE

A telephone connection equipped with scramblers or other devices so that conversations cannot be overheard.

SECURITY EXECUTIVE

The committee responsible for control of British MI5 during World War II. Headed by Lord Swinton, the Security Executive was created after Prime Minister Churchill sacked General Sir Vernon Kell as director of MI5. Churchill was bent on keeping the existence of the Security Executive secret; when several members of Parliament heard rumors of its creation, Churchill replied to Commons that the subject was "not fitted for public discussion." Privately, Churchill said he would challenge the patriotism of anyone who asked further questions, MP or not. Nothing further was ever said of the Security Executive, which to intelligence insiders soon came to be known as the "Swinton Committee," after its chairman.

SEKSOT

Russian for informer. Genrikh Grigorievich Yagoda, who ran the Soviet secret police (then the GPU) in the 1930s, once boasted, "We can turn anyone into a *seksot*...Who is eager to die of hunger? When the GPU works over somebody in order to make him an informant, we already have him under our thumb, no matter how he struggles against it. We take away his job, he won't find another one without the secret agreement of our organs. And, above all, if a man has a family, wife and children, he is forced to capitulate quickly." The network of *seksots* permeates all of Soviet society, by testimony of defected intelligence officers.

SEKTOR

A section in the KGB central office that controls illegals working abroad, or those preparing for assignment.

SEMATEX

A Czech-made plastic explosive that has long been a favorite tool for Mideastern terror organizations. According to Israeli journalist

Yossi Melman, "Dark orange in color and clay-like in consistency, Sematex can be detected by trained dogs, but apparently not by existing airport X-ray equipment."

SENSITIVE COMPARTMENT INFORMATION FACILITY (SCIF)

Rooms, vaults, or even entire buildings that are specially constructed and certified for the handling and storage of classified intelligence information known as "Sensitive Compartmented Information" (SCI), ranging from electronic intercepts to satellite images and agent reports. Pronounced "skiffs."

SERVICE, THE

KGB officers' nickname for their organization.

SETTER

A CIA mail-intercept project conducted in New Orleans in 1957 involving the screening and opening of first class international mail via New Orleans en route to and from South and Central America. SETTER started as a result of Congressional protests about the "venomous propaganda" passing through New Orleans. SETTER was abandoned within two and one-half weeks as worthless.

SEVEN "BIG P'S"

Proper Prior Planning Prevents Piss Poor Performance. A mantra taught to fledgling FBI agents at the training facility in Quantico, Virginia.

SEXPIONAGE

The use of lust as a means of gathering intelligence. Although the concept is as old as the urge itself, the term "sexpionage" comes from British journalist David Lewis, whose book by that title was published in 1976. "To use the double bed as a passport to indiscreet pillow talk is a technique of Biblical antiquity," Lewis wrote. "In the tenth century, B.C., the first recorded sex spy, Delilah, used her charms to destroy the Danite hero Samson." Beds have continued bouncing ever since, in the name of the national interest.

The *femme fatale* who seduces statesmen and generals in the service of her country is a cliche of pulp fiction—and a reality of modern intelligence. *All* intelligence agencies employ sex as an element of tradecraft. In some instances, a person is furnished with a sex partner as a means of keeping him or her happy (as was the case with the late President Sukarno of Indonesia during a state visit to the United States, and the defected Soviet diplomat Arkady Shevchenko in 1978; CIA found the latter's particular playmate, "Judy Chavez," through an escort ad in the Yellow Pages of the Washington telephone directory).

Throughout its existence, the Soviet foreign intelligence service made wide use of sex as a tool of intelligence. Loy Henderson, a veteran American diplomat, first went to the Moscow embassy in 1934; he dealt with Soviet affairs for decades. As he observed in his memoir, "A Question of Trust," published in 1987, after his death, "The [Soviet] secret police had at their disposal a number of exceptionally well-groomed and intelligent young women who apparently had been assigned the task of making friends with both the married and unmarried members of the diplomatic missions and foreign correspondents. It was quite easy for those of us who were acquainted with Soviet intelligence to spot the women who were serving the police. We knew enough about the Soviet system to realize that these young women would not be meeting foreigners or inviting them to their apartments unless they were authorized to do so."

But sexpionage can also be a brutal form of blackmail used against persons of many sexual persuasions. An oft-repeated warning given Westerners of rank, traveling to Iron Curtain countries, is "Don't go to bed with *anyone* other than your spouse, regardless of the temptation." But Eros often conquers common sense (and especially when given a boost by John Barleycorn).

The most illustrious victim was Sir Geoffrey Harrison, British ambassador to the USSR, who was seduced by a chambermaid, photographed by KGB, and withdrawn from his mission. Uncountable lesser personages have fallen victim to the same sort of trap. Several United States military sergeants served long prison terms for what began as vodka-fueled escapades with complacent women in Moscow, Warsaw, and other Eastern European capitals. Faced with blackmail photos, they agreed to spy for the Soviet Bloc. The friendly women, it proved, were what KGB and its subordinates call "swallows"—prostitutes who are programmed to seduce Western-ers. (Male prostitutes, both straight and homosexual, are known as "swans.")

The Czechs' secret service seems particularly obsessed with the use of sex as an intelligence tool. Eva Bosakova, several times an Olympics winner in gymnastics, was called by Czech defector Josef Frolik "an agent of long standing, utilized primarily for the pro-duction of compromising films of a sexual nature." Jiri Mucha, the writer, was also an STB agent, according to Frolik, who was used "to compromise members of the Prague diplomatic corps [with] sexual orgies arranged in his apartment."

According to Frolik, a strikingly beautiful international airline hostess recruited by Czech intelligence in the early 1950s used a unique approach to American officers from whom she sought infor-mation: she would casually hand them a calling card bearing her nude photograph, and suggest a "quiet meeting for a drink." She enjoyed wide popularity among American servicemen in West Ger-many before being caught and jailed for seven years. In the 1960s, Czech intelligence, acting for KGB, even managed to find a woman who had been rocket expert Wernher Von Braun's wartime lover. The Czechs sent the woman to the United States, where she tried to persuade Von Braun to share military secrets with the Soviets "in the interest of world peace." Von Braun was not interested in either the woman or her proposal, and she was turned over to the FBI.

During the 1960s, the Canadian national hockey team defeated the USSR in the semifinals of a tournament in Prague. The Czech minister of interior (i.e., secret police boss) was so miffed that he ordered subordinates to summon "all the best-looking Prague hook-ers" to the Hotel International, where the Canadian team was stay-ing. According to defected Czech agent Josef Frolik, "these hookers did such a job on the Canadian team that the next day in the finals, the Czechoslovakians very easily defeated them."

Sexual blackmail is also undertaken by Western agencies. In aptly named Operation DEEP ROOT, the Royal Canadian Mounted Police in 1968 managed to get photographs showing the wife of a Soviet diplomat having intercourse with a Canadian. RCMP agents tried to force the woman to become an informant; she refused and left immediately for Moscow.

Western agencies have their own swallows. Colonel Oleg Penkovsky, the Soviet defector-in-place, made no secret of his desire for complaisant female company during a debriefing trip to Paris. The British Intelligence Service obliged with several svelte English girls. "They did not just happen to be in Paris," acknowledges Greville Wynne, who handled Penkovsky. "We had brought them. They had been carefully selected for their quality as good companions, their expense accounts were generous, and their sole duty was to look after the gentleman from Belgrade (as Penkovsky was introduced) should he become lonely. [Penkovsky] must be kept happy, but it was far too dangerous to allow him to pick and choose for himself."

Western services also make frequent use of homosexuals. As a BBC commentator during the 1930s, Guy Burgess often did odd jobs for the British Secret Intelligence Service. An open homosexual, Burgess was once instructed to befriend Edouard Pfeiffer, *chef de cabinet* to Daladier, the French prime minister. Burgess's specific role was to act as a conduit for secret messages between Daladier and British Prime Minister Neville Chamberlain, who wished to bypass his own Foreign Office.

Sexual misconduct can backfire on a spy in unexpected ways. Geoffrey Arthur Prime spied for the Soviets for years—undetected—while working for the British Government Communications Headquarters (GCHQ), passing highly sensitive information about reconnaissance satellites. Although British security did not know it, Prime had an uncontrollable sexual interest in very young girls. His suspicious wife, looking for evidence of his sexual philandering, ran across spy material—as well as naughty photographs of prepubescent girls. Prime was sentenced to a long prison term.

Through the mid-1970s, intelligence personnel of Western agencies were advised against extramarital sexual liaisons as a prophylactic against blackmail. Anyone caught in such an affair faced censure or even dismissal.

Several prominent intelligence personalities openly defied the stricture. The late Allen Dulles, while director of central intelligence, was a notorious womanizer, to the exasperation of his wife. Mrs. Dulles once told a friend that for a while she bought an expensive piece of jewelry each time she learned of an affair. "I had to stop," she said, "because I was running through all the family fortune."

The threat of blackmail did not deter Roger Hollis, longtime head of the British MI5, from an affair with his secretary, Edith Valentine Hammond. The affair was common knowledge to other MI5 officers (and presumably KGB). In February 1968, some two years after Hollis's retirement, Mrs. Hollis sued for divorce on grounds of his adultery with Miss Hammond. Once the decree was granted, Hollis married his former mistress, and they lived together until he died in 1973.

The use of "honey pot" female agents by Mossad, the Israeli intelligence service, has received the blessing of none other than Rabbi Ari Schvat, one-time speaker of the Knesset. Writing in a 2010 paper published by the Tzomet Institute, which studies the interface between religion and modernity, the rabbi cited historical precedent. Queen Esther, who was Jewish, slept with the Persian king Xerxes circa 500 bc to save her people. Yael, wife of Hevr, slept with the enemy chief of staff Sisra to tire him and cut off his head. Rabbi Schvat did add some caveats: "If it is necessary to use a married woman, it should be best [for] her husband to divorce her... After the [sex] act, he would be entitled to bring her back.... Naurally, a job of that sort could be given to a woman who in an event is licentious in her ways."

SHAKING OFF THE DOGS

Losing a surveillance team. The subject darts out of a subway car or a bus just as it leaves; he enters a department store or other building with multiple exits; he suddenly reverses his course and walks right past the surveillance person. A CIA officer in West Berlin once disposed of a KGB surveillant by arising in a bar and shouting, "Take your goddamned hand off my knee, you pervert." The flustered KGB man fled into the night, and the CIA man went about his business.

SHAKING THE TREE

A counterintelligence term that covers a potpourri of techniques intended to bring a dormant investigation alive. The purpose is to provoke the opposition, either through disinformation or an arrest of a known agent; the opposition's panicky reaction in turn will provide further leads. For instance, word can be leaked that an agent under arrest is cooperating and giving names of other members of his ring. If a suspected accomplice bolts for the airport, he would have some interesting days ahead.

SHAMROCK

The systematic interception, by the National Security Agency (and its predecessor agencies) of millions of international telegrams sent to, from, or by way of the United States, between 1945 and May 1975. The original purpose of SHAMROCK was to obtain the enciphered telegrams of certain foreign targets. For three decades, NSA screened some 150,000 messages monthly, handled by RCA Global and ITT World Communications; Western Union International gave NSA a less thorough range of messages.

SHAVKI

"Trash-eating dogs," in Russian contraction; KGB term for low-level agents. Such a designation shows KGB's contempt for outsiders, a major flaw of Russian intelligence.

SHEEP DIPPING

Using a piece of military equipment (such as a helicopter) or a military person in an intelligence operation under civilian cover. In actuality, the equipment or person remains assigned to the military; any transfer is on paper only. For instance, CIA sheep-dipped much of the military equipment given to the *contras* fighting the Sandinista government in Nicaragua in the 1980s. In a nonmilitary context, sheep dipping refers to placing of agents in organizations in which they can become active, in order to establish credentials that can enable them to collect information of intelligence value on similar groups. For example, the agent might join a radical group in the hope that this membership would make him acceptable to a terrorist organization.

SHEPHERD

A KGB strong-arm man who accompanied Russians who traveled abroad; their mission was not companionship, but to ensure that the subject did not defect. If the subject did flee, the shepherd went to Siberia, or worse; hence his dedication to his job. (*See* NURSEMAIDS.)

SHIFR OTDEL

Soviet term for an expert code-breaker, a man capable of deciphering messages without benefit of computers.

SHOPPED

Assassinated. A British MI6 euphemism.

SHOPPING LIST

The Western industrial, electronic, and other technological equipment that the Soviet Union attempted to purchase or steal abroad on an ongoing basis. The shopping list was revised and updated at least annually. KGB and GRU kept the exact contents a close secret so as not to tip Western intelligence of their most urgent requirements.

SHOPWORN GOODS

A would-be defector's information, so dated or remote as to be worthless to the other side. The debriefing officers who screen a potential defector try to determine, as a first order of business, whether he has any useful intelligence in his baggage. That an agent or intelligence bureaucrat has slid down the ladder does not necessarily make him worthless. Some overt over-the-hill cases are given refuge because of the historical perspective they can give to past operations and policies. Others are valuable for propaganda purposes. (The British traitor Kim Philby, for instance, had no current intelligence information in 1963 when the Russians took him in; his value was publicity—the chance for the Communists to boast about one of Britain's top spymasters being their puppet for years.)

Economics alone dictate that an intelligence service not accept willy-nilly any defector who sidles into an embassy. The initial debriefing expenses are only a minor part of the cost. The defector must be relocated under a new identity and given enough training so that he can earn a living; for the first months, at least, he is guarded.

At one time the standard CIA arrangement was for a defector to become an Agency "consultant" for a number of months; after the stated period lapsed, he was on his own.

The British SIS in the postwar years went so far as to judge its defectors as "grade-one" and "grade-two." The latter were generally low-grade minor officials from East Europe, chiefly non-Communist, who either did not like the new Soviet regimes or had had some past connection with British intelligence. The system originally permitted them to enter Britain and stay, but gave them minimal or no other assistance. The Labour Government of Clement Attlee told SIS in the late 1940s that Britain was being flooded with shopworn goods, that the Eastern Europeans could do little of value; that henceforth they would not be granted political asylum simply because they were anti-Communist. SIS bided its time. When the government changed, SIS, and not the leftist Foreign Secretary Ernest Bevin, once more made decisions about which defectors should be given sanctuary.

SIB

OSS term for a propaganda rumor.

SIBLINGS

CIA term for officers of the (sometimes rival) Defense Intelligence Agency.

SIGNATURE

The individual touch used by a wireless radio operator which indicates his personal transmitting pattern. The operator has a certain interval between words and characters, he commences and ends his messages in a characteristic manner, and his touch and speed are as different from another radioman's as are his fingerprints or voice. To an experienced monitor, a change in the signature is as obvious as would be a change in the sender's voice.

SILENT SCHOOL

Individual instruction at an intelligence school, so as to avoid exposing an agent who will work under deep cover to any other persons, save the essential trainers. (KGB term.)

SINGLETON

An individual agent operating alone, rather than as a member of a net or through a chain of intermediaries. Although frequently valuable for one-time in-and-out missions, the long-range value of such solo operators is doubted by intelligence professionals. The most famed singleton ever to don cloak and dagger was the fictional James Bond. In the words of one of novelist Charles McCarry's spooks, the singleton "requires no support...he operates alone, goes where he pleases." (McCarry worked for CIA before becoming a successful professional writer.) A unilateral, as distinguished from a singleton, works under agency control. (*See* UNILATERAL.)

SINON

A Greek who was perhaps the first secret agent in history. He conceived the famous coup in Troy in which soldiers hid inside a wooden horse and were wheeled inside closely guarded gates.

SIX HUNDREDS (600s)

The financial disclosure forms that CIA are required to executive periodically.

SKATOL

A chemical in powdered form, developed by FBI laboratories, that emits an "extremely noxious odor rendering the premises surrounding the point of application uninhabitable." One use the FBI made of Skatol was to foul the San Diego printing plant that produced *The Black Panther,* newspaper of the extremist Black Panther Party. (*See* WHO, ME?)

SKUNK WORKS

A secret section of the old Lockheed Aircraft plant at Burbank, California, where engineer Kelly Johnson developed the U-2 spy plane for CIA. Working with an unlimited budget and on a tight schedule, Johnson used unorthodox techniques to design and build the plane, which snooped at will over the Soviet Union for four years before the Gary Francis Powers incident. [*See* U-2]

SLEEPER AGENT, SLEEPER

An agent put into a circumstance or situation where his sole job is to wait until it becomes possible for him to actively gather intelligence, regardless of the length of time required. The most famed sleeper story, one taught as a textbook case for years at intelligence schools, proved apochryphal once World War II documents were declassified. But the yarn, although bogus, does illustrate the principle: The Germans in the 1920s sent an agent to a coastal village near Scapa Flow, the vital British naval base. The agent worked as a watchmaker until 1939; when the war erupted, he provided information that enabled a German submarine to slip past nets and torpedo HMS *Ark Royal*. According to German intelligence files, no such sleeper existed.

A favorite "what-if?" game among CIA people concerned placing a sleeper in the USSR Politboro itself. If such did happen, what information would warrant the agent to risk blowing his cover? The consensus: nothing less than a warning of imminent war.

A sleeper is also referred to as a "back marker," or as "on ice."

SLUG

See SWALLOW.

SLUZHBA A

Russian for "Service A," an independent component within the First Chief Directorate of KGB, charged with overall management of "active measures" throughout the world.

SMERSH

The secret police units assigned to the Red Army that watch closely for signs of dissent or defeatism, created during World War II by Lavrenti Beria. Western intelligence agencies long attributed the word "smersh" to an acronym for *smert shpionam*, or "death to spies." But Kirill Khenkin, in his book *Okhotni, vverkh nogami (Hunter Upside Down)*, published in Frankfurt, says the acronym was derived from the phrase *spetsial'nie metodi razoblachenia schpinov*, which means "special methods for exposing spies."

SNAKE-EATER

Military term for a member of the Special Forces, or "Green Berets," specially trained for commando and other missions behind enemy lines. As part of their training, Green Berets learn to eat what is available; hence their jungle diet often features reptilian cuisine.

SNITCH JACKET

Neutralizing a target by labeling him as a snitch, or informant, so that he would no longer be trusted. Methods utilized range from having an authentic informant start a rumor about the target member, to anonymous letters or phone calls, to faked informants' reports. If a number of persons from a target group are taken into custody, for instance, one of them might be held several hours longer than the others, then word floated that "[subject] decided to cooperate with the cops." Such is dangerous stuff, for the person accused of being a snitch could be killed. However, despite wide use of the snitch jacket technique during COINTELPRO, the FBI claimed to the Church Committee that no one was murdered.

SNUGGLING

A black propaganda technique. A clandestine radio program is broadcast on a frequency adjacent to that of a "legitimate" station—say, that of a state-run broadcasting service. Listeners think they are hearing an official broadcast rather than artfully constructed propaganda. The British pioneered snuggling during World War II. CIA made most effective use of snuggling during the 1954 overthrow of the Marxist government of Guatemala. Under direction of CIA wizard David Atlee Phillips, rebel "announcers" broadcast such alarming items as, "It is *not* true that the waters of Lake Atitlan have been poisoned." Unwary listeners would think they were hearing a government broadcast and not believe the denial. Within hours, thousands of persons thought that the lake indeed had been poisoned.

SOFT FILES

Officially, soft files do not exist. Actually, these are maintained by every agency in the American intelligence community. They are devoted to personal information about officials and employees—sex and drinking habits, unusual hobbies or pastimes, dubious friends and associates. Because of their unofficial nature, such files are not apt to be delivered in response to a court or Congressional subpoena, or even by order of the President. One former CIA executive called them "material essential to good management—you know this stuff before someone else does, and you act accordingly."

SOFT TARGETS
Friendly or neutral nations in which CIA has only a routine interest in terms of intelligence coverage. For instance, the CIA station in Stockholm would report on Soviet attempts to steal Western technology and monitor political developments. But activities would largely be confined to reporting. (*See* HARD TARGETS.)

SOLD
An agent who has been deliberately betrayed by his own side.

SOSED
Neighbor, in Russian, meaning a complementary intelligence service; KGB, for instance, would have considered GRU or the Bulgarian service *sosed*.

SOUND MAN
Wiretapping or bugging expert.

SOUND SCHOOL
The FBI course in surreptitious bugging and wiretapping, taught at the bureau laboratory in Washington.

SPARE PARTS
The disparaging name given MI6 staff officers by field offices, as related by former SIS officer Gavin Lyall in his 1964 book, *The Most Dangerous Game*. A field officer has the somewhat more dignified nickname of "Salesman," appropriately given by MI6, which is known internally as "The Firm."

SPLIT

KGB term for forcing a confession. "Forcing" needs no further description.

SPYING

Learning things about one's adversary through guile, deceit, observation and any other stratagem that comes to mind. Persons interested in this line of work should be aware of some of the pitfalls:

The psychic cost. The U.S. Department of Energy has an "Office of Safeguards and Security," which is responsible for teaching DOE employees about security awareness, especially when it comes to the nuclear weapons program. In the 1980s it circulated a handbook that contained this admonition: "One final note: as some people proceed with their careers working for DOE, the idea of spying may cross their minds. They may be experiencing emotional difficulties, or perhaps feel that life could be more exciting. Convicted spy Christopher Boyce has described his life as a spy as '...horrendous...like having a cancer...' while he was spying, and that the KGB '...never let go; they were always there, exploiting and controlling' him like a puppet..." He warns: If people knew how badly espionage '...would poison their lives...what it would mean to them personally, as individuals...' then they would never become involved.

When "friends" are the target. Commenting on the Jonathan Pollard case, in which a civilian navy employee spied for the Israeli government, retired Mossad officer Colonel Menachem Digly likened spying to exploring for oil. "In the case of Pollard the drill hit the vein that was full of information; the hunger for that information was great, but the well happened to be in the yard of a good friend— but not good enough to have given us the information voluntarily."

SOURCE PROTECT

A warning phrase at the start of a communication that directs that the contents be tightly guarded, even within the receiving office. Since intelligence agencies operate on a need-to-know basis, with compartmentalization of information, a distant office is often unaware of an ongoing operation. If events compel the second office to take control of the case on short notice, a fairly complete case history must be forwarded for guidance. "Source protect" is intended to alert the receiving office that the case is sensitive.

SOUTH CAFETERIA

CIA's "classified" dining area. Covert employees, chiefly from the Clandestine Services, eat there, secure in the knowledge that no outsiders are permitted inside. Visitors from the "outside"—including such fellow spy agencies as the Defense Intelligence Agency and the National Security Agency—are shunted to the overt cafeteria elsewhere in the building. The food reportedly is better in South Cafeteria.

SOVBLOC GREEN

Officers and agents of MI6 who were not known to Soviet intelligence services. Hence they could be used on covert missions to Communist Bloc nations.

SOVBLOC RED

MI6 officers and agents who were known to Soviet and Bloc intelligence services and who were not eligible for clandestine assignments abroad. Their personnel dossiers carried the *SovBloc Red* stamp.

SOVETSKYAYA KOLONIA (SK)

The "Soviet colony," a catchall phrase covering all Soviets living in a foreign country or city under official or business cover. Each person in the SK is kept under KGB surveillance. KGB has the responsibility of protecting the SK against penetration by Western intelligence agencies. KGB's first line of defense in this regard is to discourage, if not outright prohibit, any contacts with Westerners outside the normal course of business; dependents and low-level personnel, for instance, are seldom permitted to leave the official compound.

In Washington, the main Soviet complex is a grouping of ugly stone buildings on a slight rise on Tunlaw Road Northwest, just west of Wisconsin Avenue. Iron fences topped with electronic devices surround the area, and on sunny days women and children mill around the grounds in a manner mindful of animals in a zoo. When the compound was under construction, residents of nearby apartment buildings complained that electronic interference was wreaking havoc with radio and TV reception, an indication that either (a) CIA and the FBI were packing the new building with surreptitious listening devices or (b) that KGB was packing the new building with surreptitious counterlistening devices. In any event, the noise cleared up soon after the Soviets occupied the building.

Years later, it was revealed that during the construction, the FBI attempted to tunnel under the site to plant listening devices that would tap into telephone and other communications lines. The FBI traitor Robert B. Hannsen told his Soviet paymasters about the operation, hence it failed.

SPECIAL ACTIVITIES DIVISION

The branch of the National Clandestine service that is essentially a paramilitary army. It was created in the post-9/11 revamping of the intelligence establishment. SAD is composed of officers who conduct deniable covert operations abroad. (*See* THE POINT.)

SPECIAL CATEGORY ITEMS FILE

Depository for the occasional embarrassing mail intercepts CIA made under its HTLINGUAL project. In March 1971, CIA agents opened and photographed a letter from Senator Frank Church, a member of the Senate Foreign Relations Committee (and later chairman of the select committee on intelligence that bedeviled CIA, the FBI, and other agencies). One alarmed supervisor suggested that any such intercepts not be put into Agency files and that mail screeners be ordered "to cease the acquisition of such materials." A formal directive in 1971 instructed HTLINGUAL teams not to watch-list or screen any mail from elected or appointed federal officials, or from senior state officials such as governors or lieutenant governors. If mail from such persons was accidentally intercepted, no reports would go to the central files; the letters themselves would go to a Special Category Items File maintained in the safe of the HTLINGUAL director. (That CIA did not simply order the destruction of such intercepts without further notice is indicative of the bureaucratic mind-set that occasionally grips the Agency. CIA was "most embarrassed" when it had to inform the hostile Church in 1974 that his mail had been read. That CIA did not try to conceal the episode is indicative of the show-it-all disclosure policy decided upon at high CIA levels when the Church probe began. Some outside friends felt this CIA attitude to be unbelievably dumb.

SPECIAL INTELLIGENCE SERVICE (SIS)

An FBI unit created in 1940 to provide the State Department, the military, and other government agencies with intelligence from Latin America regarding "financial, economic, political and subversive activities detrimental to the security of the U.S." SIS assisted several Latin nations "in training police and organizing anti-espionage and anti-sabotage defenses." Through SIS, the FBI remained dominant in Latin intelligence throughout World War II, resisting attempts of the rival Office of Strategic Services to operate there. FBI director Hoover so zealously guarded his assigned turf that he sabotaged an attempt by OSS to gain intelligence from the Spanish embassy in Washington. Hoover apparently decided unilaterally that, since both Latin Americans and Spaniards spoke the same language, he could claim Spain as "his." Hoover learned that OSS agents had broken into the embassy and photographed documents. Instead of registering a protest, he waited until OSS returned for a second surreptitious mission, then had FBI cars parked outside turn on their sirens. The OSS men scattered. The dispute reached the White House, where aides to President Roosevelt ordered OSS to turn over the Spanish embassy project to Hoover.

After the war a new agency, the Central Intelligence Group (predecessor to the CIA), was given responsibility for all foreign espionage and counterespionage operations worldwide. Hoover immediately disbanded the SIS; in some instances, SIS officers in the field burned their files rather than surrender them to the new agency.

Two other organizations with the "SIS" initials were noted earlier—the Soviet Intelligence Services and the (British) Secret Intelligence Service.

SPECIAL OPERATIONS EXECUTIVE (SOE)

The British organization founded in 1940 to raise, arm, fund, and train resistance and partisan cadres in German-occupied territories in Europe. Prime Minister Winston Churchill instructed SOE to "Set Europe ablaze!" And that it did. SOE was first a trainer of, and then a partner with, the fledgling American Office of Strategic Services (OSS). SOE's ranks included professional soldiers, academics, and paroled jailhouse thugs. (*See* STATELY 'OMES OF ENGLAND.)

SPECIAL TASKS

KGB euphemism for murders, kidnappings, and sabotage. These operations were conducted by "mobile brigades" created to carry out assassinations outside the USSR. The mobile groups were created circa 1936 by Nikolai Ivanovich Yezhov, then the Soviet secret police chief. The most famed (of many) victims was Leon Trotsky, axed to death in suburban Mexico City in 1939. Special tasks were later mostly delegated to subservient services such as the Bulgarian secret police. (*See also* MOBILE BRIGADES.)

SPETSBURO

The Bureau of Special Tasks, the Soviet intelligence unit responsible for assassinations. The *Spetsburo* was responsible for the murders of many anti-Soviet Russian emigres in Western Europe during the 1940s and 1950s. Hiring on for murder is too much for even some hardened Soviet agents to stomach. On at least two occasions, agents of *Spetsburo* defected when ordered to kill specific persons. *Spetsburo* works under direct control of the Central Committee of the Communist Party.

SPIKE MIKE

See PROBE MICROPHONE.

SPOOK

A term meaning "CIA officer" that originated in the American diplomatic corps—"sometimes pejoratively, sometimes affectionately," in the words of former CIA operative David Atlee Phillips. As Phillips noted in his memoir, *Night Watch*, "CIA officers have learned to live with the term, and occasionally refer to themselves as spooks."

SPOTTER

See SURVEILLANCE.

SPY

The intelligence historian Donald McCormick (who writes under the pen name Richard Deacon) traces the term to the ancient Chinese, where a single character in the Chinese language "had as its original meaning...that of a 'chink,' 'a crack,' or crevice." McCormick wrote (in his *Who's Who in Spy Fiction)* that "from any of these meanings one can derive the sense of a peep-hole, so it would seem that the earliest Chinese conception of a spy is very simply one who peeps through a crack."

The *Encyclopedia Britannica,* in its 1771 edition, defined a spy as "A person hired to watch the actions, motions, etc., of another; particularly of what passes in a camp. When a spy is discovered, he is hanged immediately."

SQUIRT TRANSMITTER

A device that permits an agent operating in enemy territory to punch coded messages on a tape. Through the use of a special keying device, the tape can be fed through a radio transmitter at upwards of three hundred words per minute, enabling the agent to send his message rapidly and be off the air before directional radio honing equipment can locate him.

SSD (Staatssicherheitsdient)

State Security Service, the East German political police. Low-grade, used for border duty chiefly; untrusted by KGB overseers. Western agencies called *SSD* men "rent-a-cops." *SSD* was noted for bravery chiefly when given the chance to club unarmed border crossers, particularly women.

ST. MALLARD'S

"A not quite affectionate term for the nameless private hospital that the Agency maintains at its old training center near Monterey," according to former CIA officer Roy Hayes in his novel, *The Hungarian Game.* He wrote that the name "derives from a value judgment on the quacks who practice there."

STAG

FBI code for its "Student Agitation" files.

STEGANOGRAPHY

An Internet Age means of secret spy communication. According to the indictment of ten deep-cover sleeper agents of the Russian SVR in June 2010, "Steganography is the process of secreting data in an image. Moscow Center [headquarters of the SVR] uses steganographic software that is not commercially available. The software package permits the SVR clandestinely to insert encrypted data in images that are located in publicly-available websites without the data being visible. The encrypted data can be removed from the image, and then decrypted, using SVR-provided software. Similarly, SVR-provided software can be used to encrypt data, and then clandestinely to embed the images on publicly-available websites."

According to an FBI affidavit in the case, agents seized and analyzed a computer hard drive that revealed an address book with links to various websites. Images were downloaded from them "which appear wholly unremarkable to the naked eye." But when run through a steganographic program, "some of the images have been revealed as containing readable text files," more than one hundred in all on computers seized from a Boston couple working for the SVR.

The Russian agents quickly entered guilty pleas, and the Obama Administration entered into a deal where they were sent home in return for the release of a single person who, albeit serving a prison term for spying, denied any espionage activities. FBI agents who worked the "sleeper case" for almost a decade were not happy with its disposition.

STATE COMMITTEE FOR COORDINATION OF SCIENTIFIC RESEARCH WORK

The Soviet agency, tightly controlled by KGB, that handled all scientific and technical liaison activities with foreign countries. One major function was the recruitment of foreign scientists to act as spies; hence the procurement of scientific information and equipment. Because of the euphemistic title, the "coordination" committee often duped Western scientists into believing it was in fact an independent scientific group. But Colonel Oleg Penkovsky, the intelligence officer working for the committee when he began supplying information to CIA, testified that it, in fact, was a spy group.

STATELY 'OMES OF ENGLAND
Derisive name given to the Special Operations Executive (SOE), the British sabotage organization during World War II, prompted by the organization's proclivity for commandeering lavish country houses for training sites and operational bases.

STB (Statni Tajna Bezpecnost)
The Czech intelligence service. In Western lore, STB has "the longest legs of any Bloc service." Why? "Because they have to spread their legs the widest for KGB. The exercise made their legs grow."

STAY-BEHIND NETS
Clandestine infrastructures of leaders and equipment trained and ready to be called into action as sabotage and espionage forces, generally in areas subject to enemy occupation. Organizing stay-behind nets was William Colby's first assignment when he joined CIA in November 1950. (He served with OSS during World War II, then worked as a lawyer.) CIA feared the Soviets would use the Korean War, just under way, as a pretext for grabbing all of Western Europe. So Colby, who did guerrilla operations in Norway for OSS, was assigned to establish covert stay-behind nets in Scandinavia that would resist the Soviets should they indeed invade.

Radio transmitters, weapons, safe houses, trusted agents and handlers, codes—even recordings of national music to be played over clandestine radio stations—are the stuff with which stay-behind nets are equipped. Even a friendly host government is frequently unaware of the covert apparatus set up on its borders and manned by its citizens.

STAYER
A KGB deep-cover agent working in a foreign country whose only intelligence activity was to verify the safe arrival of other Soviet operatives assigned to the country. For instance, if KGB sent an agent into the United States under the cover of, say, a reporter for a British newspaper, the stayer would screen him from afar, then make contact via a previously arranged code phrase. The stayer

enabled the new agent to avoid any contact whatsoever with his nation's more conventional intelligence apparatus.

STERILE TELEPHONE

A telephone whose location cannot be traced, even through the telephone company. CIA has access to such telephones both in the United States and abroad, through techniques that go beyond bribery.

STERILITY CODING

The use of intermediary companies or individuals to cover purchases or payments that an intelligence agency does not wish to be traced to its own doorstep. Past uses include prostitutes for the late President Sukarno of Indonesia during a visit to the United States, and Swift boats for anti-Castro Cuban exile groups. The amount and date of the expenditure will appear on the agency's books, its only stated purpose being the sterility code, the meaning of which is contained in a tightly held file elsewhere.

STOOGES

Low-level informants infiltrated into British POW camps during World War II to garner information on German and Italian prisoners. Stooges worked under the control of the "B"—or counterespionage—division of MI5.

STOVEPIPING

In the words of spyspeak aficionado William Safire, the term of "espionage argot for sending compartmentalized data directly up top. No foreign dissemination; on intra-community vetting; no coordination with law enforcement." Safire lamented, "In this way, leaders and overseers become musclebound." [Safire, "Where Is Globocop?," *The New York Times*, July 3, 1995.] CHIMNEYING is less frequently used.

STRINGER

A low-level agent who lives or works in proximity to an intelligence target and who passes along whatever information is acquired in the course of daily business. Stringers generally receive only rudimentary training and are paid a minimal stipend plus an occasional bonus for outstanding work. (The bonus, however, is frequently paid *not* for valuable information, but for trivia; to do otherwise would pinpoint the sort of intelligence being avidly sought, an unacceptable security breach. But the bonus payments keep the stringer active.) Stringers are also used for such occasional odd jobs as serving as "live" letter-drops, renting a one-time-use safe house, or aiding in a hurry-up surveillance.

The stringer in all probability does not know the true identity of the intelligence service for which he is working; in West Germany in the 1950s, for instance, CIA agents routinely passed themselves off as agents of the U.S. Army's Counter Intelligence Corps (CIC). CIC agents took the guise of operatives from either the British Secret Intelligence Service (which employs enough linguistic oddballs to make the cover plausible) or the West German Gehlen Organization. Stringers are an expendable asset: If a double agent needs "credits" to establish his worth, stringers are the first to be exposed.

STUDY CIRCLES, STUDY GROUPS

The euphemism for the Communist cells that seeded the United States government during the 1930s, particularly in Washington. In addition to listening to lectures on Marx, Russia, and capitalism, many members of the study group were persuaded to steal papers, take home secret documents for copying, and allow Soviet handlers to set up photo workshops in their homes. By the testimony of Whittaker Chambers, one of the overlords of these groups, no less than seventy-five government employees were involved in Soviet espionage in 1936–38. The American left has long claimed that many of these "study groups" were legitimate discussion organizations with no Soviet connections. However, see COMINTERN.

SUBMERGE

To disappear from sight once within the target country, usually to reappear later with new identification papers, cover story, and physical appearance.

SUCKING DRY

Soviet term for debriefing an agent after he returns from a mission.

SUITABILITY FILES

Highly personal information that might show the unreliability or vulnerability of a federal employee—with an intelligence or defense agency—which could lead to compromise of classified information. The information is highly personal (sexual proclivities, drinking habits, financial and marital problems). The National Security Agency states that it maintains suitability files to aid in providing counsel and other forms of guidance to individuals with personal problems—not to damage or threaten them. Even the highly suspicious Church Committee concluded it "has no reason to believe that information in these files has been misused."

SUPER-GRADER

In CIA parlance, a senior officer with a civil service rank of GS-16 or above. Although CIA employees are not members of the civil service system, they do work in the normal government grade structure, with GS-18 being the highest rank. Super-graders are the equivalent of flag officers (generals or admirals) in the military services.

SUPPORT AGENT

A field operator whose sole function is to act as a courier or message center for an illegal agent. Accepted tradecraft is that one support agent "handles" only a single person. Violation of this precept contributed to the roll-up of eleven Russian "sleepers" in the US in the summer of 2010 (they were promptly swapped for persons the US wished to rescue from Russian custody.

SURFACING

Publicizing a defector, either through a carefully sanitized article or through a public press conference. Understandably, a defector is not surfaced until his interrogators have extracted all information of an intelligence value. Surfacing gives an agency the opportunity to "rub the other side's nose in it."

Surfacing can be posthumous, as was the case for Colonel Oleg Penkovsky, the scientific intelligence officer who worked for CIA from April 1961 through August 1962. The Soviet state publishing house distributed some 10,000 copies of the transcript of Penkovsky's trial, denouncing him as a vile traitor. CIA had the last word, however, with *The Penkovsky Papers*, an amalgamation of reports, background material, and other information that was put into book form by *Time-Life* writer Frank Gibney.

The CIA turncoat Philip Agee, in his book *On the Run*, asserted that in the agency, surfacing is the "authorized leak of classified information in the press or another outlet, with the intent of obtaining publicity." In essence, surfacing is a "legal leak" which enables CIA or another agency to make a point in a debate without direct attribution. As Washington bureau chief of *The Philadelphia Inquirer* 1967–68, at the height of the Vietnam War, I can attest that the practice was wide-spread, with the White House, State and Defense Departments, and CIA being more or less equally adept in leaking.

SURREPTITIOUS ENTRY

FBI term for warrantless entries into a target property, both for installation of microphones and theft (and/or photography) of documents. (*See* BLACK BAG JOB.)

SURROUND

Heavy-handed surveillance in which no precautions are taken to conceal the fact that a subject is being watched. When an agent realizes that he is surrounded, his hours of freedom are few.

SURVEILLANCE

Following a subject of intelligence interest, either by foot or by vehicle. A surveillance can be either "loose" with the watchers keeping such a distance that they do not risk detection themselves, or "tight," in which instance they do not break contact, even if spotted.

Sir Robert Baden-Powell, a turn-of-the-century British intelligence officer (and the founder of the world Boy Scout movement), didn't feel that surveillance of suspected agents was overly difficult. "Spies betray themselves by their walk," Baden-Powell once wrote. "A spy may effect a wonderful disguise in front yet be instantly recognized by a keen eye from behind. This is a point frequently forgotten by beginners." Fortunately for the British services, Baden-Powell progressed further in scouting than he did in intelligence.

"Spotters" are helpful in evading surveillance by automobile. A person who wishes to shake off tails drives around a traffic circle two or three times. A couple sits in a parked car on the circle. If after his second or third circuit no tail appears, the woman draws a scarf around her head, or the man takes off his hat—a "clear signal." A bridge can be substituted for the traffic circle.

Overt officers working abroad assume that they are subjected to frequent—and sometimes constant—surveillance, something they learn to accept as a matter of course. When the adversary wishes to make plain that the subject is being followed, he is put under "close surveillance," with the watchers making no attempt to conceal what they are doing. It is not unusual for a CIA officer working abroad to give his surveillance team a friendly wave when he drives away from his home or office, in silent acknowledgement that the other guys are simply doing their job, and that he is not going to make things difficult for them by using counter-surveillance tricks.

Subjects break the "unwritten rules" at their peril. An FBI agent once told me of a "loose surveillance" that he and a colleague maintained on a Soviet "diplomat" suspected of working for the KGB as he made a long drive down the Eastern seaboard (following a route approved by the State Department). "He irritated us by making several attempts to shake us off—dumb things like getting off the highway and making sudden turns here and there." The FBI man feared the Soviet might try to "slip coverage" when he stopped for the night at a motel, by sneaking away when he thought his watchers were sleeping. "Once he checked into the motel and parked, my partner walked about half a mile to a residential street, found a parked car, hot-wired it, and drove back to the motel. He parked it so that it blocked the Russkie—the only way he could get out was for the car to be moved. Sure enough, right after midnight, when he figured we might be snoozing, he came out and obviously intended to drive away. To his visible annoyance, there was NO way he could get his car out of the space. He fumed. He went into the motel office and raised a ruckus. The motel clerk, of course, had no idea who owned the car. There was much back-for-forth—we sat a comfortable distance away and watched and laughed—and after several hours the cops showed up and called a wrecker to tow the car away. By that time, it was nearly dawn. When the Russkie drove away, we got right on his bumper and honked the horn and waved at him. He gave us the finger, but he behaved the rest of the trip."

SVOI
Russian for "he is one of us," meaning in intelligence terms a witting collaborator. Its use indicates a willingness to submit to orders and discipline. Another Russian term, *nashi*, has a parallel meaning.

SVYAZNA
In Russian, "cut-out."

SVYAZNIYE
In Russian, "go-between"—a functionary who makes direct contact with agents and thence with KGB agents assigned to a Soviet embassy.

SW (SECRET WRITING)
Writing modified, usually by chemical means, to remain invisible. Various agencies around the world invested thousands of man-years in searching for the "perfect ink" for writing invisible messages that can be brought to light by exposure to light or another liquid. Early in World War I, the British Secret Intelligence Service was eager to obtain "ink that came from a natural source of supply." The director, Commander Mansfield Cumming, made inquiries of scientists at London University. He reported to subordinates that "the best invisible ink is semen, which does not react to the main detection methods." Tests were conducted, and in fact semen did not react to iodine vapors. But the semen had to be fresh. As an SIS officer wrote, "we thought we had solved a great problem. But our man in Copenhagen evidently stocked it in a bottle—for his letters stank to high heaven, and we had to tell him that a fresh operation was necessary for each letter." (Keith Jeffrey related the story in his 2010 book, *The Secret History of MI6, 1909–1949.*)

SWALLOW
A female KGB spy. Despite specific warnings, U.S. embassy personnel in Moscow maintained a fatal affinity for offered Soviet flesh. KGB procedure was to exact payment once the target returned

to the United States—that is, "if you don't spy for us, interesting pictures and recordings will be sent to your wife and mother." Mythology is that KGB swallows were trained at a special "sex school." In actuality, the swallows attended a rather basic intelligence school, and sexual prowess did not figure in the curriculum. A swallow, in essence, was a prostitute with an IQ slightly above her sisters-on-the-street. Swallows were viewed with utter contempt both by fellow KGB agents and CIA officers against whom they were directed on occasion. (*See* SEXPIONAGE.)

SWALLOW'S NEST

An apartment or house used by a swallow (see above) for the sexual entertainment of a KGB target. The "nest" was fitted with audio and video recording equipment to put the target's sexual play onto permanent record, for use in blackmail.

SWIM

The dispatch of a KGB officer from the USSR to an assignment abroad. For example, "Boris is going to swim to London."

SYMBOL NUMBER

An FBI code number used in lieu of the words "telephone surveillance" as a cover for a wiretap.

T

TALENT-SPOTTER

A deep-cover agent responsible for spotting persons who are suitable recruits for intelligence work. The label is most commonly used to denote someone who recruits agents to work against their own country (most vividly illustrated in the instance of the Cambridge don who persuaded numerous undergraduates to become Soviet agents in the 1930s. The most famous of his "talents" were Kim Philby, Donald Maclean, Guy Burgess, and Anthony Blunt). The same term is applied, in a positive sense, to American university professors who look for students with the attributes essential to a CIA officer.

A skilled talent-spotter works indirectly: Seldom does he state at the outset exactly what he expects of the target. Anthony Blunt, under interrogation, quoted the approach used on him by Guy Burgess: "Anthony, we must do something to counter the horrors of Nazism. We can't just sit here and talk about it.... I am already committed to work secretly for peace. Are you prepared to help me?" Only later was the recruit informed he was working for the Comintern and for Soviet intelligence.

The term is also applied to trusted academics in both American and European universities, who would spot students with a seeming aptitude for intelligence work in their classes. In the instance of the CIA, the actual recruitment pitch would be made by an active-duty officer, not the professor.

TANK, THE

A sound-secure room in the larger CIA stations around the world. Novelist David Wise described the London tank in his book, *Spectrum:* "The tank, which resembled a streamlined railroad car on stilts, was actually a room within a room. It rested on steel legs above the floor. A speaker had been mounted on the outside, and when the tank was in use, a noisemaking tape emitted a loud, steady sound of whirring machinery." (A tape made in a cotton mill in North Carolina, according to station lore.) Tanks are bugproof—but also windowless; they tend to get stuffy.

TARGET STUDY

A compilation of all available information on a person being considered for recruitment as an intelligence source. Sources include existing file material, surveillance for as long as two months to check the person's associations and movements, and whatever information can be garnered from other intelligence agencies. The "vulnerability paragraph" of the target study outlines why the person might be receptive to an offer to work for a foreign intelligence agency—money, ideology, vulnerability to blackmail; the reasons are limitless.

TARGETED KILLING

A post-9/11 counterterrorism term meaning the assassination of al-Queda or Taliban insurgents in Afghanistan or Iraq [see, for instance, *The New York Times*, August 1, 2010, for the Obama Administration's reliance on this form of counterterrorism.]

TASK

An assignment for intelligence personnel.

TASS

The official Soviet news agency, whose correspondents abroad doubled as espionage agents. Although TASS "reporters" protested their independence of government control, on at least one occasion they have been forced to fly their true colors. In 1949 a TASS reporter somehow became president of the Foreign Press Association in London, a position for which government officials are not eligible. A Czech refugee named Krajina, living in London, claimed he had been libeled in a TASS dispatch and filed a civil action in court. The Soviet embassy intervened with a declaration that the TASS employees were Russian officials and hence entitled to diplomatic immunity. A British appeals court upheld the Soviet position—but in doing so shattered the myth of TASS "independence."

In Washington, TASS correspondents enjoyed many of the same

privileges as do American reporters. But there are exceptions: TASS men, for instance, are not included in the "deep background" sessions at which officials, such as the Secretary of State or Defense, explain policy issues off-the-record. Further, TASS employees are subjected to the same FBI surveillance as are formal members of the Soviet diplomatic mission.

TAYNIK (or Tainik)
See DUBOK.

TECHNICAL COVERAGE
FBI euphemism for a wiretap or bug.

TECHNICAL SERVICES
The division of MI5 responsible for electronic and other forms of non-human surveillance.

TECHNOLOGY COLLECTION OFFICER
A KGB or GRU agent assigned to steal or buy Western technology, either in the form of plans or actual working items. Beginning in the late 1970s, the Soviet emphasis was on computer and microchip technology. Technology collection officers worked under the Directorate of KGB (more formally, the Scientific and Technical Directorate). The department known as "Line X" was specifically responsible for foreign field operations.

TECHNOLOGY TRANSFER ASSESSMENT CENTER
A CIA branch that documented the use the Soviet Union and its allies made of technology acquired from the West; also, the clandestine methods used to obtain the items. During 1983–84, according to William J. Casey, director of central intelligence, the center played a role in the expulsion of "well over 150 Soviet agents" from 20 countries for "technology theft." Casey noted in a 1984 speech, "Successes have also been achieved in recovering stolen technology, blocking shipments, and breaking up the technology smuggling rings."

TELEGRAPH

A prearranged signal that tells an agent he should pick up material from a "dead drop." Reino Hayhanen, a Soviet spy in the United States from 1952 through 1957, used as his telegraph to other agents a childlike chalk scrawl on a wooden fence. Hayhanen came to the United States under deep cover, posing as the American-born son of Estonian parents who had taken him to Estonia before World War II. He defected to American intelligence in 1957. His information led, in turn, to the seizure of Colonel Rudolf Abel, the highest-ranking spy ever caught in the West.

TELINJECT VARIO AIR PISTOL

As described by reliable spy fiction writer Alex Berenson, CIA's Directorate of Science and Technology patterned this device on "chemical stun guns" used by ranchers and veterinarians to sedate unruly animals. The core is a syringe filled with katamine—"the drug that club kids and other fun-seekers called Special K"—and Versid, a liquid sedative similar to Valium. The syringe is fitted into an air pistol. Targets experience feelings ranging from "out of body" to unconsciousness, with no lasting ill effects.

TELL-TALE

A form of talcum powder, invisible on white paper; examination under an ultraviolet light will reveal whether the documents on which it is placed have been disturbed.

TERMINATE WITH EXTREME PREJUDICE

Murdering an agent who has outlived his usefulness, per spy novelists and movie writers. In fact, the term has never been used by any American intelligence professional, espionage mythologists notwithstanding, as an euphemism for murder. When employed by CIA officers, it means simply, "Get this guy off our payroll and out of sight; we want nothing else to do with him." (*See also* DISPOSAL, EXECUTIVE ACTION.)

TERRORISM

"The unlawful use of force or violence against persons or property to intimidate or coerce a government, the civilian population or any segment thereof, in furtherance of political or social objectives." Such is the formal definition adopted by the FBI in 1982 and followed by other U.S. government agencies.

THIRD COUNTRY OPERATIONS

Using a base in one country as a means of gaining access to intelligence of other countries, and of conducting operations elsewhere in the geographical area. The host country is either friendly or neutral, and is itself of no special intelligence interest. Both the KGB and CIA have used Mexico City as an outpost for "third country operations" throughout Latin America and maintained large stations there. As a traditional haven for "political" exiles, Mexico hosts revolutionaries of every leftist hue, the one ground rule being that they do not get involved with local dissidents. Cuba's DGI *(Direccidn General de la Inteligencia,* or General Intelligence Directorate) is prominent in Mexico because of the ease of travel to other Latin countries. As a resident journalist in Mexico City in the 1960s, I could make contact with Castroite groups with considerably more ease, say, than I could make a dental appointment.

TIT FOR TAT

A Reagan Administration strategem intended to subject official Soviets working in Washington to the same strictures as the USSR imposed on the American diplomatic community in Moscow. The order, issued April 1, 1983, required Soviets to make travel arrangements—plane tickets and hotel reservations—through a new Office of Foreign Missions, under the State Department. To ensure that the office was run by "someone meaner than the normal diplomatic type," the White House selected a former FBI senior officer, James E. Nolan, to be its director.

In the old Soviet Union, foreign diplomats had to deal with an agency known as *Upravlrniye po Obsluzhivaniyu Diplomaticheskogo Korpusa,* or the Administration for Serving the Diplomatic Corps, known widely as the UPDK. Although officially a part of the Foreign Ministry, UPDK was widely accepted as a branch of the KGB, tasked to keep track of what foreigners wee doing. It provided apartment leases, household help, piano teachers and even gave driving lessons. Many Americans working in Moscow—journalists as well as Foreign Service officers—complained for years that UPDK seemed to delight in subjecting them to petty annoyances.

TIRE SPIKE

A crude sabotage device developed by the OSS during World War II, still in wide use. The spike is a piece of one-eighth-inch-thick steel, cut in the form of a four-pointed star. The star is three inches in diameter, and the points are alternately bent up and down at an angle of 45 degrees from the horizontal. The tire spike is used to puncture rubber tires of vehicles or airplanes; it is most effective when scattered in the gravel or ruts of unpaved roads, or on airplane runways. Because of the angle in which the points are bent, one of the points will always be in a vertical position, regardless of how the spike is dropped.

OSS doctrine was for liberal use of the spikes, which were shipped to field units in 125-pound lots packed in wooden kegs (2,160 one-ounce spikes per keg).

The KGB and its subsidiaries made frequent use of tire spikes to discourage surveillance or pursuit in operations involving cars. For instance, on July 8, 1952, Soviet agents grabbed the West German anti-Communist lawyer Walter Linse from a street near his home in a suburb of West Berlin. A brave citizen drove in chase, only to have his tires ruined by spikes thrown from the kidnap vehicle. Despite his flattened tires, the citizen pursued Linse's captors to the border of the Soviet zone—where guards raised the barrier gate with precision timing as the kidnap car roared into view.

"TONGUE," CAPTURING A

Soviet military intelligence term for kidnapping individual officers and enlisted men who are apt to have information of value. During World War II, tongue operations were conducted chiefly by partisan bands with Chekist advisors; among the tongues caught by these raiding groups was the German puppet minister of defense in Slovakia and the commander of the Slovakian land forces. In the postwar period, the Soviets frequently used kidnapping to silence enemies, particularly nationalist exiles from the Sovietized puppet regions within the USSR.

TONGUE-TANGLER

Speech alteration device developed by CIA's Technical Services Division. A thin layer of flesh-colored plastic, it causes the wearer to speak with a slight lisp. Normal speech intonations are also changed. The tongue-tangler is not popular because it is uncomfortable.

TOSS

To enter and search, surreptitiously (and perhaps illegally), the living quarters or office of a person who is a suspect in an espionage or criminal case.

TRADECRAFT

The methods by which an intelligence agency conducts its business. "Tradecraft may be mysterious to outsiders," writes CIA veteran William Hood, "but it is little more than a compound of common sense, experience, and certain almost universally accepted security practices—The fact is that tradecraft is like arithmetic: it has been around for centuries. The basics are easy to learn and good texts can be found in any library. Although it is easy to make mistakes under pressure, only the advanced subjects—like multiplying fractions or manipulating double agents—are particularly complex."

Tradecraft can be learned in practical fashion. During World War II, David Atlee Phillips, an air force officer, escaped from a German POW camp. Making his way toward Allied lines, Phillips was helped by a friendly French farmer. "Give me your name and address," Phillips said, "I want to do something nice for you once the war ends." The farmer shook his head. "No," he said, "*you* give me *your* name and address." As Phillips commented later—after retiring from a quarter century service as one of CIA's top clandestine officers—"that was my first grass roots lesson in tradecraft. Had I been caught with the farmer's name in my pocket, he would have been a dead man."

TRAITOR

A person who sells or otherwise divulges his own country's secrets, be it for monetary or other reasons.

TREASON

As defined in Article III, Section 3, of the U.S. Constitution, "Treason against the United States shall consist only in levying war against them, or in adhering to their enemies, giving them aid and comfort."

TREFF

A German espionage term of World War II origin, meaning a meeting between an agent and his controller in a neutral country. *Treff* was used widely by both Western and Soviet agencies.

By CIA practice, the first item discussed in a *treff is* the timing and location of the next meeting, in the event the meeting in progress must be broken off suddenly.

Good tradecraft calls for sensitive *treffs* to be made in a country where the agents do not live or normally work. For instance, KGB controls in London regularly met British informers in France or Belgium, where close surveillance was more difficult.

TREE-SHAKER

See AGENT PROVOCATEUR.

TRIANGULATION

In signals intelligence, a technique of locating secret radio transmitters. Three radio receivers have revolving antennae that permit them to take bearings on a radio signal. The bearings are plotted on a map; their point of intersection gives the general locale of the radio. A mobile receiver (concealed in a van) then roams the locale until it is in audible proximity to the signal. The Germans used triangulation with deadly accuracy during the first part of World War II; "squirt transmissions" that were on the air for just minutes, or even seconds, helped counter the technique.

In counterintelligence, triangulation is a technique for locating the source of leaks of classified material. Classified information is put in reach of suspect persons; each receives it in slightly altered form (for instance, aircraft production figures are varied). "Feedback" as to what information is being leaked—obtained either by radio intercepts or human sources—points toward the persons who were entrusted with the specific figures divulged. In the next round, each of these persons is again given slightly variant forms of information. When the information emerges again, its source is usually evident. Triangulation is not unlike trout fishing: it requires a steady hand, patience, and the willingness to stand around in cold and uncomfortable water while waiting for something that might never happen.

TURN

To persuade an enemy agent to go to work for one's own intelligence service, either through persuasion or coercion. An agent so persuaded is said to be "turned."

TWENTY COMMITTEE

The British unit charged with convincing German intelligence during World War II that its Abwehr agents, although captured, were still actively spying. Through aggressive counterintelligence and radio intercepts, the British systematically caught every German agent dispatched to the United Kingdom during the war. The radios of many of these agents were used to send back spurious—but plausible—intelligence. Since the operation was a double-cross (XX), the British restated the Roman numerals as Twenty; hence the committee's designation.

TWO GIRLS, THE

German Communist slang for the separate Soviet spy organizations working in their country before World War II. "Grete" was the KGB predecessor: "Klara" was the Red Army.

TWISTED BALLS

According to Donald McCormick, in his *Who's Who in Spy Fiction*, "originally a Russian expression to indicate an agent who had at some time previously been given electric shocks in the genitals. Such a man was considered relatively an easy subject for further interrogation."

Safe House Interlude Ten

The Female of the Species

Until well into the 20th Century, intelligence agencies world-wide shunned the use of female officers, the exceptions being chiefly instances where they were tasked with sexual exploitation of sources. (*See* SEXPIONAGE.)

A classic misogynist was Oreste Pinto, an Allied counterintelligence officer. Among other things, he trained agents to be parachuted into occupied Europe. Several Dutch women who had escaped from Holland asked to be permitted to volunteer for the dangerous missions. In his memoir, *Spy-Catcher*, Pinto recollected, "They were obviously sincere and deeply patriotic. To each one I would say, 'What risks are you prepared to take?'

"Each would invariably reply, simply and without false heroics, 'I am prepared to give my life for my country.'

"My automatic reply was, 'That is the last thing we want. Dead, you are useless to us. But are you prepared to give your body?'

Pinto was serious. "In my opinion the only limited use a woman spy has is to gain information for her country by seducing a senior official...on the other side and subsequently blackmailing him into giving further information by threatening to report him to his security officers or, worse still, perhaps, to his wife. This is why I always asked the Dutch women...whether they were prepared to give their bodies for their country. The woman who would be prepared to sleep with a stranger, often a physically repulsive stranger, in order to worm secrets out of him needs the soul of a harlot. And harlots are notoriously unreliable. Thus, as potential spies, women do not rate very high in my opinion."

The same attitude was expressed by Richard Sorge, the Comintern agent who was a Soviet spy in Japan before and during part of World War II, in the guise of a German journalist: "Women are absolutely unfit for espionage work. They have little understanding of high politics or military affairs. Even if

you use them to spy on their husbands, they do not really understand what their husbands are talking about. They are too emotional sentimental and unreliable."

But women received a somewhat qualified endorsement from
Colonel David Henderson, a British intelligence officer, in his
1904 text, *Field Intelligence: Its Principles and Practice:* "When
women are employed as secret service agents, the probability of
success and the difficulty of administration are alike increased.
Women are frequently very skilful in eliciting information; they
require no disguise; if attractive, they are likely to be welcome
everywhere, and may be able to seduce from their loyalty those
whose assistance or information may be of use. On the other
hand, they are variable, easily offended, seldom sufficiently
reticent, and apt to be reckless. Usually they will work more
consistently for a person than for a principle, and a lover in the
Intelligence Corps makes a useful intermediary."

Recruiting a woman as a spy, however effective she might
prove to be, can carry unexpected consequences. The spring
1962 issue of *Studies in Intelligence*, CIA's in-house journal, carried an account by a man identified only as a "prewar European
intelligence chief" under the title, "A Dim View of Women."

In the pre-war period, he wished to penetrate "the Nazi and
front organizations in our country that were working to subvert
us." A talent spotter recruited a secretary in the local Nazi headquarters who "for reasonable pay," delivered copies of everything
she typed. All went well for several months.

"Then her case officer brought a letter she'd insisted be delivered to the chief. It was a very long one, giving the history of
her love life in lurid and unnecessary detail. From the time she
was a teenager, it seems, she had been ugly and fat. Men had
not been interested in her, and so she began to take care of her
own sexual needs. Eventually she had to spend a year in a sani-
tarium to be cured of her onanism. The cure was successful,
all right, but she emerged a nymphomaniac. Now, when desire
came upon her she was unable to control herself.

"'I am now in your service,' she wrote. 'You should have the greatest interest in my reliability. If you do not want me to get mixed up with the wrong kind of people you will have to keep my hunger satisfied. Otherwise I cannot guarantee that in my weak moments I would not divulge my connection with you to an unauthorized person, of which there are many in this office.'

"What could I do? The information she supplied was too important to the nation's security to think of getting rid of her. I called several of my bachelor officers together, explained the situation in strictly professional terms and instructed them to alternate in taking care of her. It was hardship duty—she was not only unattractive but terribly demanding—but it saved the day. She continued to work for us until the Germans overran the country. Later I heard that she was discovered by the Gestapo and executed."

Modern intelligence agencies are far more amenable to women in their ranks, even at the upper level (although the male/female balance is nowhere near 50/50 in CIA and other U.S. organizations). But CIA has named several women to the important post of Chief of Station (the very first being my late Georgetown neighbor Eloise Page, who served in Athens.) The British Security Service (MI5) has had two female director-generals.

Affirmation of the value of women in intelligence came at the climax of the case of infamous Aldrich Ames, a Clandestine Service office who spied for Moscow. He was identified through the painstaking work of counterintelligence offices Jeanne Vertefeuille and Sandra Grimes. Ames treated the women with disdain during his interrogation. "He thought the mole hunt was being led by two dumb broads...and that he was smarter than we were," Vertefeuille said afterwards. Ames is serving a life prison term for espionage. (Should you visit the International Spy Museum in Washington, seek out a video interview with these two remarkable women.)

U

UNCLE

KGB, as referred to the Communist Bloc intelligence services. For example, "Uncle is coming around tomorrow."

UNILATERAL

A CIA representative or source who operates in a foreign country without visible ties either to the Agency or the U.S. embassy. He might or might not be a formal employee. But his cover is constructed so that he can be officially disavowed if one of his operations goes awry. Unilaterals are used in risky recruiting efforts when the target is, say, an official of the host government and apt to complain if asked to supply information about his nation's politics. A unilateral differs from a singleton in that he works under Agency control; the latter is a freewheeler.

UNSUB

FBI abbreviation for "unknown subject." When the bureau opens a dossier on a person whose name it is unable to determine, he is given this designation plus a code affix—to wit, UNSUB JOHN.

USEFUL IDIOT

A phrase supposedly used by Vladimir Lenin to describe misguided liberals who help advance the Communist cause outside the Soviet Union. Although Lenin scholars have been unable to find an exact quotation using the phrase, "useful idiots" has long been accepted as the definition of left-liberals and European social democrats who, wittingly or not, advocated Moscow's causes. According to wordologist William Safire of *The New York Times*, European socialists revived the phrase in 1981, and by 1987 it had come to replace "unwitting dupe" and "fellow traveler," two anti-Communist epithets of earlier years. Former CIA counterintelligence officer

Kent Clizbe coined another term for the claque, "Willing Accomplices," the title of his 2011 book.

U-2

Arguably the most important achievement of CIA during the entire Cold War. U-2 was the designation of an aircraft—part plane, part glider—capable of flying thousands of miles at an altitude approaching thirteen miles. The Defense Department estimated that some 90 percent of the "hard data" on the USSR military was derived from U-2 aerial reconnaissance.

The U-2 (the "U" is used by the air force to designate a "utility plane," hence its employment for this craft was for cover purposes) was conceived by intelligence and military officers, chiefly civilian, who from the 1950s on desired more detailed information on the Soviet Union than could be obtained by conventional aircraft on dangerous (and illegal) overflights.

The U-2 had many "fathers," but perhaps the most important, at the beginning, was Air Force Colonel Richard Leghorn, who envisioned a craft that could fly above the USSR high enough to be immune to air defenses.

General Curtis LeMay, commander of the Strategic Air Command, wanted nothing to do with such a plane; he walked out of an early meeting where it was discussed, storming that he was "not about to waste space in my bombers with a damned camera."

In stepped Trevor Gardner, a Danish-born aeronautical expert serving as a special assistant to the secretary of the Air Force. Described as "abrupt and abrasive, and also tireless and determined," Gardner argued for the project with CIA's Directorate of Science and Technology. DCI Allen Dulles was initially dubious, pointing out that any overflight, even by an unmanned craft, could lead to a war with the Soviets. Dulles was also wary of CIA intruding on air force turf. But when powerful scientific advisers—notably Edwin Land, developer of the Polaroid camera—pushed the U-2 concept to the Oval Office, President Eisenhower gave his approval, although cautiously. He directed that the work be done outside the Pentagon bureaucracy and approved giving Lockheed Corporation $225 million to build twenty U-2s.

At this juncture, the U-2 became the ward of Richard Bissell, director of CIA's Clandestine Services. An economist by training, Bissell served as a shipping expert during World War II and then helped direct the Marshall Plan in post-war Europe.

As his hands-on manager, Bissell worked with Kelly Johnson, of Lockheed, who had developed a number of sophisticated aircraft during the war. Johnson's crews, housed in a top-secret Lockheed facility known as "the Skunk Works," worked on a crash basis—80 hour weeks were the norm—and had a plane ready for a test flight on August 4, 1955. Several pilots died on subsequent test flights—the U-2 was unstable both in the air and during take-offs and landings—but air force pilots (detailed to the CIA and "sheep-dipped" to cover their military backgrounds) persisted.

The first operational flight came July 4, 1956, over East Germany and Poland. A flight over Moscow followed the next day. Soviet protests were immediate and heated, but just as Dick Leghorn had predicted, the flights were out of range of Soviet air defenses.

President Eisenhower insisted on approving all flights; despite the Soviet anger, he considered the U-2 intelligence to be a valuable tool. For instance, its photography dashed the contention that the U.S. was endangered by a so-called "missile gap" that Democrats made a political battle cry during the late 1950s. (But the U-2 intelligence was so sensitive that it could not be used to rebut the critics, and Ike suffered the criticisms in seething silence.)

Then, disaster. On May 1, 1960, on the eve of a summit conference between Ike and Soviet Premier Nikita Khrushchev in Paris, the Soviets finally succeeded in knocking a U-2 out of the air with a rocket. Pilot Francis Gary Powers parachuted to safety. The Soviet craftily concealed the fact that he survived for several days during which U.S. officials claimed he was on a "weather flight" that went astray because of navigational failures. Then the Soviets produced a very live Power—and spy gear from his plane—in a move designed to cause maximum embarrassment to the President. The summit collapsed. (Critics roasted Eisenhower, and CIA, for launching a flight at such a sensitive time. But given Soviet behavior during other high-level meetings during the period, it is doubtful that the Paris talks would have produced any meaningful results.)

Ike did order an end to overflights of the Soviet Bloc. But in October 1962 the U-2 produced hard evidence that the USSR had based long-range ballistic missiles in Cuba, leading to a crisis that threatened world war. U-2 craft saw extensive service in Vietnam and elsewhere until they were replaced by another CIA creation, the SR-71 Blackbird, in the early 1960s. (A good account of the U-2 can be found in a book-length paper by the Center for the Study of Intelligence on the CIA web site.)

USTASHI

A Croatian nationalist group of fascist origin, connected in later years with KGB. *Ustashi* agitated for independence for the Yugoslav province of Croatia. KGB supported its activities as a means of punishing the Yugoslav regime for not swearing allegiance to the Soviet Bloc. *Ustashi* terrorists gunned down and blew up numerous victims in Europe; they also claimed credit for a bloody 1975 bombing at LaGuardia Airport in New York.

V

VACUUM CLEANER

An informant who provides an intelligence agency with details of every aspect of the activities of a target organization, regardless of their relevance to his assignment.

VEVAK

The Iranian secret police.

VIDEM

FBI code for its "Vietnam Demonstration" security files.

VLADIMIR

A Soviet jail for important political prisoners, located 150 miles east of Moscow. Originally constructed by the czar in the 1910s, Vladimir became infamous as a way station for prisoners forced to march to the steppes and salt mines of Siberia, many hundreds of miles further east. KGB made it a major prison in the 1920s. A Russian saying has it that fortunate prisoners died before reaching Vladimir, the less lucky die thereafter, and the *really* unlucky make it to the salt mines. There is no recorded instance of a prisoner escaping from Vladimir and few instances where a person is released: if he survived his original term, he was simply resentenced. Some German and Japanese generals imprisoned soon after World War II were said to still be in Vladimir in the 1970s.

V-MEN

Agents of the West German Gehlen Organization who worked behind the Iron Curtain. Despite the illegality of their primary mission, the commercial firms which gave cover to V-Men were most proper in their daily operations: they obtained business licenses, they paid taxes, they insured their employees, and they registered their motor vehicles. They also grabbed up useful information by the crateful.

Safe House Interlude Eleven

When Disaster Strikes

"Don't he look like a spy?
Let's hang him up to a tree."
His eyes roved looking for a suitable branch,
His mouth seemed pleased....
"It ain't so bad. You won't have
To fight no more."
> —Stephen Vincent Benet, *John Brown's Body.*

∾

The first German spy caught by the British during World War I was named Carl Lody, "a really fine man," in the estimate of Vernon Kell, the head of MI5. "I suppose you will not shake hands with a spy?" Lody remarked to the officer commanding the firing squad. "No, but I will shake hands with a brave man," the officer replied. And he did.

"As I appear to be going to stay here all night, could you find me a good chess player?"
> —Gordon Lonsdale, to his British jailer after
> his arrest as a deep-cover Soviet spy.

∾

"I am reconciled to my fate, but not to the mode."
> —Major John Andre, a convicted British spy of
> the Revolutionary War, upon learning that he was
> to be hanged, not shot, as he had requested. As he
> wrote General George Washington, "If aught in my
> character impresses you with esteem toward me...
> I shall experience the operation of these feelings
> in your breast by having informed that I am not
> to die on the gibbet." He wished "to be indulged
> in a professional death." Washington refused to
> change the accepted means of execution of spies.

∾

"Levity and passion have destroyed me. Pray for me. I pay with my life for my sins. 1:15 a.m. I will die now. Please do not permit a post-mortem examination. Pray for me."
—Suicide note penned by Afred Redl, the chief of Austrian intelligence who also was a Russian spy before being detected in 1911. Fellow officers gave the disgraced Red a revolver and left him alone in his room.

∾

"To hell with mankind."
—Soviet spy Richard Sorge's shout from the gallows as he was hanged by the Japanese in 1944.

WALK-INS

Persons who volunteer their services to an espionage agency. Contrary to popular mythology, agencies in fact do accept such volunteers, and make wide use of them. In the words of former CIA operative William Hood, "'It's the walk-in trade that keeps the shop open' is one of the first bits of operation wisdom that is impressed on newcomers to the business." While in Vienna in the 1950s, Hood was responsible for "running" one of the most valued walk-in informants ever recruited by CIA—Pyotr Popov, an officer of GRU, the Soviet military intelligence service.

Other walk-ins who have been valuable over the years include Fritz Kolbe, an anti-Nazi career diplomat in the German foreign office, who suddenly appeared at Allen Dulles's OSS office in Geneva in 1943; Oleg Penkovsky, a Soviet scientific intelligence officer who sabotaged Khrushchev's attempt to frighten the United States out of Berlin in 1961; and Arkady Shevchenko, a top-level Soviet diplomat at the United Nations in the late 1970s.

Because intelligence agencies tend to be skeptical of volunteer defectors until they establish their *bona fides* (because of the ever-present danger of a double agent) walk-ins can have difficulty persuading anyone to take them seriously. The most extreme example involved Igor Gouzenko, who in 1945 was a GRU cipher clerk in the Soviet embassy in Ottawa...Angered that the USSR was simultaneously taking Canadians' aid and stealing their secrets, Gouzenko one night bundled up a suitcase of confidential dispatches, took them to a newspaper, announced he was defecting, and offered the story. As corroborating evidence, Gouzenko offered documents naming Canadian officials who were spying for the Soviets. "Come back tomorrow," a subeditor told him.

Gouzenko the next day visited other newspapers and a number of government agencies, but could persuade no one to listen to him or read his papers. Not until Soviet security officers wrecked his

246

apartment that evening, in a search for the purloined documents, did officials recognize he was serious. His disclosures—the first hard evidence of the Soviets' cold war intentions—shocked Western nations. They also led to the cracking of a multi-nation spy ring stealing atomic secrets both in the United States and Great Britain, plus the arrests of Alan Nunn May, a British nuclear physicist, and Klaus Fuchs, a German-born British scientist. (Gouzenko thereafter lived in hiding—with a KGB price on his head; he died in 1982 at age 65.)

WALKERS

KGB term for low-level agents sent across the border between East and West Germany.

WALK-PAST

The appearance by an illegal agent working abroad, at a set time and place, so that he or she can be observed by an officer of the illegals' support staff working in the area. No contact is made. The walk-past enables the intelligence agency to know that the illegal has arrived and is ready to go to work. It also enables the support officer to check whether the illegal is under surveillance. The illegal might be required to do a walk-past in key cities en route to his ultimate destination; thus, if he is detected and arrested en route, his agency has at least a general idea of where his mission went awry.

WASH

The recycling of a valid passport—one obtained either by theft or purchase from a tourist—to remove all traces of writing and to reissue it with a new photograph and name. Penniless American students who sell their passports in Paris or the Middle East have unwittingly provided authentic cover for uncountable KGB agents. Since the 1970s, KGB technicians have also washed documents for use by the Palestine Liberation Organization and other international terrorist groups.

WATCH LIST

A compilation of names of persons considered of interest to the intelligence community. The most common usage is at border-crossing points. One's presence on a Watch List is not evidence of subversion or espionage, but only that the person named has contacts that deserve close scrutiny. For instance, a government officer in a sensitive job who regularly received mail with a return address known to be a KGB letter-drop could expect to have his life fairly closely monitored. The Secret Service maintains an extensive Watch List of persons considered threats to the President of the United States.

One Watch List detailed publicly was that of persons whose mail was to be given particular scrutiny during CIA's HT-LINGUAL screening of mail to and from the Soviet Union, beginning in the 1950s. The criteria for inclusion on the Watch List were succinctly defined to include persons from the "Denied Area" of Europe (i.e., Soviet Bloc nations) who had gone to work for CIA or other intelligence agencies; who had been repatriated to either the United States or Canada; who had or would return to the USSR or other Denied Areas; who were suspected Soviet intelligence agents resident in the U.S.; or who were foreign nationals from the USSR being utilized by CIA in any capacity. The original Watch List, of some twenty names, by 1956 had expanded to more than six hundred, with additions being suggested regularly by both CIA and FBI counterintelligence officers. It came to include persons who had communicated with individuals already on the Watch List and those selected for scrutiny by random sampling of Soviet mail.

Between them, CIA and the FBI included on the Watch List such individuals and organizations as the American Friends Service Committee; authors Edward Albee and John Steinbeck; numerous scientific organizations and their members; and various political activists. One peculiar target was Frederick A. Praeger Publishers—which had produced many books with covert Agency support.

WATCHER SERVICE
The department of MI5 responsible for surveillance of suspects, either by car or on foot.

WEEDER
A security officer responsible for screening British state papers for embarrassing material—before they are put into the public record

after passage of the statutory declassification period. One subject automatically excised—supposedly—is any mention of MI5 operations. There is an occasional slip. In early 1982, a careless weeder permitted passage of a document about illegal MI5 wiretaps of Frederick Kuh, late London correspondent of the *Chicago Sun,* that had been conducted in 1946, after he wrote a story about the government's atomic energy bill; and of Paul Enzig, political correspondent of the *Financial Times* of London, for a critical story on government economic planning. John Drew, former Cabinet functionary whose office handled the matters in the 1940s, was aghast when *The Economist* informed him his files were now in the National Archives in Kew. "This sounds really a bit near the bone," Drew said. "In fact, it's more than that: you're digging near the bone."

WEEDING

The process of reviewing files and discarding those no longer considered important enough to warrant storage space. Computerization of files in such agencies as CIA and DIA during the more recent years means that file information is now retained permanently.

WESTPOINTER

A CIA mail intercept project based in San Francisco during brief periods between September 1969 and October 1971. Mail to and from a single Asian nation was examined—first, surface only; later, opened and photographed. In WESTPOINTER, postal officials were not privy to the fact that mail was being opened. CIA people would surreptitiously place envelopes in their pockets when no one was watching, and take the letters to a Technical Services Division laboratory in the San Francisco area for examination. Although the Church Committee report did not name the "Asian nation" targeted, the quoted memoranda suggest the People's Republic of China. (CIA's Plans Directorate, also involved in the project, code-named it KMSOURDOUGH.)

WET SQUAD

A special KGB assassination group, controlled by and dispatched from KGB Central in Moscow. CIA credited the wet squad with no less than three assassinations of major Afghan leaders during the two years preceding the 1979 Soviet seizure of that country. Another victim was President Ahmed Hussein Ghashmi of North Yemen, a staunch foe of the Soviets. The method used in this instance was particularly dastardly. An envoy of the pro-Soviet rival state of South Yemen visited President Ghashmi, ostensibly to discuss peace. When he opened his briefcase, it exploded violently, blowing both envoy and Ghashmi to bits. CIA specialists said manufacture of such a sophisticated device was far beyond Yemeni capability; they concluded the incident was planned in Moscow and carried out via the wet squad.

WET WORK

An operation involving the shedding of blood. KGB term.

WHITE CROW

KGB term for someone who stands out in a crowd, a situation to be avoided by a covert agent.

WHITE INTELLIGENCE

Information gleaned from such overt sources as foreign publications and broadcasts. The United States Government Printing Office, which publishes hundreds of thousands of words annually on Congressional hearings on defense plans, had no counterpart in the USSR. The Soviet embassy in Washington receives some 1,700 pounds of mail daily, by FBI scales, the bulk of it governmental and other publications. Countless other pounds went to various KGB mail drops and convenience addresses around the country.

WHITE PROPAGANDA

Statements or publications that make no attempt to conceal authorship, source, or point of origin. (*See also* GRAY and BLACK PROPAGANDA.)

WHO, ME?

A "psychological harassing agent" the Office of Strategic Services developed for use in Asia during World War II. As an OSS manual stated, "It is to be squirted directly upon the body or clothing of a person a few feet away. The odor is that of Occidental feces, which is extremely offensive to Orientals. Very good use of this agent can be made by native patriots in crowded markets and bazaars to create disturbances, attack morale of enemy guards, and to divert attention from other activities." *Who, Me?* consisted of a soft metal tube with a screw cap on a projecting tip. When the cap was removed and the tube squeezed, it squirted a liquid chemical that OSS described as being of "violent, repulsive and lasting odor." *Who, Me?* tubes weighed half an ounce and were slightly less than three inches long; OSS distributed them five to a carton.

WICKET GATE

Soviet term, circa World War II, for a place where agents could cross a military front line into enemy territory.

WITTING

A person who knowingly cooperates with an intelligence agency. The word first came to public view in garbled form in the mid-1960s, when *Ramparts Magazine* exposed CIA links with the National Student Association. One of the magazine's informants said that NSA officers who knew of the arrangement were *"witty,"* and two decades later this corrupted version of *"witting"* still shows up in spy novels. (*See* BIGOT LIST, NOT WITTING.)

WORK NAME

An alias used by an officer or support person in the field. (*See* FALSE NAMES.)

WRATH OF GOD

An Israeli counterterrorist group formed after the massacre of Olympic athletes in 1972. "WOG"—also known as "Israel's long arm"—has as its mission to identify, search out, and destroy Arab terrorists in Europe; the chief target was the Black September Palestinian group which claimed credit for the Munich murders. In two years, Wrath of God killed more than a dozen Black September leaders. It was "officially" disbanded in late 1974 after Western European governments protested its freebooting activities within their boundaries. Whether WOG truly was disbanded is a matter of conjecture.

YAVKA
Soviet name for a safe house.

YEZHOVSHCHINA
Russian for "The Great Purge," the period during the late 1930s when Stalin decimated Soviet society of its leading generals, scientists, physicians, and politicians. Named for the chief of Soviet state security, Nikolia Ivanovich Yezhov.

Z

Z-COVERAGE

The first and longest-running FBI mail intercept program, initiated in 1940 to cover Axis diplomatic offices in Washington. Z-Coverage later extended to diplomats of various Communist nations, with the purpose "to detect individuals in contact with these establishments who might be attempting to make contact for espionage reasons, for purposes of defecting, or who might be illegal agents."

Z-Coverage, as it evolved, aimed at tight targets, screening incoming mail in urban postal zones where foreign agents were believed to be living. According to Church Committee testimony, coverage included, at various times, postal zones 10023, 10024, and 10025 in New York; zone 48231 in Detroit and the suburban Hamtramck area; and, finally, all mail sent to San Francisco from New York and Washington.

The Z-Coverage was fruitful. In July 1964 the program intercepted a letter from "an employee of an American intelligence agency" to a foreign embassy in which he "offered to sell information relating to weapons systems...and also expressed an interest in defecting." Three illegal agents were detected in Washington alone. And Z-Coverage monitored the demands laid upon Chinese-born scientists who were ordered to return to the Mainland lest their relatives suffer reprisals. The queries sent to these scientists—information they were expected to bring back to the Mainland—alerted U.S. intelligence to the areas of particular interest to the Communist Chinese.

ZENITH TECHNICAL ENTERPRISES

Cover corporation for CIA's covert war against Castro's Cuba during the early 1960s (code-named JMWAVE). Zenith was located on the University of Miami's South Campus, adjacent to the abandoned Richmond Naval Air Station, mostly destroyed by a hurricane; it supposedly did classified "government research."

Zenith had the outward appearance of a functioning business. A notice to salesmen, pinned on an outside doorway, listed calling hours for various departments. On the wall of the reception room was a certificate from the United Way thanking Zenith for "outstanding participation" in its annual fundraising.

ZODIAC (for Spies)

Mercury is the most favorable planet for a spy, with Gemini as the sign of the zodiac (birthdays May 21 to June 21). As an astrologer told the British espionage expert Bernard Newman, "Spies are significant in dreams. If you dream that you are a spy in the service of your own country, this indicates that you will be elected to some position you do not desire. If you dream that you are being spied on, this is a warning to be more circumspect in your behaviour."

Sources

Among the printed sources for *The Dictionary of Espionage* were the following volumes: Joseph Burkholder Smith, *Portrait of a Cold Warrior* (New York, 1976); Christopher Felix, *A Short Course in the Cold War* (New York, 1963); David Atlee Phillips, *The Night Watch* (New York, 1977), and *Careers in Secret Operations* (Frederick, Maryland, 1985); William Hood, *Mole* (New York: 1982); A. I. Romanov, *Nights Are Longer There* (Boston, 1972); E. Howard Hunt, *Give Us This Day* (New Rochelle, 1973); Harry Rositzke, *The KGB: The Eyes of Russia* (New York, 1981); David J. Dallin *Soviet Espionage* (New Haven, 1955); Chapman Pincher, *Dirty Tricks* (New York, 1980), and *Too Secret Too Long* (New York, 1984); Donald McCormick, *Who's Who in Spy Fiction* (New York, 1977); Bradley Earl Ayers, *The War That Never Was* (Indianapolis/New York, 1976); James Bamford, *The Puzzle Palace* (Boston, 1982); Louise Bernikow, *Abel* (New York, 1970); Anthony Cave Brown, *Bodyguard of Lies* (New York, 1975); William Colby, *Honorable Men* (New York, 1978); Thomas Coulson, *MataHari: Courtesan and Spy* (New York, 1930); Richard Deacon, *A History of the British Secret Service* (New York, 1969), and *The Chinese Secret Service* (New York, 1976); Peer de Silva, *Sub Rosa: The CIA and Uses of Intelligence* (New York, 1978); James B. Donovan, *Strangers on a Bridge* (New York, 1976); Brian Freemantle, *KGB: Inside the World's Largest Intelligence Network* (New York, 1984); Reinhard Gehlen, *The Service* (New York, 1972); Anatoliy Golitsyn, *New Lies for Old (New* York, 1984); Anatoli Granovsky, *I Was An NKVD Agent* (New York, 1962); Louis Hagen, *The Secret War for Europe: A Dossier of Espionage (New* York; 1969); Baruch Hazan, *Soviet Impregnational Propaganda* (Ann Arbor, 1982); Allison Ind, *A Short History of Espionage* (New York, 1963); Nikolai Khikhlov, *In the Name of Conscience,* New York, 1959); David Lewis, *Sexpionage* (New York, 1976); Fitzroy Maclean, *Take Nine Spies* (New York, 1978); Pawel Monat, *Spy in the United States* (New York, 1961); Alan Moorhead, *The Traitors* (London, 1974); Bernard Newman, *The World of Espionage (New* York, 1962);

Liam O'Flaherty, *The Informer* (New York, 1961); Oleg Penkovsky, *The Penkovsky Papers,* (New York, 1965); Walter Pforzheimer, editor, *Bibliography of Intelligence Literature* (Washington, Defense Intelligence College, 1985, eighth edition); Francis Gary Powers, *Overflight* (New York, 1970); Gordon W. Prange, *Target Tokyo: The Story of the Sorge Spy Ring* (New York, 1984); Harry Howe Ransom, *The Intelligence Establishment* (Cambridge, 1970); Anthony Read and David Fisher, *Colonel Z* (New York, 1985), and *Operation Lucy* (New York, 1981); Jeffrey T. Richelson, *The U.S. Intelligence Community* (Cambridge, 1985); Vladimir Sakharov, *High Treason* (New York, 1980); Ronald Seth, *Encyclopedia of Espionage* (London, 1972), and *Unmasked: The Story of Soviet Espionage (New* York, 1965); Bradley F. Smith, *The Shadow Warriors* (New York, 1983); John J. Stephan, *The Russian Fascists* (New York, 1978); Steven Stewart, *The Spymasters of Israel* (New York, 1980); Viktor Suvorov, *Inside Soviet Military Intelligence* (New York, 1984); Edward Van Der Rhoer, *The Shadow Network* (New York, 1973); Nigel West, *The Circus* (Briarcliff Manor, New York, 1983), *MI5* (London, 1981), *MI6* (New York, 1983), and *A Thread of Deceit* (New York, 1985); David Wise, *Spectrum* (New York, 1981); Thaddeus Wittlin, *Commissar: The Life and Death of Laventry Beria* (New York, 1972); Greville Wynne, *Contact on Gorky Street* (New York, 1968); and Allen Dulles, *The Craft of Intelligence* (New York, 1963). Government publications of value included Book One, "Foreign and Military Intelligence," of the Senate Select Committee to Study Governmental Activities with Respect to Intelligence Activities, 94th Congress, Second Session, Report 94-755, April 14, 1976 (The Church Committee, popularly); "Soviet Active Measures," House Permanent Select Committee on Intelligence, 97th Congress, Second Session, 1982; and "Communist Bloc Intelligence Activities in the United States," internal security subcommittee of the Senate Judiciary Committee, 94th Congress, First Session, 1975 (the testimony of Josef Frolik). The best overall volume on the history of intelligence remains Richard Wilmer Rowan, *The Story of Secret Service* (New York, 1937). And, finally, anyone who writes on the subject owes gratitude to Allen Dulles, *The Craft of Intelligence* (New York, 1963); Sherman Kent, *Strategic Intelligence for American World Policy* (Princeton, 1966, revised edition); and Lyman B. Kirkpatrick, Jr., *The US. Intelligence Community* (New York, 1973).